The Meaning of More's "Utopia"

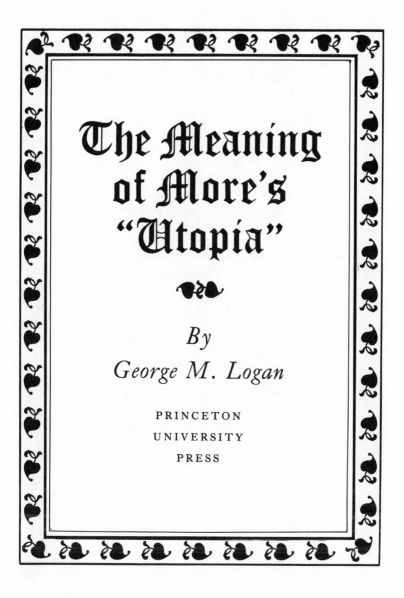

The Meaning of More's "Utopia"

By

George M. Logan

PRINCETON
UNIVERSITY
PRESS

Library of Congress Cataloging in Publication Data will be
found on the last printed page of this book

This book has been composed in Linotron Caslon

Clothbound editions of Princeton University Press books
are printed on acid-free paper, and binding materials are
chosen for strength and durability.
Paperbacks, while satisfactory for personal collections,
are not usually suitable for library rebinding

Printed in the United States of America by Princeton
University Press, Princeton, New Jersey

Designed by Laury A. Egan

To my sister Lenore
and the memory of our parents
Lucile Meredith Logan
Rex A. Logan

Contents

꩜

Preface

The principal antecedents of this study are a number of works that identify *Utopia* as a product of Renaissance humanism and undertake to interpret it by specifying as precisely as possible its position in the development of that tradition. Above all, I am indebted to the studies of J. H. Hexter and the late Edward Surtz, S.J., debts that I hope are not obscured by my criticism of some of their views. Like these scholars and the other exponents of what Father Surtz called the "humanistic interpretation" of *Utopia*, I am convinced that More's book is, despite the wit and indirection of its manner, a serious work of political philosophy, and that it embodies More's profound sympathy with the ideals of Erasmian Christian humanism.

I do not, however, share with this school the view that *Utopia* is essentially a recapitulation, partly direct and partly disguised, of the normative suggestions of Christian humanists, a view that in effect consigns More's book to a backwater of political theory, where most historians of that discipline have been content to leave it. Quentin Skinner, who is the most recent and authoritative historian of Renaissance political thought, and whose work provides indispensable background and interpretive perspectives for this study, alters the usual judgment somewhat. According to Skinner, More, though largely recapitulating humanist views, also questions the comfortable conservatism of humanist political thought by following out the implications of some of its themes. I endorse the notion that *Utopia* embodies a critique of other works of political theory, but Skinner's view of the means and the extent of that critique seems to me too narrow.

Skinner usefully distinguishes two traditions in early Renaissance political theory, a humanist tradition affiliated with Roman Stoic thought and a scholastic tradition that represents a revival of Aristotelian theory. He defines the significance of the brilliant

Italian theory of More's own time largely in terms of its attempt to fuse these traditions. I argue that More is engaged in a parallel, though substantively very different, attempt. *Utopia* is, first, an object lesson in the methodology of Greek theory (Platonic as well as Aristotelian), a methodology that it significantly refines, and, second, an attempt to bring this methodology to bear in a critique of the substantive conclusions of both the Stoic and the Greek traditions. In particular, *Utopia* not only suggests the preconditions for the implementation of Stoic norms and the mutual incompatibility of some of them, but also questions some *realpolitisch* conclusions of theorists in the Greek tradition. A profound rumination on central themes of classical and Renaissance political thought, *Utopia* deserves a place among the most advanced and creative political writings of its era.

Most interpretive failures in the criticism of *Utopia* stem from taking parts of it out of context—both the context of the book itself and that of the history of political theory. This seems a particularly grave and ironic failing in the case of a humanist work, since the humanists' own critical method, which forms the origin of our most common approaches to literary texts, has at its heart the principle that works must be regarded as wholes and in all their relevant contexts. To avoid this failing, I have treated the three sections of *Utopia*—the Letter to Giles, Book I, and Book II—consecutively and, I believe, comprehensively, and I have also attempted to replace the book in its context in the history of political thought. This attempt necessitates drawing back sometimes from the text. My rule has been to incorporate the resulting sections at what seem to me the earliest points where the reflections they embody can be fully clear to the reader.

The study begins with brief prolegomena, which identify the traditional deficiencies in criticism of *Utopia* and show why we are in a better position than earlier readers to supply them. I pay particular attention to findings of the humanistic interpreters that serve to establish fundamental critical guidelines and, in Hexter's reconstruction of the composition of *Utopia*, to provide vital clues to More's intentions—and to raise a serious question about the unity of his book.

The following chapter, on the Letter to Giles, shows that this letter indicates not only that *Utopia* is a product of Renaissance humanism but also that it is directed primarily to a humanist audience. The latter fact undermines previous interpretations, which have either ignored the indications of intended audience or misconstrued their implications. The chapter concludes with an examination of the enigmatic hints that the letter offers as to the concerns of the book.

The chapter on Book I opens with an explication of the introductory pages and of Hythloday's account of his conversation at Cardinal Morton's table. The *structure* of this account serves to confirm (for the most part) Hythloday's claim that it is futile for a humanist philosopher to enter practical politics. The second section of the chapter shows how the *substance* of the account introduces other topics, especially the question of the relation between the politically expedient and the moral, and a particular method of social analysis. This method stems from a holistic approach to social problems and emphasizes rationalistic causal analysis, the value of comparative study and experiment, and the utility of constructing imaginative models as a way of testing social theories. The section concludes with an explication of Hythloday's next speeches (those culminating in his accounts of imaginary council meetings), which extend the several considerations introduced in the earlier episode. The third section of the chapter investigates the relation of More's method to those of other political theorists, both of the Renaissance and of the classical era. A final section explicates the heated exchange between Hythloday and More and Hythloday's consequent introduction of the subject of Utopia, passages that serve to conclude Book I and to indicate its relation to Book II.

The chapter on Book II is also divided into four sections. The first gives a brief account of the steps of the exercise developed by Plato and Aristotle for determining the best form of the commonwealth and suggests the relation of the Utopian construct to that exercise. The second section identifies Hythloday's account of Utopian moral philosophy as the crucial first step of the exercise—the determination of the best life of the individual—and offers a detailed explication of the tortuous arguments of the account and a reconstruction of More's polemical intentions in developing them. The third section shows how the conclusions of the Utopian moral philosophers underlie More's handling of the subsequent steps of the best-commonwealth exercise—in which the theorist determines the goals of the commonwealth and the array of physical and institutional features that will best promote the realization of these goals—and how his handling of these steps completes his critique of the conclusions of the Greek theorists (and their followers). The final section turns to the problem presented by the discrepancies between Utopian practices and the ideals of Christian humanists and shows that the proper explanation of these discrepancies lies in More's strict adherence to the rules of the best-commonwealth exercise, and that his subtle emphasis on these discrepancies reflects the fact that his book is designed partly as a corrective to the naive idealism of Christian humanists.

Finally, the epilogue recapitulates the central conclusions of the study and attempts to account for the surprising modernity of some aspects of More's thought by reexamining, in the light of the current understanding of Renaissance humanism, the relation of *Utopia* to that tradition.

A study of this kind requires reference to a good many other works. I have tried to fulfill this requirement in the least irritating and space-consuming way. Authorities and the sources of quotations are indicated parenthetically in the body of the text, and I have included in these references the minimum amount of information compatible with clarity—often simply a page number. They will guide the reader, when he wishes, to the bibliographical data in the list of Works Cited.

It would be unrealistic to quote *Utopia* in Latin, though I have included the Latin wherever it reveals something obscured in translation. Every new interpreter covets a new translation. He constantly feels that another version of a particular phrase, a version that is equally or, as it seems to him, more justified by the Latin, should replace the rendering in the translation he employs. In a sense he is right, since any previous translation is biased by the critical view of its creator, a view that the interpreter's own, being later, presumably transcends. At the same time, the use of an existing translation precludes misshaping one's own to accommodate one's interpretation and thus distorting the data that the reader needs in order to assess it. With such considerations in mind, I have quoted from the translation in the Yale edition of Surtz and Hexter, which, though unsatisfactory in several respects (cf. Prévost 1964; Miller 1966; Skinner 1967, pp. 165-68), is standard and likely to remain so for some time. A number of departures from it are noted and explained at the points where they occur.

In choosing editions of other primary sources, I have considered both authority and accessibility. In particular, I normally quote the Greek and Latin classics in the editions and translations of the Loeb Classical Library. Four central Greek works, however, are quoted in translations that seem to me superior to those of the Loeb Library, whether because their more recent date means that they incorporate scholarly advances unavailable to the Loeb editors or because of the extraordinary perspicacity of the translator. These works are Plato's *Republic* (quoted in the translation of H.D.P. Lee) and *Laws* (Trevor J. Saunders), and Aristotle's *Nicomachean Ethics* (W. D. Ross) and *Politics* (Ernest Barker).

In addition to my debts to others' work, there are more personal ones that I am happy to acknowledge. Those of longest standing are to Professor Douglas Bush of Harvard University (Emeritus) and Professor Herschel Baker, also of Harvard, who introduced me to the study of Renaissance literature and in great part determined the lines along which my views have developed. Their unstinting generosity to me over the years instances the kindness they have always shown their students. No such historical connection, however, helps to account for the generosity of Professors

Paul Oskar Kristeller of Columbia University (Emeritus), William J. Bouwsma of the University of California, Berkeley, and Quentin Skinner of the University of Cambridge, all of whom read my typescript with scarcely credible care and offered invaluable suggestions and corrections. Moreover, this study would have been impossible without their published work, on Renaissance humanism, on the history of political thought, and on *Utopia*. Professor Robert M. Adams of the University of California at Los Angeles (Emeritus), whose admirable Norton Critical Edition of *Utopia* has been at my elbow throughout the writing of the monograph, gave me encouragement and wise counsel at a crucial point. Professor Thomas I. White of Upsala College not only assisted me greatly by his publications but also shared his thoughts on *Utopia* with me in correspondence and allowed me to see typescripts of his forthcoming study of Plato and *Utopia*. I am also pleased to recall the generosity of Professor Jay Robinson of the University of Michigan, who secured me library privileges and an office during the summer of 1977, when I began writing. When I finished, everyone at Princeton University Press was splendid to me. I can single out Marjorie Sherwood, Marilyn Campbell, Laury Egan, and Harriet Hitch; I wish I knew more names.

I have also incurred local debts. I am grateful to the Department of English of Queen's University, Kingston, Canada, which has given me, through the continuance of an undergraduate program that must now be unique in its faithful adherence to the traditional curriculum of my subject, the opportunity to teach *Utopia* to undergraduate, as well as graduate, students for a dozen years. George Whalley, as Head during several of those years, encouraged me not just to write but to try to write something worth reading. Professor Whalley also read the typescript and gave me extensive and valuable comments on it. A. C. Hamilton, our senior professor of Renaissance literature, has always been generous to me, and, though he may be surprised to hear it, I have profited greatly from his advice (on this and many other matters) and his example. Professor Phillip W. Rogers read the typescript and helped me with a number of difficult points. Professor Catherine R. Harland read the typescript and discussed many matters in it and about it with me. Her help of all kinds has been invaluable. I have often discussed *Utopia* with my fellow admirer of More, Professor W. J. Barnes. John Tinkler gave me valuable insights into the relation between *Utopia* and the rhetorical tradition. Michal Ben-Gera discussed many of the ideas in the book with me and read parts of early drafts, commenting incisively on them. My son Adam remarked enthusiastically on the growing number of pages. My former student and former colleague Peter Sabor, now of the University of Calgary, was the first person to whom I dared show the penultimate, barely legible, form of the typescript, and his heroic fortitude in reading it, as well as his astute comments, constitute a signal proof of his dedication to scholarship and his friendship. The only other person who suffered through that version was my typist (and sometimes cryptographer and editor), Kathy Goodfriend. Our preparation of the final typescript was assisted, thanks to Dean J. C. Beal, by a grant from the Discretionary Fund of the Graduate School of Queen's.

The Meaning
of More's
"Utopia"

Prolegomena

Utopia is a designedly enigmatic book, but we cannot doubt that More meant it to be comprehensible to his intended audience; meant, that is, that an intelligent, appropriately educated person reading through it should grasp its import. The book has not, however, proved to be thus comprehensible. From the time of its first publication to the present, responses to it have varied widely, and even the best of them, however illuminating with respect to particular aspects of the book, prove reductive in one way or another when tested against *Utopia* as a whole.

The failure to achieve consensus about the meaning of a book that has been scrutinized for nearly five centuries can stem from either or both of two causes: defects of coherence in the book itself, or an excessive gap of sophistication between it and its readers. The first cause may well obtain, but obviously we should fall back on interpretation in such terms only as a last resort. The operation and importance of the second cause are beyond doubt. *Utopia* has proved to be too sophisticated for its readers, both in substance and in literary method.

The most insightful early readers of *Utopia* that we can identify are the group of More's fellow humanists represented in the commendatory letters prefixed to the early editions. These letters, as Hexter says, embody "interpretations of *Utopia* by a highly select group of More's contemporaries[,] . . . all in close rapport with his intellectual ideals" (1952, p. 44).[1] Some modern scholars rely heavily on the letters (e.g., Hexter, pp. 43-48; Caspari, p. 91; Avineri, p. 285; Schoeck 1969, pp. 281-82). Yet the obvious interpretive failures of these first critics of *Utopia* suggest that we ought not to accept their views incautiously. Budé's letter is the most substantial, and it contains a number of perceptive

---

[1] For biographical sketches, see P. R. Allen, pp. 92-99.

remarks. In particular, Budé calls attention to the harmony between some Utopian practices and "the customs and the true
wisdom of Christianity" and observes that the behavior of the
Utopians shames "those regions which hold fast and cling to the
surname of Christian" (*Ut.*, p. 11). But when he goes on to
conclude from the points of congruence between Utopian practices and Christian ideals that Utopia is "Hagnopolis" (p. 13),
the Holy City, and that the account of it is intended as "a nursery
of correct and useful institutions from which every man may
introduce and adapt transplanted customs to his own city" (p.
15), he ignores not only some questionable and dubiously Christian Utopian institutions but also the criticisms of a number of
these institutions that More attributes to himself (p. 245)—criticisms that need not be taken at face value but must be taken
some way. Nor, though aware of the learned jokes of the book,
does he appear to understand that these jokes (and other features)
create an ironic distance between More and the views of Hythloday, the "expert in nonsense" (see *Ut.*, p. 301n). The same
failure to acknowledge the flaws of Utopia or More's partial
dissociation of himself from the practices of that commonwealth
characterizes all the other letters. In general, these readers seem
determined to find a book that embodies their own social and
religious ideals. Insomuch as *Utopia is* that kind of book, their
criticism is perceptive; insomuch as it is not, they seem blind.[2]

In the present century More's sophistication, whether as ironist
or as political theorist, still seems greater than that of his readers.
Recognition of the interpretive significance of his ironic method
is for the most part confined to students of imaginative literature.
Historians routinely treat *Utopia* as if it were a simple manifesto,
unambiguously a presentation of More's ideal commonwealth.
Hexter, for example, writes that

---

[2] It is possible that this blindness is, at least in some cases, simulated.
Simulated or real, it renders the letters insufficient guides to *Utopia*, although
a proof of simulation would undercut the claim that the book was too sophisticated for its early readers.

More truly believed that the Utopian commonwealth as he had framed it was the Best Society. That he did indeed believe this he indicates time after time, but never more emphatically than at the beginning of the summation . . . [near the end] of *Utopia*: "Now I have declared and described to you, as truly as I could, the form and order of that commonwealth which verily in my judgment is not only the best, but also that which alone of good right may claim and take upon it the name of a commonwealth or public weal." (1952, p. 57)

But of course "I" here is Hythloday, not More—a fact to which Hexter nowhere alludes.[3] For their part, students of literature remain on the whole remarkably impercipient about the relation of *Utopia* to the tradition of political theory. At worst this impercipience takes the form of the unpardonable sin of trivializing More's impassioned, profoundly reflective, and enormously learned book as a *jeu d'esprit*. In his volume of the Oxford History of English Literature, C. S. Lewis describes *Utopia* as "a book whose real place is not in the history of political thought so much as in that of fiction and satire. . . . It becomes intelligible and delightful as soon as we take it for what it is—a holiday work, a spontaneous overflow of intellectual high spirits, a revel of debate, paradox, comedy and (above all) of invention, which starts many hares and kills none" (pp. 167, 169).[4] Or the book may, as in a number of recent studies, be regarded as serious but as concerned with political theory in only a general or secondary way. Warren Wooden notes the development of a new interpretive tradition, in which *Utopia* is regarded "as primarily

[3] Ward Allen calls attention to the interpretive implications of Hexter's confusion of Hythloday and More (pp. 110-12). For surveys of views on the relation between Hythloday's opinions and those of the author, see Caspari, pp. 129-30, n. 7, and Avineri, pp. 278-83.

[4] To be sure, the view of *Utopia* as *jeu d'esprit* is not confined to literary professionals. Cf. Knox, pp. 43-44; Campbell, p. 24; Jenkins, pp. 19-20; Ross, pp. 54-55; Morris, p. 19. In refutation, see Surtz 1952, pp. 157-58; Coles; and White 1978, pp. 143-45.

and generically a conscious and consistent work of satire. This satiric approach has inevitably generated a good deal of controversy in critical circles, denying as it does the basic assumption of Catholic and Marxist critics alike that the *Utopia* is essentially and fundamentally a serious socio-philosophical document tinged only occasionally with topical satire" (1977, p. 29).[5] In the readings of this school, some of which R. M. Adams fairly characterizes as "suspicious and diminishing" (p. 202), it often appears that what is most important in *Utopia* is not the complex fabric of Utopian institutions, with its innumerable points of contact with previous works of political theory, or the brilliant analyses of the problems of Europe, but Hythloday's character. Harry Berger, Jr., suggests that More's primary purpose is to criticize "Hythloday's radical idealism," which is "that of a closed inner world: it is pure and monologal, not open to time, to correction, compromise or the interplay of perspective made possible by dialogue and conversation" (p. 63). Even R. S. Sylvester, a superb literary historian whose services to More were of the highest order, came disturbingly close to suggesting that *Utopia* is a sort of dramatic monologue designed to expose the foibles of Hythloday.[6]

[5] As representatives of this approach, Wooden lists Traugott, Heiserman, Elliott, Berger, Barnes, Dorsch, Sylvester 1968, and Johnson. One may add, in addition to Wooden himself (1972, 1977), Stevens; Weiner; Kinney 1976, 1979; Rudat 1981a, b; and Schaeffer. Actually, where Hythloday is regarded (as by Heiserman and Elliott) primarily as the vehicle of satire rather than as its target, the satiric approach results in a view of the themes of *Utopia* not much different from that of more traditional critics.

[6] Sylvester 1968, pp. 298-99: "We do not go wrong if we see Book II as an extended image of Hythlodaeus' own personality: Utopia enshrines his ideals and virtues, but it also—and he himself is completely unaware of this—hints at the defects in his thinking and at the moral flaws in his character. Utopia is made, like all famous creations, in the image and likeness of its creator." Cf. Kinney 1976, p. 443, n. 34; Rudat 1981a, p. 57; Schaeffer, p. 18. Similarly, Berger diminishes the exchanges of the Morton episode of Book I: "Morton humors Hythloday as he humors the lawyer, friar and parasite—a Chaucerian gallery eminently qualified to bring on an attack. He amuses himself with them, is amused by them, allows them to vent their vanities and theories at his table,

At the same time, the fact that we are able to recognize these deficiencies in early and recent interpretations of *Utopia* suggests that if we can peer over the fences that separate our particular academic disciplines we are in a better position than any of our predecessors to produce an adequate reading of *Utopia*. The literature of our time is pervaded by irony and its attendant ambiguity, and crucially concerned with the relativity of truth to point of view. Correspondingly, our criticism has developed sophisticated insights into the bearing of irony and narrative point of view on meaning. If these insights have sometimes been applied to *Utopia* with an enthusiasm too narrow, it is nonetheless clear that they are vital to a full understanding of More's book. Similarly, developments in political theory have rendered some aspects of *Utopia* more understandable than they could have been to earlier readers. Kautsky's *Thomas More and His Utopia* (1888) is for the most part invalidated by ideological special pleading and appalling anachronism, but when Kautsky applied Marxist theory to *Utopia* one aspect of the book—the relation between economic arrangements and other elements of Utopian society— came suddenly into focus. In the same way, Hexter's insights into the rationalistic and holistic nature of More's approach to social problems (see below, pp. 58-59) reflect the fact that the

---

and dismisses them when it is time 'to heare his sueters' " (p. 64). For a critique of such readings, see White 1978, pp. 145-49.

In general, one may say that although *Utopia* partakes of many of the standard features of satire (see especially Heiserman), the book as a whole cannot be adequately characterized as satire—as, indeed, some members of Wooden's list would agree. The satiric interpreters frequently cite *The Praise of Folly* and the writings of Lucian as generic parallels. Certainly More was influenced, in *Utopia* and elsewhere, by both (see, most recently, Duncan, pp. 52-76). But the insufficiency of labeling *Utopia* a satire is driven home by a moment's consideration of the substantive and tonal differences between any passage of *The Praise of Folly* (except the last, where Erasmus leaves the territory of satire) or—a fortiori—any passage of Lucian and such passages of *Utopia* as Hythloday's discussion of theft and poverty in England, his final remarks on Europe vis-à-vis Utopia, his exchange with More about the political role of the philosopher, and any number of all-too-sober passages in the account of Utopia.

social thought of our own time has developed an essentially similar approach. Moreover, as some remarks of Chambers (1935) suggest, clearer understanding of *Utopia* is a function of developments not only in political theory but also in political fact:

> The changes which are taking place should make it easier to appreciate More, by ridding us of some of the prejudices which have hampered his admirers for four hundred years. . . . apologies for the "political chimeras" of *Utopia* are beginning to look unnecessary. In the course of one lifetime *Utopia* has passed out of the realm of fantastic "poetry," as Tyndale called it, and has become a text-book of practical politicians. (pp. 372-73; cf. pp. 125, 143)

This process continues. In one of Hexter's recent remarks on *Utopia*, we find that his confidence in the ideal nature of More's imaginary commonwealth has been undermined by contemplation of political events: "Since I wrote the above [a passage in his section of the introduction to the Yale edition], the way of life of the Chinese as prescribed by Chairman Mao has forced itself on my attention. It sounds uncomfortably like Utopia in a number of significant respects" (1973, p. 125n). Similarly, Sylvester observes that "the defects in the Utopian system . . . are no longer escaping notice, perhaps because so many of them have become grim reality in our own century" (1968, pp. 299-300).

To be sure, we labor under one great disadvantage relative to earlier, especially the earliest, readers of *Utopia*: we do not participate in the social and intellectual milieu of the book. But this disadvantage has in part been obviated by recent scholarship. Indeed, the recognition of the need to reconstruct the milieu of *Utopia* forms the basis of the central modern interpretive tradition, that which Surtz called the "humanistic interpretation" (1957a, pp. 2-8; 1957b, p. 12; cf. 1952, pp. 157, 161-74), and which may be regarded as including the work of Surtz himself and of Russell Ames, Hexter, R. P. Adams, Fritz Caspari, R. J. Schoeck, and Skinner, to name only the most conspicuous figures. Although there are wide divergences among the positions of these scholars, they all share a thesis originally developed by Frederick Seebohm (1867): that the primary affiliation of *Utopia* is with the tradition of Renaissance humanism and that the best approach to the interpretation of the book accordingly lies in placing it as accurately as possible in the context of humanism and of the wider currents of thought and action of which that movement forms a part.[7]

In addition to illuminating individual passages, the researches of the humanistic interpreters have served to establish fundamental guidelines for the interpretation of the book as a whole, by proving beyond any reasonable doubt that *Utopia* is a careful and essentially serious work, and that its primary disciplinary affiliation is with the tradition of political theory. These points have been established, first, by the demonstration that, far from being a revel of unconstrained invention, *Utopia* reflects More's painstaking collection and fusion of ideas from a wide range of books, especially serious works of political thought. This is the case not only with large, conspicuous features of the work, such as the communistic institutions of Utopia (Surtz 1957a, pp. 151-91), but also with small, seemingly arbitrary or whimsical details,

---

[7] Brief as Seebohm's treatment of *Utopia* is, it anticipates several of the major themes of twentieth-century criticism. The purpose of Book II of *Utopia* lies in "the contrast presented by its ideal commonwealth to the condition and habits of the European commonwealths of the period" (p. 217). Demonstrating the harmony of the law of nature and the law of God, *Utopia* is a response to the *realpolitisch* theory of its time (pp. 230-31). Book I embodies More's reasonings on the question whether he should accept Henry's offer of a place at court (pp. 238-44). Some of Seebohm's insights were developed further in Chambers's highly influential *Thomas More* (pp. 125-44)—although Chambers acknowledges no debt to Seebohm, only sneering at him at one point (p. 66). Seebohm's book was recalled to the attention of postwar scholars largely by Ames, who modestly claimed that his own *Citizen Thomas More and His Utopia* (1949) only "revived, expanded, and documented" the ideas of Seebohm and Kautsky (pp. 6-7).

One should note that the "satiric approach," too, is humanistic, in the sense that its premise (perfectly valid in itself) is that *Utopia* exemplifies the development of increasingly complex ironic and satiric writing by humanists of the later Renaissance.

such as the fact that the Utopian constitution was 1,760 years old at the time of Hythloday's visit, a circumstance that embodies an allusion to Plutarch's "Agis" (Schoeck 1956, pp. 277-78). Second, the humanistic interpreters have narrowed the spectrum of possible ironic readings of *Utopia* by showing that most of the social, political, and religious ideas of the book were regarded with genuine approval by More. This fact is implicit in the large number of parallels that has been adduced between ideas in *Utopia* and those espoused by More in others of his works, or attributed to him by close acquaintances. A passage in More's Letter to a Monk (1519-20), for example, notes that God originally "instituted all things in common" and that Christ "made the attempt to recall mortals again from what was private to what was common" (trans. Surtz 1957a, p. 175).[8] More goes on to comment, in a way that reminds us of Hythloday's closing remarks (*Ut.*, pp. 243-45), on the fact that

> our fallen human nature . . . [is] desperately in love with its own private pursuits to the detriment of the common cause; that fact is everywhere obvious. Everyone loves his own premises, his own money; everyone is interested only in his own profession, or his own corporation; anything at all which we can call our own attracts our attentions to itself and away from common interests. (*Sel. Let.*, p. 130; *Cor.*, pp. 195-96)

Surtz (1957a, p. 79) remarks the striking similarities between passages in More's letter to William Gonell (1518?) and the views of the Utopians on true and false pleasures:

> warn my children . . . not to be dazzled at the sight of gold; not to lament that they do not possess what they er-

---

[8] Elizabeth F. Rogers, in More's *Selected Letters*, gives a very different translation: "God foresaw many problems in decreeing that all things were to be a matter of common interest; so too did Christ when He in turn endeavored to urge men to turn away from provincial interests back to universal interests" (pp. 129-30). Cf. *Correspondence*, p. 195: "Multum prouidit Deus, cum omnia institueret communia, multum Christus cum in commune conatus est rursus a priuato reuocare mortales."

roneously admire in others; not to think more of themselves for gaudy trappings, nor less for want of them; . . . to put virtue in the first place, learning in the second; and in their studies to esteem most whatever may teach them piety towards God, charity to all, and Christian humility in themselves. By such means they will receive from God the reward of an innocent life, and in the assured expectation of it, will view death without horror. (trans. Surtz 1957a, p. 79; *Cor.*, p. 122; cf. *Ut.*, pp. 167-71)

Erasmus' letter to Ulrich von Hutten of 23 July 1519, which contains a biographical sketch of More, is another valuable document in this connection. Erasmus says that More, like the Utopians, prefers "to dress simply and does not wear silk or purple or gold chains, excepting where it would not be decent not to wear them." Like them, too, he is averse to "cards and gambling, and the other games with which the ordinary run of men of rank are used to kill time"; yet also like them, he is "otherwise . . . by no means averse to all sources of innocent pleasure, even to the appetite" (trans. Flower, pp. 233, 234; *EE*, 4:15, 16; cf. *Ut.*, pp. 167, 129, 145). Such parallels, which can be multiplied indefinitely, render untenable the interpretation of the account of Utopia as merely a satire of a "repellent" state (Dorsch, p. 362) and do considerable damage to the view of *Utopia* as an exposé of the folly of "radical idealism."[9]

Moreover, one of the most important accomplishments of recent scholarship, Hexter's reconstruction of the stages of More's composing *Utopia*, allows us a perspective on the book that was denied to all More's earlier readers except his close associates. Starting from Erasmus' remark that More wrote the second part of *Utopia* first,[10] Hexter asked what, precisely, the later-written

[9] It is also possible to multiply quotations that suggest that More disapproved of various Utopian practices (see, e.g., Dorsch). This fact would constitute a problem if one were attempting to prove that Utopia is More's ideal commonwealth. But I am here interested in showing only that Utopia embodies at least some of More's own ideals and practices.

[10] Erasmus to Hutten (23 July 1519): "He had written the second book first

segment included. The answer cannot be simply Book I. The opening pages of this book form in effect an introduction to Book II, which must always have had some such introduction, since it assumes the reader's familiarity with "Raphael" and with the occasion of his monologue (1952, pp. 15-18). In fact, there is strong internal evidence to suggest that the beginning of the later-written segment comes in the passage that leads into the debate on councilorship. This passage concludes the narrator's initial summary of Hythloday's account of his travels, and it appears to be designed to funnel directly into the description of Utopia:

> What he said he saw in each place would be a long tale to unfold and is not the purpose of this work. Perhaps on another occasion we shall tell his story, . . . above all, those wise and prudent provisions which he noticed anywhere among nations living together in a civilized way. . . .
>
> To be sure, . . . he rehearsed not a few points from which . . . [we] may take example. . . . These instances, as I said, I must mention on another occasion. Now I intend to relate merely what he told us of the manners and customs of the Utopians. . . . (*Ut.*, pp. 53-55)

As Hexter argues, the fact that the last sentence now suddenly changes direction—"first, however, giving the talk which drew and led him on to mention that commonwealth"—together with the fact that Hythloday in the ensuing debate *does* describe "wise and prudent provisions which he noticed" among other nations, suggests that at this point More opened a seam in an earlier form of his work to insert new material (1952, pp. 18-21).[11] The validity of the claim seems incontestable: More's patchwork here is quite crude.

---

in his leisure hours, and added the first book on the spur of the moment later, when the occasion offered" (trans. Flower, p. 238; *EE*, 4:21: "Secundum librum prius scripserat per ocium, mox per occasionem primum adiecit ex tempore").

[11] Hexter acknowledges (1952, p. 14n; *Ut.*, p. xxn) that his argument had been anticipated by Hermann Oncken (1922b, pp. 11*-12*).

Hexter also shows that at least a portion of the brief conclusion (*Ut.*, pp. 245-47) that follows the peroration (pp. 237-45) of Hythloday's monologue in Book II must form part of the later-written segment. In this section, More says he refrained from challenging Hythloday's ideas partly because he remembered that Hythloday had censured "others on account of their fear that they might not appear to be wise enough, unless they found some fault to criticize in other men's discoveries" (p. 245). But Hythloday had reprehended this failing "at a point somewhat *after*" the seam in Book I (1952, p. 26).

Hexter recapitulates and extends his argument in the Yale edition. Here he points out that there is some reason for thinking that Hythloday's peroration forms part of the later-written segment:

> Its tone . . . as well as its intensity is more in harmony with the Dialogue [of Book I] . . . than with the Discourse [of Book II]. Indeed if we read *only* the somewhat diffuse and rambling, occasionally gay and sportive Discourse we are not wholly prepared for the sharp focus, the consistently intense tone, the steady drive of the peroration. Only because we have read Book I and thus have already become accustomed to the forcefulness and firmness of Hythlodaeus' social grasp, do we sense no dissonance between the peroration and the rest of *Utopia*.[12] (p. xxi)

[12] It is not necessary to endorse Hexter's description of Book II in order to feel that his point about the similarity of tone between the dialogue of Book I and the peroration of Book II is valid.

I have suppressed by elision one of Hexter's subdivisions of the text—"the exordium [*Ut.*, pp. 103-9] which concludes Book I and introduces the Discourse in Book II" (p. xx)—since the analytic separation of these pages from what precedes them seems artificial. I have also declined to follow Hexter in calling the dialogue of Book I a "Dialogue of Counsel," since I think this term specifies only one, and not the central one, of the concerns of the section (see Chap. 2).

In this second discussion of the matter Hexter detected yet another seam in Book I. More, having already treated the subject of counsel in the first addition to the earlier-written segment, subsequently became interested in the subject of

One should add that *Utopia* includes, in addition to Books I and II, a third section, and that this section was apparently written last of all. The prefatory Letter to Giles must be regarded as an integral part of *Utopia*, since it opens the fiction of the book by giving the initial characterizations of the main speakers and the first references to the island of Utopia.[13] The letter to Erasmus (3 September 1516) that accompanied the manuscript of *Utopia* suggests that this preface was the final addition: "I am sending you my *Nowhere*. . . . I have added a prefatory epistle to my friend, Peter" (*Sel. Let.*, p. 73; *EE*, 2:339: "Nvsqvamam nostram . . . ad te mitto: praescripsi epistolam ad Petrum meum").

The composition of *Utopia*, then, fell into two discrete phases. In phase one, More produced an ur-*Utopia*, which he evidently regarded as a complete work, and which included an introduction more or less like the opening pages of Book I, the discourse of Utopia, and some sort of peroration and conclusion, perhaps considerably different from those in the present form of the book. At some later time, More added the dialogue of Book I, revised, however extensively, the peroration and conclusion of Book II, and wrote the Letter to Giles.

"the condition of England": "so again he opened a seam in his book—this time in the Dialogue of Counsel—to insert an addition, the dialogue on the condition of England" (p. xxxviii). (The section referred to is Hythloday's account of the conversation at Morton's table [pp. 59-87].) It is difficult to understand why Hexter thought this hypothesis necessary or how he imagined it was sufficiently supported (cf. Miller 1965-66, p. 306). Although this section of Book I is formally discontinuous with its context—being a dialogue within a dialogue—it embodies a kind of discontinuity that is twice repeated—in Hythloday's accounts of a meeting of the French privy council and the council of "some king or other" (*Ut.*, pp. 87-97). More important, the episode is thematically continuous with its context. Like the two reported council meetings, it is introduced explicitly as an illustration of the validity of Hythloday's claims about councilors and kings, which launch the debate of Book I (pp. 57-59). In this case, Hythloday means to illustrate the self-serving sycophancy and conservatism of councilors: "Such proud, ridiculous, and obstinate prejudices I have encountered often in other places and once in England too. . . ." (p. 59).

[13] In the first edition, the letter is headed "Prefatio in opus de optimo reipublicae statu" (*Ut.*, p. 38n).

This reconstruction of the composition of *Utopia* provides valuable clues to interpretation. In the first place, as Hexter notes, it makes it more plausible that the interpretive problems of the book stem in part from defects of coherence:

> Critics have tended to see in the published book a unified literary design, and to treat it as if it were the consistent working out of a preconceived plan; but our breakdown of its construction suggests another possibility. The part of *Utopia* that More composed first is itself a consistent, coherent, and practically complete literary work. This implies—what I believe to be true—that in More's original intent the first-written part of *Utopia* . . . *was* a finished work, that only . . . [later] did he feel impelled to add anything to it, that the published version of *Utopia* falls into two parts which represent two different and separate sets of intention on the part of the author. (1952, pp. 27-28)

Indeed, in *More's "Utopia"* Hexter offers a thoroughly disintegrative reading—one that has been widely accepted (cf. Bradshaw, p. 1). The earlier- and later-written sections of the book make up "a hodgepodge of discourse and dialogue" (Hexter 1952, p. 27). The transition at the end of the inserted dialogue is as shoddy as that at its beginning: Hythloday "suddenly takes off at an angle from the course he had set in his previous remarks" and "abruptly launches . . . into a eulogy of the community of all things as practiced in Utopia" (pp. 22, 24). These stylistic flaws are explained as consequences of disunified substance. The dialogue "disturbs the esthetic unity" of the book because its "impulsion . . . was external, extrinsic to the work itself" (p. 29). The abrupt transition at the end of the dialogue was necessary "to allow Hythloday to come around to the point from which he was diverted many pages earlier" (p. 25). In the remainder of his book, Hexter goes on to specify the different impulsions of the two sections. The discourse was the product of a period of leisure in the Netherlands, when More was moved to consider large questions of the nature of the truly Christian state. The impulsion of the dialogue was Wolsey's offer of a place on Henry's council, which provoked an internal debate in More to which he gave expression in the debate on counsel.[14]

In the Yale edition Hexter downplays the theme of disunity. The episode at Morton's is still a "digression" (p. xx), the discourse of Utopia still "wanders discursively" (p. xxxix), but at least all the individual sections except the discourse—even, surprisingly, the dialogue with its digression—are said to be unified (ibid.). The book as a whole, however, is still regarded as the incongruous result of two separate and unrelated impulsions. Perforce, the greatness of such a book "lies not in its harmony but in its intensity" (p. xxvii).

But the charge of disunity remains to be proved. It is true that the later-written portion of *Utopia* reflects More's immediate concerns at the time when he wrote it, and that these concerns must have been different in part from those of the period of the earlier-written portion. But this fact, which would help to account for a disunified book, does not necessitate one. The concerns of different periods may be, and often have been, integrated perfectly in books a long time in the making. Nor does the fact that individual sections of *Utopia* are themselves unified and able to stand alone as important treatments of their subjects imply that these sections cannot fit together to form a unified whole. And the carelessness of the narrative transition at the beginning of the dialogue of Book I does not imply that the materials thus joined do not belong together. Moreover, the other stylistic flaws that Hexter cites may turn out not to be flaws at all if one correctly understands the argument of the book. We must still, then, take as our working assumption that More knew what he was doing,

[14] Jerry Mermel's recent study of the process of More's entry into royal service shows that "early in his career More had committed himself to an active public life, that his actions during the period in which he was at work on *Utopia* indicate not so much an aversion to court service as a serious and interested consideration of it, and finally, that his decision to become a member of Henry VIII's government came within a few months after he had completed *Utopia* in 1516" (p. 54). See also Elton 1972, pp. 87-92.

that if he reopened a completed book he did so to make it better, not to conflate it with a different one.

The second interpretive clue that Hexter derives from his reconstruction in fact suggests how this may be the case. This clue lies in the realization that the later-written segment of *Utopia* represents, at least in part, More's second thoughts about the earlier-written segment:

> In a loose sense the part of any book which its author writes first becomes the milieu of what he writes later. In the *Utopia*, however, this is the case in a peculiar and exceptional way. The peculiarity results from the odd circumstances of the composition of *Utopia*. . . . From these circumstances it follows that More had the opportunity to reflect on the substance of the Discourse on Utopia for a while before he wrote the Dialogue . . . and the peroration. Indeed in order to decide how he wanted to integrate the Dialogue with the Discourse, he had to reflect considerably on the latter. The sum of the matter is that those points of view, opinions, modes of thinking and feeling that occur in both the Discourse and the Dialogue cannot be dismissed as passing fancies or ill-considered trifles. If they do not embody More's ultimate convictions and concerns, they do embody his deepest convictions and concerns as of 1515-16. (*Ut.*, p. xxvi; cf. p. cxxii, and 1952, pp. 35-43)

These observations call attention to the interpretive significance of pairs of related passages in Book I and Book II. Taken together with the fact that More placed the largest chunk of the later-written segment—the dialogue—*before* the account of Utopia, they suggest another important interpretive guide: whatever else the dialogue may be, it was evidently intended as an *introduction* to the account of Utopia. This is, indeed, the function assigned the dialogue by the narrator (in terms consistent with the decorum of the fiction): he will include only that part of the talk with Hythloday "which drew and led him on to mention" Utopia (p. 55). In turn, the Letter to Giles, written last of all and placed first, is presumably the kind of foreword that Eric Erikson characterizes as enabling "an author to put his afterthoughts first. Looking back on what he has written, he can try to tell the reader what lies before him" (p. 15). Such considerations make it seem likely that examining the sections of *Utopia* consecutively—that is, in the order in which More meant them to be read—is the best critical procedure.

Chapter
One
❧
The Letter to Giles

What does the Letter to Giles tell us about the book it introduces? First, it suggests strongly, in every aspect of its substance and manner, that *Utopia* belongs to the tradition of Renaissance humanism. The letter is addressed to the humanist Peter Giles, a friend of Erasmus. Its Latin is humanist Latin; its informal, semi-fictional mode is characteristic of the humanist approach to philosophical topics. The letter takes much of its substance from standard humanist *topoi*. Claiming, especially in a dedicatory letter, that a work was composed in odd hours or inopportune circumstances had been a convention (sometimes corresponding to facts) of humanist prose since Petrarch's "Ascent of Mont Ventoux"—a virtuoso piece that Petrarch claims he scribbled while waiting for supper in an inn after a long day of mountain-climbing (p. 46)—and his treatise *On His Own Ignorance and That of Many Others*—supposedly written "quickly on a hasty journey" (p. 47). Erasmus begins his dedicatory letter to More in *The Praise of Folly* with the same *topos*—he composed the book on horseback—and later has Folly mock this convention, as she refers to "the common run of orators[1] . . . [who], when they bring out a speech they have been working on for thirty whole years, and sometimes not their own at all, will swear it was written in three days, for pastime, or even that they merely dictated it"

[1] "Orators," like "rhetoricians" in the passage quoted below, refers particularly to humanists—as the allusion to these rhetoricians' knowledge of Greek confirms. On rhetoric as the central professional skill of the humanists, see Kristeller 1961, pp. 10-11.

(p. 9). More's highminded identification of himself with learning (*Ut.*, p. 39) and the corresponding elitist contempt of the views of the crowd (pp. 43-45) also embody favorite humanist *topoi*.[2] The humorous Greek coinages in the letter—Utopia, Hythlodaeus, Amaurotum, Anydrus—constitute a stylistic feature associated specifically with the humanism of the later Renaissance, being an affectation that reflects the fact that knowledge of Greek was only in this period becoming widespread among humanists. Erasmus exemplifies this habit in *The Praise of Folly* and, through Folly, comments shrewdly on it:

> It has seemed well, you note, to imitate the rhetoricians of our time, who believe themselves absolutely to be gods if they can show themselves bilingual (like a horse-leech), and account it a famous feat if they can weave a few Greekish words, like inlay work, ever and anon into their Latin orations, even if at the moment there is no place for them. (pp. 10-11)

At the same time that these Grecisms serve to establish More's affiliation with humanism, they clarify the nature of his intended audience. Greek coinages (like the constant indirect classical allusions in the body of *Utopia*) are included for the sake of those readers—exclusively humanists—who can understand them.[3] The

---

[2] On other humanist elements in this self-characterization, see Weiner, pp. 4-6. See also Nagel, pp. 177-79. On More's humanism, see Nelson; Sylvester 1966; Schoeck 1967; Kristeller 1980.

[3] Cf. More's elaborately ironic second letter to Giles (printed in the 1517 edition), where he says that "if I had determined to write about the commonwealth" in fictional form,

> I should certainly have tempered the fiction so that, if I wanted to abuse the ignorance of common folk, I should have prefixed some indications at least for the more learned [*litteratioribus*] to see through our purpose.
>
> Thus, if I had done nothing else than impose names on ruler, river, city, and island such as might suggest to the more learned that the island was nowhere, the city a phantom, the river without water, and the ruler without a people, it would not have been hard to do and would have been much wittier than what I actually did. (*Ut.*, p. 251)

Commenting on the Letter to Giles, Robbin Johnson observes that "unlike many 'political' treatises of the time . . . , *Utopia* is not intended ultimately

knowing, self-congratulatory approbation of the book embodied
in the commendatory letters in the early editions confirms its
impact on this audience. As Folly says, exotic antiquarian references "spread darkness" over the ordinary reader: but "those
who understand will be vastly pleased with themselves" (p. 11).

The letter also contains evidence of another kind that *Utopia*
is a book by a humanist directed primarily to his fellows. In this
letter More has already adopted the pretense that *Utopia* records
conversations with Hythloday. Modern readers have been so
ready to effect the invited suspension of disbelief that they have
failed to recognize that most of what is attributed to Hythloday
here in fiction is to be attributed to More in fact. As a result,
some of what More tells us about the book and his feelings about
it escapes notice.

More says that

> there was no reason for me to take trouble about the style
> of the narrative, seeing that his [Hythloday's] language
> could not be polished. It was, first of all, hurried and im-
> promptu and, secondly, the product of a person who, as
> you know, was not so well acquainted with Latin as with
> Greek. Therefore the nearer my style came to his careless
> simplicity the closer it would be to the truth, for which
> alone I am bound to care under the circumstances and ac-
> tually do care. (p. 39)

The main purpose of this passage is to acknowledge that the
Latinity of the book does not come up to the highest humanist
standards, a purpose that becomes clearer with a sentence a little
farther on: "If it had been required that the matter be written

---

for the instruction of rulers. The subtle revelation of its fictional character
through the names, and the consequent irony which develops, demand an
audience of men trained in literature, acquainted with the classics, and profoundly sensitive to the elusive tone of many of its passages" (p. 12; cf. Herbrüggen, p. 252; Greene and Dolan, pp. 154-55; Manuel and Manuel, p.
131; Kinney 1979, p. 34). Judith Jones (1979) observes that "Erasmus's letters
of 1516 and 1517 are full of comments encouraging—even begging—his
friends to contribute letters to More's book, then to read it and share it with
their friends" (p. 60).

down not only accurately but eloquently, I could not have performed the task with any amount of time or application."[4] The remark that Hythloday was "not so well acquainted with Latin as with Greek," in addition to its function in characterizing Hythloday, offers a respectable excuse for the lack of polish of the book's style: the narrative really *was* "the product of a person who" had been immersed in Greek studies. In fact, More's only substantial publication (apart from the *Life of Pico*) before *Utopia* had been the translations from Lucian that were printed with those of Erasmus.

Deprecation of one's style is another humanist convention, and often an especially pained display of it is designed to call attention to the excellence of the style, as in the disclaimer that Poggio attaches to a collection of his letters: "This book, although it may seem to represent a man who is unlearned and of no great account, . . . may be . . . a sort of incentive . . . by which you may be stimulated to greater endeavors, that is, to imitating the literary style of the ancients from which I am very far away" (p. 22). But in More's case the deprecation surely reflects genuine anxiety. He was, after all, a provincial humanist in "ultima Britannia" (Catullus XXIX.4) and nervous like all provincials in offering himself to the great world. His nervousness about the book (presumably on several scores) is also recorded in a number of letters written around the time of its issue (*Cor.*, nos. 20, 22, 26, 28-32, 34).[5] Moreover, Erasmus' remark that there is some "unevenness" in the style of *Utopia* (Erasmus to Hutten, *EE*, 4:21), together with the list of More's solecisms and barbarisms compiled by his enemy Brixius, confirm that More had reason for uneasiness in this matter.[6]

---

[4] These allusions to the ineloquent style of the book may also be intended, as Heiserman argues (p. 166), to suggest a link with satire, which traditionally employs a low style. But Surtz points out that in fact More "uses few 'low' words, and never without necessity" (*Ut.*, Appendix B, p. 582).

[5] Cf., e.g., *Sel. Let.*, p. 73 (*EE*, 2:339): "I am sending you my *Nowhere*, which is nowhere well written."

[6] Erasmus offered another, more favorable, assessment of More's style in

The letter tells us, then, the kind of reader for whom *Utopia* was designed. This information is significant for interpretation in two ways. First, it suggests the range of learning we need in order to be adequate readers: familiarity with the classical, patristic, and Renaissance books that form the common intellectual property of humanism and with the ideas and concerns that characterize the humanists, especially those of More's generation and the immediately preceding period. Second, the fact that *Utopia* is addressed primarily to a humanist audience implies that we should anticipate and accept as themes of the book only those that More could plausibly be expected to address to such an audience, and that we should be correspondingly reluctant to accept any reading of *Utopia* that suggests that the book is designed to tell humanists either things that we cannot imagine them (or More) being interested in or things that they already knew (though, indeed, works of less serious humanists often simply repeat humanist commonplaces).

Unfortunately, almost all criticism of *Utopia* embodies such implausibilities. In particular, the most influential recent commentators, the humanistic interpreters, tell us that More is rehashing, albeit in eloquent and mystifyingly indirect form, the shared political ideals of Erasmian humanists. *Utopia* is seen, that is, as essentially a *speculum principis*, a book more or less identical in substance to such works as Erasmus' *Education of a Christian Prince*—although in form it is (unlike the relentlessly simple and direct *specula*) obviously designed for an audience of sophisticated literary scholars. Seebohm had in fact characterized *Utopia* as having "a very similar object" to that of *The Education*

Ciceronianus (p. 104). On More's style in relation to the humanist norm, and on Brixius' censures, see *Ut.*, Appendix B, pp. 579-82. "Three months before the completion of the *Utopia*, Erasmus had praised More's growing powers of expression . . . [*EE*, 2:243]. In his reply, More shows great embarrassment. His legal affairs allow him no time for thought or composition. Erasmus is inviting him to keep silent if he continues to weigh every word and to estimate his rhetorical abilities, that is, to count his solecisms and barbarisms [ibid., 259]" (p. 579).

of a Christian Prince (p. 229; cf. p. 217), and there are like statements in the works of most of his successors. Caspari, for example, says that "in *Utopia*, More drew a picture clearer and fuller than anything his friend Erasmus had produced, of a humanistic state, of a society which was inspired by the central ideals they held in common" (p. 90; cf. pp. 91, 101, 117), while Schoeck tells us that the purpose of *Utopia* is "the creation of a model or mirror," "a model by reference to which reforms might be achieved" (1969, pp. 285, 287). Skinner says that the interpretation of *Utopia* "simply as a contribution to a more general 'programme' of humanist reform . . . helps to capture much of the spirit of More's book," although in some respects More's pattern of "a virtuous and harmonious commonwealth" differs from the prescriptions of other northern humanists (1978, pp. 255-56, 261; cf. Elton 1977, pp. 43-44; Bradshaw, p. 20).

It is a little surprising that these writers have been so pleased to conclude that *Utopia* is closely affiliated with the *speculum principis*, a genre that is accurately characterized by Hexter as "wretched and dreary" (1952, p. 103). In a period that witnessed the brilliant beginnings of modern positive theory, the late *specula* (except for Machiavelli's radical reformulation) appear, to historians of the development of political thought, as uninteresting survivals of an outmoded tradition. And indeed it is in this way that *Utopia* is usually regarded by these historians (with the notable exception of Skinner), who share with the humanistic interpreters the view that *Utopia* is only a sort of disguised *speculum*. J. W. Allen allots *Utopia* four pages in his *History of Political Thought in the Sixteenth Century*. He is impressed, as almost all readers are, by the descriptive and analytic power of Hythloday's account of England in Book I, but he views Book II as only a "fairy tale" (p. 154) pieced together of ideals that More knew would remain unrealized and whimsical elements "calculated rather to amuse than to suggest" (p. 156). George H. Sabine's admirable *History of Political Theory*, the standard survey, devotes two pages to More (as compared to twenty-two to Machiavelli). Sabine also praises the account of England in Book I, but "this attack upon the economics of business enterprise . . . was really motivated by a longing for the past" (p. 436)—a view that reflects the influence of Chambers. Although *Utopia* embodies "a worthy moral idea," the book is (as to Allen) "pitiable," expressing "the reasonableness and open-mindedness of humanism, and withal the futility of a moral aspiration that cannot make its account with brute fact" (p. 437). *Utopia* is thus "an isolated and unimportant episode in the political philosophy of its time. It illustrated rather the dying utterance of an old ideal than an authentic voice of the age that was coming into being."

Fortunately for More's reputation as a political theorist, the view of *Utopia* as a disguised humanist *speculum* is untenable, not only because (as we shall find in Chapter Three) the reading of Book II that it entails is rendered insupportable by discrepancies between Utopian practices and humanist ideals, but also because it is incompatible with the fact that *Utopia* is addressed to a humanist audience. Why should More write a book to tell his fellow humanists what they already knew and to recommend to them what they already approved? Indeed, the very means used to establish that *Utopia* is a restatement of humanist orthodoxy—citing the numerous parallels between ideas in *Utopia* and those in other humanist works—is self-defeating, since the more these ideas are shown to be humanist commonplaces, the less plausible it appears that so serious and brilliant a thinker as More should write a book merely for the purpose of reiterating them. To be sure, the humanistic interpreters sometimes claim that More's intended audience is some other group, even though their own researches clearly imply that *Utopia* is designed primarily for humanists. Although Surtz at one point says that "*Utopia* is . . . addressed to humanists filled with dislike and disdain for the old order," and that "Hythlodaeus is giving their common idealism classic utterance" (*Ut.*, pp. cxlvii, cxlviii), he also constantly echoes Chambers's thesis that *Utopia* is designed to move Europeans in general, and their leaders in particular, to reform (e.g., 1957a, p. 199; 1957b, pp. 7, 19-20). Similarly, R. P. Adams says that *Utopia* is "a 'mirror' not merely for a magistrate but for all Englishmen" (1962, p. 141), while Skinner links *Utopia* with Italian "civic humanist" works addressed "not merely to the leaders of society, but also to the whole body of the citizens" (1978, p. 215). But if *Utopia* is addressed to this less erudite audience, why did More make it so difficult, so cliquish—in a word, why did he aim it so far over the heads of most Europeans and their rulers? Humanist rhetorician that he is, More is quite conscious of the need to choose a literary mode appropriate to his intended audience. When he addressed a more general audience, as in his defenses of humanist learning or in the English version of *The History of King Richard III*, he used a different style and often a different language—the vernacular (which is also employed, for the same reason, in the civic humanist treatises cited by Skinner).

Rejecting the idea that *Utopia* is a disguised rehash of humanist prescriptions, we are forced to confront afresh the fundamental interpretive question about the book: if it is political theory (and yet is not simply a summary of More's and other humanists' political ideals), what kind of political theory *is* it? The Letter to Giles, which presumably is designed to tell what lies before us, offers two clues, both, however, tantalizingly enigmatic.

First, just as the letter suggests an aspect of *Utopia* about which More was especially anxious (its Latinity), so also it suggests an aspect in which he took particular pride. To apprehend this suggestion, we must again apply what More says about Hythloday to himself.

The letter begins with an apology for More's delay in completing the book. Giles will be surprised that a book that he "looked for . . . within a month and a half" has arrived only after almost a year:

> Certainly you know that I was relieved of all the labor of gathering materials [*inueniendi laborem*] for the work and that I had to give no thought at all to their arrangement

[*dispositione*]. I had only to repeat what in your company I heard Raphael relate.[7] (p. 39)

Hexter argues that this passage tells us that Book II and its introduction were essentially complete when More returned from the Netherlands in 1515, and that Book I was an afterthought (1952, pp. 28-29; *Ut.*, p. xxii).[8] But the primary intention of the passage is surely to remind Giles and other readers that a good deal of reflection and much collecting and arranging of materials from many sources *were* necessary in order to turn into a book the conversations with Giles that presumably gave rise to *Utopia*. More again alludes to this fact, in the same indirect fashion, a few lines farther on: if he were not simply reproducing Hythloday's remarks (which of course he is not), "the gathering or the arrangement [*uel excogitatio, uel oeconomia*] of the materials could have required a good deal of both time and application even from a talent neither the meanest nor the most ignorant." There is a related boast a little later. Asking Giles "to remind me of anything that has escaped me," More goes on to say that "in this respect I do not entirely distrust myself. (I only wish I were as good in intelligence and learning as I am not altogether deficient in memory!)" (p. 41). In addition to its function in establishing fictional verisimilitude (rendering it plausible that More should recall Hythloday's talk more or less verbatim), this

---

[7] *Inventio* and *dispositio* are the first steps of rhetorical composition. "Excogitatio" and "oeconomia" in the passage quoted below are more or less equivalent to *inventio* and *dispositio*, though *oeconomia* includes style in addition to arrangement (Quintilian III.iii.9; Kennedy, pp. 304, 314).

[8] Heiserman suggests that the passage implies that More did not actually write down *any* part of *Utopia* until he returned to London: "More's use of . . . [*inventio* and *dispositio*] controverts the tradition that he wrote Book II . . . in Flanders; in fact, he claims to have explored the idea and outlined its 'disposition' in Flanders, and to have written it down in London" (p. 166). The letter does not, as Heiserman claims, demand this conclusion, but neither does it preclude it. In any case, it remains certain—from Erasmus' testimony and the existence of the compositional seam near the beginning of Book I— that the *order* of composition was as Hexter says (above, pp. 11-13).

remark is designed to call attention to the astonishing powers of memory that the eclectic and synthetic procedure of the book illustrates.[9]

At this point, it is impossible to know just what to make of these hints. Is More merely boasting about his accomplishment in two parts of rhetorical composition (having conceded his deficiency in the third—style), or is he, more interestingly, suggesting that there is something truly special about the way learning is used in his book? The latter possibility seems strengthened by the fact that the prefatory contributions of Giles, the commentator of greatest authority,[10] clearly hint at the importance of *method* in *Utopia*. In his Utopian hexastich Giles emphasizes the connection between *Utopia* and the *Republic* and calls attention to an advance embodied in More's book: Utopia is "a rival of Plato's republic, perhaps even a victor over it," because "what he [Plato] has delineated in words" Utopia alone has "exhibited in men and resources and laws of surpassing excellence" (p. 21). This is praise, within the fictional decorum of *Utopia*, not just for More's conclusions but, especially, for his way of presenting them (cf. Fleisher, pp. 3-4). Similarly, in Giles's "translation" of a "quatrain in the Utopian vernacular" the personified Utopia draws a distinction between the usual methods of political philosophy and More's method: "Alone of all lands, without the aid of abstract philosophy, I have represented for mortals the philosophical city" (p. 19). (Moreover, the poem acknowledges that Utopia, though

---

[9] Sylvester demonstrates the power of More's memory, and quotes a contemporary tribute to it, in his Introduction to *The History of King Richard III*, pp. lxxxv-lxxxvii. Erasmus told Hutten that More "has a present wit, always flying ahead, and a ready memory; and having all this ready to hand, he can promptly and unhesitatingly produce whatever the subject or occasion requires" (trans. Flower, p. 238; *EE*, 4:21). See also Nagel, pp. 178-79.

[10] The Letter to Giles and the opening pages of Book I suggest that *Utopia* grew out of conversations with Giles. In his letter commending *Utopia* to Busleyden, Giles says More's book sets the island of Utopia before his eyes more vividly "than when, being as much a part of the conversation as More himself, I heard Raphael Hythlodaeus' own words sounding in my ears" (*Ut.*, p. 21).

a very good commonwealth, is not a perfect one: "Ungrudgingly do I share my benefits with others; undemurringly do I adopt whatever is better from others.")

Second, the letter indicates the literary mode of the book, which is a curious one. On the one hand, the book is a fiction, and one in which the author goes to such lengths to establish verisimilitude that it may appear for a moment not to be fiction at all. On the other hand, the elaborately-established verisimilitude is undercut even as it is established, so that the fiction mocks its own pretense of factuality.

The peculiar nature of the letter in this regard emerges when we compare it with the letter to More that prefaces *The Praise of Folly*. In this letter Erasmus has not yet assumed the pretense that the following oration is delivered by Folly. Discussing the ensuing work from outside, he acknowledges explicitly that it is a *declamatio*, a fictitious speech (p. 2). But in the Letter to Giles More claims that *Utopia* records an actual conversation and offers elaborate circumstantial details to reinforce this claim. Raphael has already a definite character: his speech is hurried and informal; he knows Greek (the language of philosophy) better than Latin; he may be irritated that More is publishing a book about a subject that is rightfully his own (*Ut.*, pp. 39, 43). Three real people— More, Giles, John Clement—heard his discourse. Two of them have different recollections about one point in it (p. 41). An English theologian is anxious to go as a missionary to the new island (p. 43).[11] Moreover, Raphael's comic surname is withheld in the first part of the letter, as is the name of the island he visited.[12] If it were not for the presence of these names on the title page and in the commendatory letters, the reader might well

[11] This detail should surely be taken as part of the fiction—a characteristic humanist gibe at scholastic theologians or an allusion to the joking proposal of some friend (cf. *Ut.*, p. 292n)—rather than (as it nearly always is taken) as a record of a real occurrence.

[12] On the thoroughly positive associations of his given name, which suggests, by linking him with the archangel Raphael, that he is a guide and healer, see McCutcheon 1969 (cf. Chap. 2, n. 85).

at first believe that the book recorded an actual conversation about a real place.[13]

Near the middle of the letter, however, we come to a curious passage that at once contributes to the circumstantiality that helps create the verisimilitude of the fiction and to undermining that verisimilitude. More and John Clement remember differently one point in Raphael's discourse: how wide did he say the river bridge is in the principal city of the new island? Is it three hundred paces or five hundred? But in the very sentence in which this question is introduced, we learn that Raphael's last name is Hythlodaeus, that the island he visited is "nowhere," and that the city through which this "waterless" river flows is itself only a "mirage" (*Ut.*, pp. 41, 392n, 388n).

The mode of this work of political theory, then, is not merely fiction but self-mocking fiction. As in the case of More's oblique boasts about the invention and disposition of materials in the book, we cannot at this point know how to use what the letter tells us—in this case, what to make of More's choice of such an eccentric mode. To be sure, the very fact that the carefully-created and carefully-undermined verisimilitude produces an enigma suggests a partial explanation for this choice. Enigmatic indirection was highly fashionable among More's fellow humanists and, apparently, constitutional in More himself.[14] In the pref-

---

[13] As Schoeck points out (1969, p. 629n), the careful establishment of verisimilitude was in accordance with Erasmus' advice: "If entirely fictional narratives are introduced as if they were true because they will help us to get our point across, we must make them as much like the real thing as possible" (*De copia*, p. 634).

[14] Cf. the well-known remark in the *Dialogue Concerning Heresies*, where the messenger says of More that "ye vse . . . to loke so sadly whan ye mene merely that many tymes men doubte whyther ye speke in sporte whan ye mene good ernest" (pp. 68-69). See also Stapleton, p. 121.

Edgar Wind probes the significance of paradox and irony in humanist writing. "Unless we allow for a certain ingredient of deliberate paradox, which qualified the imitation of antiquity by Renaissance humanists, we may misjudge altogether the atmosphere in which the pagan mysteries were revived. They were sponsored by men of letters who had learned from Plato that the deepest things are best spoken of in a tone of irony" (p. 236).

atory letter of *The Praise of Folly*, Erasmus suggests that his own elaborately indirect book will be especially acceptable to More, who is "wont to enjoy to the full jokes of this kind, that is, those that are somewhat learned" (p. 1). The Letter to Giles includes a passage that makes the usual humanist distinction between the elite tastes of humanist readers and the variously crude palates of others, which include those incapable of savoring literary wit: "This fellow is so grim that he will not hear of a joke; that fellow is so insipid that he cannot endure wit" (*Ut.*, p. 45).

But the particular kind of joke that More chooses to indulge in in the letter acts not only to create a piquant enigma for sophisticated readers but also to dissociate him to some extent from his principal speaker and principal subject.[15] More's fiction is detailed and careful, but he holds it at arm's length. The reader who perceives this distance is of course invited through it to adopt a similar attitude toward Hythloday and Utopia. The fact that Utopia is nowhere and its spokesman an expert in nonsense is bound to make us wary of that commonwealth. But the enigma of why More chooses to establish this distance must remain unresolved until we reach Book II.

[15] On jokes in the letter and elsewhere in *Utopia*, and on various inconsistencies in Hythloday's account of Utopia (which, if intentional, must also have been designed to dissociate More from Utopia and its spokesman), see Heiserman, p. 171; Nagel; Kinney 1976, pp. 427-28; and R. M. Adams's annotations to the Norton edition, *passim*. It is unwise to lay much interpretive stress on inconsistent details, since they may reflect not intention but oversight. Plato's account of the Republic is full of them, but no one, as far as I know, has suggested that this fact implies that his design of an ideal *polis* is not seriously intended.

Chapter
Two
Europe

I

Book I of *Utopia* opens with a brief account of More's mission to the Netherlands. The passage serves to distribute compliments: to Henry VIII ("a model monarch" [p. 47]), Cuthbert Tunstal, and Georges de Themsecke, head of the delegation from the Prince of Castile. Considering what *Utopia* goes on to suggest about kings and councilors in general, More perhaps felt it especially important to compliment the particular king and councilors with whom he was personally associated. An opening in these terms also serves, like the Letter to Giles, to increase the verisimilitude of the ensuing fiction and thus to enhance its interest. Moreover, the passage, by prefacing the conversation with Hythloday with an allusion to actual European politics—"certain weighty matters" disputed between monarchs—helps to create a climate for serious political discussion.

The following passage, on More's introduction to Giles and on Giles's character, serves not only to laud More's friend but also to introduce the first of the three speakers of the ensuing dialogue. Actually, this characterization of Giles does not correspond very well to his figure in the dialogue itself. Here More says of Giles that "in conversation he is so polished and so witty without offense that his delightful society and charming discourse largely took away my nostalgia and made me less conscious than before of the separation from my home, wife, and children" (p. 49).[1] But the Giles of the dialogue says little, and what he says

[1] Cf. the similar characterization of Giles in More's letter to Erasmus, c. 17 Feb. 1516 (*Correspondence of Erasmus*, 3:235; *EE*, 2:197). On Giles's role in *Utopia*, see Bevington, pp. 499-500.

is neither very witty nor very profound. The explanation of this discrepancy lies, presumably, in the fact that in the original version of *Utopia* the portrait of Giles was only the most elaborate of the opening compliments and not a characterization of an interlocutor in a dialogue: in the ur-*Utopia* there *was* no dialogue.

The characterization of the other two speakers involves the same kind of discrepancy. In the case of Hythloday, there is no hint of the problematic aspects of his personality that become apparent in the dialogue. Here, in fact, Hythloday is a completely attractive, if completely stock, figure. His credentials for speaking about politics are, from a humanist point of view, impeccable. Surtz points out that More characterizes Hythloday largely in terms of traditional attributes of the philosopher. The "careless simplicity" of his style, alluded to in the Letter to Giles (p. 39), may reflect Quintilian's recommendation that the philosopher avoid "most of the ornaments of oratory" (p. 290n; *Inst.* XI.i.33). In the present passage, the description of Hythloday shows him to be as unconcerned with appearance as with prose style: he is "a man of advanced years, with sunburnt countenance, a long beard, and a cloak hanging loosely from his shoulders,[2] while his appearance and dress seemed to me to be those of a ship's captain" (p. 49). This description fits Hythloday's actual experience as a voyager, and the long beard, as well as the contempt for externals that the passage suggests, is a stock attribute of the philosopher. His age, too, betokens wisdom. Giles's remarks confirm and supplement the visual image. Hythloday, Giles says, has been a voyager, but his voyaging has not been like that of Palinurus, Aeneas' sleepy pilot, but like that of those students of men and governments, Ulysses and Plato (cf. p. 301n; Baker-Smith, p. 4). We are then hardly surprised when Giles adds that Hythloday has "devoted himself unreservedly to philosophy" (p. 51).[3]

[2] The phrases about Hythloday's beard and cloak are from R. M. Adams's translation (p. 6). Yale has the beard also hanging from Hythloday's shoulder.

[3] At the same time, More presumably does not mean us to forget entirely that Ulysses is also a notorious liar. As W.E.H. Rudat points out (1981a, pp.

Moreover, it is clear that Hythloday embodies a specifically humanist conception of philosophy, like that found in Erasmus' definition at the beginning of *The Education of a Christian Prince*: "By 'philosophy' I do not mean that which disputes concerning the first beginnings, of primordial matter, of motion and infinity, but that which frees the mind from the false opinions and the vicious predilections of the masses and points out a theory of government according to the example of the Eternal Power" (pp. 133-34). As the allusion to his travels tells us, Hythloday's career reflects the humanist ideal of combining contemplation with action and learning with practical experience (cf. Rice). We know from the Letter to Giles that Hythloday also exhibits the linguistic accomplishments of a humanist: he is "no bad Latin scholar, and most learned in Greek" (pp. 49-51). Various details, such as the allusions to Ulysses and to "certain treatises of Seneca and Cicero," suggest that Hythloday's particular field is moral philosophy—the branch of philosophy to which political theory is traditionally attached, and the branch included in the *studia humanitatis*.[4]

But the opening pages of *Utopia* hint at more specific models for Hythloday and his career. The clue to these models lies in Giles's remark that Hythloday's sailing has been like that of Plato. This comment suggests that More's philosophic traveler is based partly on Plato, who, according to Diogenes Laertius (III.6, 18-

41-42), this association is reinforced by the mention, in the same sentence, of Raphael's surname.

[4] Cf. Kristeller 1961, pp. 9-10; 1980, p. 7. Later we learn that Hythloday is contemptuous of scholastic dialectic (*Ut.*, p. 159).

Hythloday's admiration for Cicero and Seneca suggests that some of his moral views derive from Roman Stoicism—a suggestion immediately confirmed by the fact that the "two sayings . . . constantly on his lips" (p. 51) are Stoic (see *Ut.*, p. 303n; Arnold, p. 278) and, as we shall see, confirmed in more important ways in what follows. His opinion that in philosophy "there is nothing valuable in Latin" except works of Cicero and Seneca is echoed in More's Letter to Oxford: "If you leave out Cicero and Seneca, the Romans wrote their philosophy in Greek or translated it from Greek" (*Sel. Let.*, p. 100; *Cor.*, p. 117). See Surtz 1957a, pp. 127-29; *Ut.*, p. 302n.

19), traveled to Cyrene, Italy, and Egypt, and three times to
Sicily.[5] Moreover, there are close parallels to the fictional situation of *Utopia* in Plato's *Sophist*, *Statesman*, and *Laws*. In the
Sophist Theodorus and Theaetetus introduce an "Eleatic Stranger"
to Socrates. The Stranger, whose opinions are clearly Plato's, is
treated with great deference by the other speakers, and he entirely
dominates both the *Sophist* and the ensuing *Statesman*. In the
latter he discusses the best form of government. A similar figure
dominates the *Laws*. Here an "Old Athenian," a visitor to Crete,
is deferred to by two local sages, who question him as to his
views on the perfect constitution. Hythloday is also a "stranger"
(p. 49), newly returned to Europe. His resemblance to Plato's
two travelers is obvious, as is the resemblance between the dramatic situation of *Utopia* and those of the *Statesman* and *Laws*.[6]
In sum, Hythloday seems designed for the role Plato's spokesmen
play in these dialogues: that of a completely reliable commentator
on comparative politics and a highly authoritative political theorist. Presumably this is the simple and straightforward role that
he played in the original form of *Utopia*.[7]

[5] Plato gives a detailed account of his Sicilian experiences in Epistle VII.
(More would not, like many modern scholars [most recently, Ludwig Edel-
stein], have doubted the authenticity of this work.) Hythloday's career was
obviously also influenced by Vespucci's account of his voyages to the New World
(publ. 1507). Cf. Baker-Smith, p. 4: "for Raphael as for Plato, the most
important feature of travel is its power to detach the mind from the pressures
of normal life and focus it on essential forms. Travel to the Americas as described
in Vespucci's *Mundus Novus*, travel to the ancient world made possible in
imagination by the salvage operation of humanism, travel to a realm of pure
ideas supported by a revived platonic philosophy: all these could serve to sharpen
awareness of the discrepancy between individual aspirations and institutional
facts."

[6] For additional parallels between Hythloday and Plato and Plato's spokesmen, see below, pp. 100-2. Baker-Smith (p. 4) compares the opening of More's
dialogue, where the speakers meet after Mass, with that of the *Republic*, where
the speakers assemble after a religious festival in the port of Piraeus. He also
argues plausibly (pp. 13-14) that More's admired Pico may have provided a
model for Hythloday. Cf. *Ut.*, p. 310n.

[7] It is, then, misleading to describe Hythloday as "a version of a conventional

If Hythloday is presented as a bundle of stock attributes, the characterization of More in this passage is much subtler. Since this third speaker in the dialogue is the narrator, he cannot be characterized by direct description. Instead, his character is established by the autobiographical disclosures in the Letter to Giles and the opening of Book I and supplemented by the nature of his responses to Hythloday in the passage just discussed. It is easy to overlook the fact that the passage on Hythloday also characterizes More, but we must remember that this passage, unlike the description of Giles, reflects not More's response to a real person but his imaginary response to a fictitious character: thus not only the terms of the description but also those of the response could be freely chosen and were presumably chosen in accordance with More's purposes.

The view of More that emerges from this passage is not entirely flattering and, as in the cases of Giles and Hythloday, not entirely consistent with the role that he plays in the dialogue. Nor does it consort well with the self-portrait in the Letter to Giles. Again the explanation would seem to lie in the fact that More did not, when he wrote this introductory section, contemplate a dialogue or an elaborate prefatory letter. The delicate self-mockery here, then, was only the kind of joke at his own expense that Erasmus several times inserts into *The Praise of Folly*.

More, says Giles, is "always most greedy to hear" accounts of unknown peoples and lands (p. 49)—indeed, the reception and recapitulation of such an account was his only function in the ur-*Utopia*. But it is also suggested that More is somewhat worldly and snobbish, and that he is apt to leap to conclusions—characteristics not apparent in the dialogue. He responds coolly to Giles's offer to introduce him to this fellow who looks like a sea captain: " 'He would have been very welcome,' said I, 'for your sake.' " Unlike Hythloday, then, More is not uninterested in outward appearances. When Giles tells him that in fact Hythloday

satiric persona: the missionary who returns from a journey through strange places to report the unadorned truth about society, the court, the clergy, the times" (Heiserman, p. 167).

has, as More had inferred, been a voyager, More's response is self-congratulatory—and wrong:

> "Well, then," said I, "my guess was not a bad one. The moment I saw him, I was sure he was a ship's captain."
> "But you are quite mistaken," said he. . . .

But after Giles has clarified what sort of man Hythloday is, More is eager to talk with him, and, following an exchange of civilities, the three adjourn to a garden—the *locus amoenus* of the humanist dialogue—where they sit down to converse.[8]

The dialogue is prefaced by a detailed summary of Hythloday's account of his travels (pp. 51-55). The title page tells us that the book deals with "the best state of a commonwealth"; this passage makes clear that More is particularly interested in the bearing of customs and institutional arrangements on the attainment of that state (cf. Fleisher, p. 8). Hythloday and his companions found "towns and cities and very populous commonwealths with excellent institutions" (p. 53: "oppida atque urbes aiebat reperisse se, ac non pessime institutas magna populorum frequentia respublicas"). It is precisely such "wise and prudent provisions"

---

[8] Cicero's *De oratore* is the prototype of the dialogue in which the speakers are seated in a garden. Cf. Huizinga, *Erasmus of Rotterdam*, p. 104: "The whole Renaissance cherished that wish of reposeful, blithe, and yet serious intercourse of good and wise friends in the cool shade of a house under trees, where serenity and harmony would dwell. . . . In Erasmus's writings that ideal wish ever recurs in the shape of a friendly walk, followed by a meal in a garden-house."

Kinney (1976, pp. 430-31) discerns darker shades in this garden. Hythloday's "discussion with the character-More is . . . surreal: amidst sickness and starvation, poverty and disease, they hold a teatime conversation in a garden which, given the darker tones surrounding their talk and the immensity of the issues at hand, cannot help but remind us of other gardens in literature: Eden, where the language of persuasion initiated the Fall of Man; Vergil's pastoral gardens, unreal because enclosed, shut off from life; medieval gardens, where man's vision of the City of God proved to be only a dream." This is a considerable improvement on More, who says only that "we went off to my house," where "in the garden, on a bench covered with turfs of grass, we sat down to talk together."

("ea . . . . recte prudenterque prouisa") that interest More and Giles, because these institutions contribute to the development of civic virtue:

> on these subjects we eagerly inquired of him, and he no less readily discoursed; but about stale travelers' wonders we were not curious. Scyllas and greedy Celaenos and folk-devouring Laestrygones and similar frightful monsters are common enough, but well and wisely trained citizens are not everywhere to be found.

Raphael "compared the wiser measures which had been taken among us as well as among them [i.e., the inhabitants of the New World]; for he remembered the manners and customs [*mores atque instituta*] of each nation as if he had lived all his life in places which he had only visited" (p. 55). In particular, "he told us of the manners and customs of the Utopians" ("de moribus atque institutis narrabat Vtopiensium"). It is also clear that these studies in comparative politics take their primary interest from their possible bearing on the improvement of European society: "just as he called attention to many ill-advised customs [*multa . . . perperam consulta*] among these new nations, so he rehearsed not a few points from which our own cities, nations, races, and kingdoms may take example for the correction of their errors."

The emphasis in this passage on the bearing of institutions on the state of the commonwealth provides a clue both to the nature of the instruction More is directing to his humanist audience and to the position of *Utopia* in the tradition of political theory. For, as we shall see, the institutional approach to the problem of securing good government had been, up to More's time, almost wholly foreign to humanist political thought. Humanists, and especially the northern humanists with whom More was affiliated, were strongly committed to a personal rather than an institutional view of politics. They characteristically regard the welfare of the polity as a function of the virtue of its citizens and especially its leaders, and they infer from this principle that moral instruction and moral examples are the crucial factors in achieving good government—hence the heavy emphasis in their political writings on the education of the prince, the importance of his choosing virtuous subordinates, and the exemplary role of leaders. If More is going to stress instead the importance of nonpersonal factors—"mores and institutions"—in securing good government, his book will indeed tell members of his humanist audience things they do not already know.

The summary of Hythloday's travels constitutes the final part of the introductory segment of *Utopia*. When we move into the dialogue—into the later-written segment of the book—we find that it immediately confirms the suggestion of a radical discrepancy between More's approach to the problem of securing good government and that of his fellow humanists.

The dialogue is launched by Giles's recommendation that Hythloday "attach . . . [himself] to some king": "you are capable not only of entertaining a king with . . . [your] learning and experience of men and places but also of furnishing him with examples and of assisting him with counsel. Thus, you would not only serve your own interests excellently but be of great assistance in the advancement of all your relatives and friends." After Hythloday's first brief reply, Giles repeats the suggestion, this time making it clear that service to a king is commendable because it amounts to service to the community as a whole: "this mode of life . . . is the very way by which you can not only profit people both as private individuals and as members of the commonwealth but also render your own condition more prosperous."

These remarks serve to introduce, in a way that accords with More's fictional decorum, what Hexter calls the "problem of counsel" (1952, p. 111; *Ut.*, p. lxxxiv)—the problem of ensuring that rulers receive and follow appropriate advice. Counsel is, as Skinner shows, a standard topic of humanist, especially northern humanist, political writing. It may be approached either from the point of view of the ruler, in which case the focus is on "the importance of choosing good councillors and learning to distinguish between true and false friends," or from the point of

view of the prospective councilor, in which case the focus is on
the advisability of the scholar's entering practical politics in this
way (Skinner 1978, pp. 216-17). One may note that the prototypal treatments of the problem from each side are found in
two of Plutarch's *Moralia*: "How to tell a Flatterer from a Friend";
"That a Philosopher ought to converse especially with Men in
Power." Viewed in the second perspective, it is an aspect of the
ancient question of the relative merits of the active and contemplative lives.[9] Since, as Skinner says, humanists "tended to see
themselves essentially as political advisers" (1978, p. 216), the
problem of counsel is, inevitably, the single most interesting
political topic to them. Its introduction as the first topic of *Utopia*
is well-calculated to engage the attention of More's humanist
audience.

Giles's remarks embody the two possible reasons for becoming
a councilor: personal profit (whether in terms of honor and power
or in terms of financial gain) and public profit. Hythloday's
response concentrates exclusively on the first: he himself is not
attracted by the perquisites of office, and neither he nor his family
is in financial need (pp. 55-57). A response in these terms signifies
that More is using the exchange between Giles and Hythloday
to clear away those aspects of the problem that he has no interest
in discussing. It evidently seems obvious to him that a philosopher
not constrained by financial considerations would be foolish to
sacrifice his liberty purely for the sake of the personal rewards
of office.[10]

[9] Cf., e.g., Cicero, *Off.* I.xx.69-xxi.73. Hythloday's declaration that he now
lives as he pleases (p. 56: "Atqui nunc sic uiuo ut uolo") echoes the oft-quoted
definition of philosophic liberty in this passage ("sic vivere, ut velis"). The
declaration and the passage in which it is embedded should hardly be taken as
evidence of Hythloday's bad character—as by Sylvester (1968, p. 297) and
Johnson (pp. 33-34). See also pp. 100-4 below.

[10] Cf. Bevington, p. 500. Hexter says that Hythloday "may be taken as a
sort of ideal type of Christian humanist: he personifies the literary interests,
the educational views, and the moral and religious commitments of the group,
free of all the limitations that the circumstances of actual living Christian
humanists imposed on the perfect expression of those interests, views, and
commitments" (*Ut.*, p. lxxxiv).

The question whether Hythloday should become a councilor is thus reduced to that whether a philosopher serves the public interest by taking such a course. After the exchange between Giles and Hythloday has cleared the ground for an unencumbered discussion of this topic, the suggestion that Hythloday should affiliate himself with a king is pressed again, this time by More. More acknowledges that the argument from personal profit has no force with Hythloday, and that this fact confirms his "truly philosophic spirit" (p. 57). But at the same time he suggests that the very fact that Hythloday *is* a true philosopher should impel him to join a council, since the highest duty and privilege of such a philosopher is to counsel princes:

> you will do what is worthy of you . . . if you so order your life as to apply your talent and industry to the public interest, even if it involves some personal disadvantages to yourself. This you can never do with as great profit as if you are councilor to some great monarch and make him follow, as I am sure you will, straightforward and honorable courses. From the monarch, as from a never-failing spring, flows a stream of all that is good or evil over the whole nation.

This position is in all respects the orthodox humanist one. In the first place, the general insistence that learning, in order to be justified, must be brought to bear on the improvement of human life is a central part of the legacy of Petrarch.[11] In ad-

---

[11] See Logan, pp. 21-31. Petrarch's views on the proper relation of learning to life are perhaps most powerfully expressed in *On His Own Ignorance and That of Many Others*. See also the selections from *De remediis utriusque fortunae* translated by Conrad Rawski as *Four Dialogues for Scholars*—e.g., p. 51 (I.44): "A knowledge of literature is useful only when it is translated into action and proves itself through deeds and not through words. Otherwise, we often discover to be true, as it is written, that *knowledge puffeth up*. To grasp clearly and quickly many things and especially those that are noble, to remember them firmly and to expound them brilliantly, to write with skill and to recite agreeably—unless all these relate to our life, what else are they but tools of empty ostentation, of useless work and clamor?" Cf. More's letter to Gonell: "Among all the benefits that learning bestows on men, I think there is none more excellent than that by study we are taught to seek in that very study not praise, but

dition, More's remarks embody standard themes of humanist political writing. From its beginnings in thirteenth- and fourteenth-century Italy, humanist political thought had stressed the importance of the pursuit of the public interest in preference to private interests, the crucial relation between the virtue of the ruler and the health of the city, and the importance of good counsel in fostering that virtue (see Skinner 1978, pp. 38-48). The conclusion that the philosopher should offer himself as a councilor is also completely orthodox. In the dedicatory epistle of *The Education of a Christian Prince* Erasmus cites Plutarch: "not without reason did Plutarch say that no one serves the state better than he who imbues the mind of the prince, who provides and cares for everyone and everything, with the best of ideas and those most becoming a prince" (p. 134; "That a Philosopher ought to converse especially with Men in Power," 778D). Skinner notes that humanist debates on counsel were normally "resolved in favour of the idea of involving oneself actively in the business of government" (1978, p. 218).[12]

Hythloday's position, however, is the opposite. By joining a king's council, he states flatly, "I should not promote the public interest." It is important to note that he does not deny that a criterion of public utility should govern the philosopher's application of his learning. The ensuing debate is intramural, conducted within the framework of shared humanist values. Hythloday simply denies that the criterion of utility has, in this particular case, the application that More claims.[13] Again More's rhetorical

---

utility" (*Sel. Let.*, p. 104; *Cor.*, p. 121). This utilitarian criterion for evaluating works of the mind has Roman Stoic as well as Biblical sources. Cf., e.g., Cicero, *Off.* I.vi.19.

[12] More's fellow humanist Elyot is perfectly clear on this point. "The end of all doctrine and study is good counsel, whereunto as unto the principal point, which geometricians do call the centre, all doctrines (which by some authors be imagined in the form of a circle) do send their effects" (*Governor* III.xxix). The passage is quoted and discussed by K. J. Wilson in his edition of Elyot's letters, p. x.

[13] Cf. Fleisher, p. 125. What Hythloday thinks the application of the criterion of utility *is* in this case becomes clear later. See p. 102 below. On the

strategy is clear. It is difficult to imagine a more effective way to open a book directed primarily to humanists than by the assertion—by such a man as Hythloday, a humanist moral philosopher of impeccable credentials—of a position diametrically opposed to the orthodox position on a matter of central interest to humanists.

Most of the remainder of Book I is devoted to Hythloday's defense of his position. His argument is based on two propositions, which he immediately states:

> In the first place almost all monarchs prefer to occupy themselves in the pursuits of war—with which I neither have nor desire any acquaintance—rather than in the honorable activities of peace, and they care much more how, by hook or by crook, they may win fresh kingdoms than how they may administer well what they have got.
>
> In the second place, among royal councilors everyone is actually so wise as to have no need of profiting by another's counsel, or everyone seems so wise in his own eyes as not to condescend to profit by it, save that they agree with the most absurd saying of, and play the parasite to, the chief royal favorites whose friendliness they strive to win by flattery. . . .
>
> If anyone, when in the company of people who are jealous of others' discoveries or prefer their own, should propose something which he either has read of as done in other times or has seen done in other places, the listeners behave as if their whole reputation for wisdom were jeopardized and as if afterwards they would deserve to be thought plain blockheads unless they could lay hold of something to find fault with in the discoveries of others. (pp. 57-59)

In sum, both the nature of kings and the nature of councilors preclude the possibility of an individual's doing much for the public good as a member of a council.

---

precedent for Hythloday's disengagement provided by Pico, see Baker-Smith, pp. 13-14.

Exhibiting the usual humanist distrust of mere dialectics, Hythloday attempts to establish the validity of these claims primarily through vivid examples rather than formal argument.[14] The first of these is a lengthy account of a dinner conversation at the table of More's mentor, Cardinal Morton. It is followed by a pair of additional examples, two imaginary meetings of the privy councils of European monarchs.

For Hythloday, the function of the account of the conversation at Morton's table is to support his claims about the nature of councilors. He identifies this function explicitly at the end of the episode: "Though I ought to have related this conversation more concisely, still I felt bound to tell it,[15] to exhibit the attitude of those who had rejected what I had said first yet who, immediately afterward, when the Cardinal did not disapprove of it, also gave their approval. . . . From this reaction you may judge what little regard courtiers would pay to me and my advice" (p. 85).

It is the *structure* of the conversation that illustrates this point, which in no way depends on the particular *subject* discussed. Even before Hythloday had concluded his first speech (on the causes of theft), the lawyer with whom he was arguing was "busily preparing himself to reply and had determined to adopt the usual method of disputants who are more careful to repeat what has been said than to answer it, so highly do they regard their memory" (p. 71). When at the conclusion of his next speech Hythloday suggests that the Polylerite system of criminal justice might be adopted in England, the lawyer replies in equally self-serving and vacuous fashion, and the collective response of the other members of Morton's entourage is of the same pompous, mindlessly conservative kind:

"Never [says the lawyer] could that system be established in England without involving the commonwealth in a very

[14] For a detailed exploration of More's characteristically humanist (i.e., rhetorical) methods of argument in his political writings, see Fleisher, pp. 71-121.

[15] For the first part of this sentence, I have substituted Miller's more accurate translation (1966, p. 60) for the version in Yale.

serious crisis." In the act of making this statement, he shook
his head and made a wry face and so fell silent. And all
those who were present gave him their assent. (p. 81)

As soon as the Cardinal suggests that the Polylerite system might
in fact be workable, however, and that its application might be
extended to include vagrants in addition to thieves, "they all vied
in praising what they all had received with contempt when suggested by me, but especially the part relating to vagrants because
this was the Cardinal's addition." The curious following episode
of the friar and the clownish hanger-on illustrates the same point:
the company flatters the Cardinal "so much that they even smiled
on and almost allowed in earnest the fancies of the hanger-on,
which his master in jest did not reject" (p. 85). The account thus
illustrates both aspects of Hythloday's second reason for thinking
that joining a council would not be useful: the vain and self-
serving nature of councilors, and their consequent lack of interest
in the sincere intellectual give-and-take of true counsel.

There is, however, a problem with this example as an illustration of Hythloday's claims. Although the behavior of Morton's
"councilors" supports these claims, the figure of Morton himself
seems to undermine them. Morton, after all, is the only actual
royal councilor present, and Hythloday's account of his nature
and his part in the conversation hardly tends to support the
contention that "among royal councilors everyone is actually so
wise as to have no need of profiting by another's counsel, or
everyone seems so wise in his own eyes as not to condescend to
profit by it" (cf. Sylvester 1968, p. 298; Weiner, pp. 13-14).
Instead, as Hythloday acknowledges, Morton was a man "who
deserved respect as much for his prudence and virtue as for his
authority" (p. 59). This truly wise man is perfectly willing to
profit from the advice offered him. Eager to learn what punishment Hythloday would suggest for theft, Morton cuts off the
lawyer and returns the floor to Hythloday. He is receptive to
Hythloday's claim that the Polylerite system of criminal justice
is superior to the English, and, describing how this system might
with proper safeguards be experimentally implemented, he ex-

hibits what is surely the ideal response to a new idea. At the same time, the fact that this wise student of domestic affairs is the principal councilor of the English king, who "placed the greatest confidence in his advice," indirectly undermines Hythloday's first proposition, which includes the claim that rulers are relatively uninterested in "how they may administer well what they have got."

It may be that this problem arose because More wanted an illustration that would perform several functions. First, he required an English example here, because he wished to use the episode to discuss the problem of theft and poverty in England as well as the general European problem of counsel. But, having begun by calling Henry VIII a "model monarch"—a characterization that More could perhaps still intend sincerely in 1516 (see R. P. Adams 1962, pp. 120-22)—he could hardly use a contemporary English example to illustrate the folly of kings and councilors. (No such restrictions inhibit Hythloday's later scathing descriptions of the councils of other kings.) The substitution of the conversation at Morton's table for a council meeting appeared to provide a good solution.[16]

Moreover, this choice allowed the episode to perform another function: to pay tribute to a man whom More greatly admired. That this is one of its purposes is clear from More's response to Hythloday's speech:

> "To be sure, my dear Raphael," I commented, "you have given me great pleasure. . . . while listening to you, I felt not only as if I were at home in my native land but as if I were become a boy again, by being pleasantly reminded of the very Cardinal in whose court I was brought up as a lad.

---

[16] We can see More preparing this route in the formulation of Hythloday's second proposition. Hythloday's claim about the nature of councilors would seem to call for illustration from a royal council. But More phrases the proposition in such a way as to render the episode at Morton's table an acceptable substitute. Councilors "agree with the most absurd saying of, and play the parasite to, the chief royal favorites whose friendliness they strive to win by flattery"—one would expect "king" here rather than "chief royal favorites."

Since you are strongly devoted to his memory, you cannot
believe how much more attached I feel to you on that account, attached exceedingly as I have been to you already.
. . ." (pp. 85-87)

Again we must remember that much of what is applied to Hythloday in fiction applies to More in fact. It is More who is "strongly
devoted to" Morton's memory.[17]

The trouble is that the intention to pay tribute to Morton
clashes with the intention of illustrating Hythloday's claims about
councilors. Of course this problem disappears if we decide that
the passage has yet another intended function, that of raising a
counterargument to Hythloday's claims. The passage suggests,
in fact, the most appropriate counter: even if kings and councilors
are for the most part as Hythloday characterizes them, does not
the fact that a man like Morton can, if only occasionally, rise to
power mean that it is worthwhile, in at least some cases, for an
intellectual to enter the political arena? This is one part of the
truth about the problem of counsel, even as Hythloday's claims,
which certainly apply to most cases, are the other. To be sure,
if More intended Hythloday's example to undermine itself in the
way I have described, then he is deliberately undermining Hythloday's authority. In view of the wholly favorable way in which
Hythloday is introduced, this would be a surprising thing for
him to do. But in fact we will find that other items in the later-
written segment of *Utopia* have this same effect (a circumstance
that is clearly significant for interpretation), so that it is not
implausible to attribute such an intention to More in the present
passage. One may, however, feel that it is likelier that More,
trying to do too much at once, simply lost track of one of the
implications of the passage. This explanation gains plausibility
from the fact that Hythloday's other major examples in Book I
(the imaginary privy council meetings) constitute perfect illustrations of his claims.

[17] The episode also *begins* with a eulogy of Morton (pp. 59-61).

II

Up to this point we have considered only the functions of the structure of the episode at Morton's table, those that could have been performed in the same way whatever the particular subject of discussion. Meanwhile, other functions are performed through the substance of the episode, the treatment of theft and poverty in England.

The treatment of this subject opens with the lawyer's wonderment at the failure of the harsh English method of dealing with thieves:

> he began to speak punctiliously of the strict justice which was then dealt out to thieves. They were everywhere executed, he reported, as many as twenty at a time being hanged on one gallows, and added that he wondered all the more, though so few escaped execution, by what bad luck the whole country was still infested with them. (p. 61)

From its beginning in this stark imagery of multiple executions,[18] the episode moves, in Hythloday's first speech, into a scathing indictment of a system of "justice"—found not only in England but also in "a great part of our world"—in which the poor are "under . . . [the] terrible necessity first of stealing and then of dying for it." Exploring the causes of this state of affairs, the indicting voice ranges over all the estates. Noblemen "live idle themselves like drones on the labors of others" and "also carry about with them a huge crowd of idle attendants who have never learned a trade for a livelihood" (p. 63).[19] These retainers think themselves "far above everybody" and too good for honest work— nor is it the case, as the lawyer claims, that such fellows make

[18] Cf. p. 59, where Hythloday dates his visit to England by saying that it took place "not long after the disastrous end of the insurrection of western Englishmen against the king, which was put down with their pitiful slaughter."

[19] Donald W. Hanson describes the "depredations of roving armed bands" that plagued England in this period. Some of these were "collections of brigands, ruffians, and poor folk driven from their land," while others were "the armed retainers of those who could afford them" (p. 182).

good soldiers. The custom of keeping retainers "is common to almost all peoples"; in France, moreover, there is a related plague. The mercenaries that the French keep for war gravely endanger France itself in peacetime. England has its own special plague: "noblemen, gentlemen, and even some abbots, . . . not content, by leading an idle and sumptuous life, to do no good to their country[,] . . . must also do it positive harm" by the enclosure of land for pasturage. This practice results in a situation in which "your sheep, . . . which are usually so tame and so cheaply fed, begin now, according to report, to be so greedy and wild that they devour human beings themselves and devastate and depopulate fields, houses, and towns" (pp. 65-67). The withdrawal of land from cultivation drives up the price of food. Even the price of raw wool has risen, "for all sheep have come into the hands of a few men, and those already rich, who are not obligated to sell before they wish and who do not wish until they get the price they ask" (p. 69). Finally, a taste for luxury pervades society: "all classes alike . . . are given to much ostentatious sumptuousness of dress and to excessive indulgence at table." In sum, however difficult it may be to determine what More thinks of Utopia, it is perfectly clear what he thinks of the present condition of England and Europe. The heavy ironies of this section are not the kind that obscures meaning but the mordancies of the harshest social criticism. The indictment is important in itself—witness its frequent citation by historians[20]—and, by underlining the gravity and urgency of European problems, it forms a perfect starting point for an exploration of the possibilities for reform.

Another function of the discussion of theft is to introduce a particular claim about the relation between politics and morality. Both Hythloday's speeches in the episode heavily emphasize the point that, in a true view, the English system of criminal justice is not only immoral but also inexpedient. His first speech begins

[20] This is not to say that Hythloday's analysis is wholly accurate. For some points where his assessments differ from those of twentieth-century historians, see *Ut.*, pp. 335-36n, 339-40n; Elton 1977, pp. 44-45; Kinney 1979, p. 28.

with a triple iteration of this claim. One should not be surprised that hanging does not reduce theft, Hythloday says,

> for this manner of punishing thieves [1a] goes beyond justice and [1b] is not for the public good [supra iustum est, & non ex usu publico]. [2a] It is too harsh a penalty for theft and yet [2b] is not a sufficient deterrent. Theft alone [3a] is not a grave offense that ought to be punished with death, and [3b] no penalty that can be devised is sufficient to restrain from acts of robbery those who have no other means of getting a livelihood. (p. 61)

At the end of the speech he restates the point: "Your policy may look superficially like justice, but in reality it is neither just nor practical."[21] Moreover, Hythloday's second speech, in which he suggests an alternative system of punishment, begins with an elaborate restatement of the same contention:

> "Certainly," I answered, "most reverend and kind Father, I think it [1] altogether unjust that a man should suffer the loss of his life for the loss of someone's money. . . . If they say that this penalty is attached to the offense against justice and the breaking of the laws, hardly to the money stolen, one may well characterize this extreme justice as extreme wrong [quid ni merito summum illud ius, summa uocetur iniuria]. . . .[22]
>
> "God has said, 'Thou shalt not kill,' and shall we so lightly kill a man for taking a bit of small change? But if the divine command against killing be held not to apply where human law justifies killing, what prevents men equally from arranging with one another how far rape, adultery, and perjury are admissible? . . .
>
> "These are the reasons why I think this punishment un-

[21] The translation is from R. M. Adams's edition (p. 16). Yale has "Such justice is more showy than really just or beneficial" (p. 71). Cf. the Latin: "iustitiam, nempe speciosam magis, quam aut iustam aut utilem."

[22] The adage "summum ius, summa iniuria" has a long history in discussions of equity. See *Ut.*, p. 341n. Cicero quotes it in *Off.* I.x.33.

lawful. Besides, surely everyone knows [2] how absurd and
even dangerous to the commonwealth it is that a thief and
a murderer should receive the same punishment. Since the
robber sees that he is in as great danger if merely condemned
for theft as if he were convicted of murder as well, this
single consideration impels him to murder the man whom
otherwise he would only have robbed. In addition to the
fact that he is in no greater danger if caught, there is greater
safety in putting the man out of the way and greater hope
of covering up the crime if he leaves no one left to tell the
tale. Thus, while we endeavor to terrify thieves with excessive cruelty, we urge them on to the destruction of honest
citizens. . . ." (pp. 73-75)

Hythloday argues, then, that accurate analysis shows that the
English policy, which certainly cannot be justified on moral or
religious grounds, also cannot be justified on the ground of expediency. From the heavy emphasis on this theme in his speeches
in this episode, we gather that for Hythloday this was the main
point of his remarks at Morton's table, even as his point in
recapitulating to More and Giles the conversation that included
these remarks is to illustrate the validity of his claims about
counsel.[23]

The theme of the relation between the moral and the expedient
recurs, in one form and another, throughout *Utopia*, and it is
evidently one of More's central concerns. The seminal treatment
of this theme is found in Book III of Cicero's *De officiis*, where,
however, it is treated primarily on the individual—ethical—level
rather than on the political level. The relation of *honestas* and
utilitas is also a key issue in discussions of the deliberative oration
in the classical rhetorical manuals: the function of this type of
oration is to advise as to the advantages or disadvantages of a
particular policy; fundamental topics are the relation of the policy

---

[23] It is noteworthy in this connection that Hythloday's opening tribute to
Morton praises him for his combination of "prudence and virtue" (p. 59;
above, p. 45).

to *honestas* and *utilitas*.[24] The fact that the relation of the moral and the expedient loomed so large in works of central importance to humanists meant that this had always been a standard topic of humanist writing. It was a particularly lively topic—thus especially appropriate in a book addressed to humanists—in the early years of the sixteenth century, both because some Italian humanists had embraced the notion of a political necessity that sometimes demands immoral policies, and because northern humanists, to whom such claims were detestable, were interested in ways of

[24] My student John Tinkler called my attention to the relevant passages in the manuals (Aristotle, *Rh.* I.1358b-1360a; Cicero, *Inv.* II.li.156-58; *Part. Or.* XXIV.83-89; *De Or.* II.lxxxii.334-36; *Rhetorica ad Herennium* III.ii.3; Quintilian III.viii.1, 14, 22-25) and pointed out to me the centrality of *honestas* and *utilitas* in "the fundamental grid of issues upon which deliberative oratory was plotted" (unpubl. paper). Hythloday's speeches at Morton's table constitute, in effect, a deliberative oration advising against the English policy for punishing thieves on the ground that it is inconsistent with both *honestas* and *utilitas* (and advocating a different policy—that of the Polylerites—as being consistent with both). As we shall see, his imaginary privy council speeches are plotted on the same grid. It is also clear that considerations of *honestas* and *utilitas* inform the positions of all three speakers in the debate on counsel.

According to Augustine, Cicero treated the question of the relation of the moral and the expedient on the political level in *De re publica*: "Philus . . . puts in a plea for a more detailed treatment of the subject of justice because it was at that time popularly supposed that some injustice was inevitable in the government of any country. Scipio . . . [maintains] the falsity of the statement that injustice is inevitable in government, and, further, the truth of the assertion that complete justice is the supreme essential for government. . . . Philus . . . contends energetically for injustice against justice, asserting its superior utility for the country, and striving to prove his point by plausible arguments and illustrations. Then Laelius, by general request, undertakes the defence of justice, and asserts with all possible emphasis that nothing is so inimical to a community as injustice, and that a country cannot be governed, and cannot continue in being, without a high degree of justice" (*CG* II.21, summarizing *Rep.* II.xlivff.). This account, in which the authority of Cicero is reinforced by that of Augustine, would also help to draw humanists' attention to the question. (*De re publica* itself was not recovered until 1820.) Cf. Chap. 3, n. 52. More lectured on *The City of God* about 1501, treating it, according to Stapleton, "not . . . from the theological point of view, but from the standpoint of history and philosophy" (pp. 7-8).

countering them.[25] Indeed, at about the same time that he wrote *Utopia*, More was also protesting against nonmoral statecraft in his *History of King Richard III*, which constitutes a powerful object lesson in the destructive and self-destructive nature of the pursuit of supposedly expedient immoral policies.

Some commentators have concluded that More means to suggest in *Utopia* that there is (as Cicero argues in *De officiis*) complete identity between the moral and the expedient. Marie Delcourt claims that "l'éthique politique de l'*Utopie* rejette précisément toute distinction entre la morale privée et la morale publique" (p. 102; cf. Caspari, p. 104). As we shall see, this is in fact *Hythloday's* position. But Hythloday did not write *Utopia*: More did, and he uses Hythloday for purposes that transcend Hythloday's own. We must reserve judgment as to More's position on this matter.

Hythloday supports his claims about the real inexpediency of the supposedly expedient English criminal justice by a sophisticated analysis of the problem of theft. This circumstance brings us to the final function of the episode at Cardinal Morton's table, which is the provision of an object lesson in the proper method of social analysis. We are, I believe, meant to infer several principles from this lesson; that is, features of the method that Hythloday employs are emphasized so strongly that one feels that it is not merely *means* but *subject* in the book.

At the core of this method is the realization that social problems

---

[25] Like the question of the relation between *honestas* and *utilitas*, the idea that necessity overrides other political considerations has important sources in rhetorical theory. In *De partitione oratoria*, Cicero says that necessity "must take precedence in public policy of all the remaining considerations, alike of honour and of profit [*et honestatibus . . . et commodis*]" (XXIV.83; cf. Quintilian III.viii.22-25). On Italian and northern humanist attitudes to political necessity, see Anglo, pp. 172-94; Skinner 1978, pp. 248-54; and below, pp. 107-10. Schoeck says that the "view of *Utopia* as a reaction against the ideas of Machiavelli in *Il Principe* was first put forth by Hermann Oncken in his lecture on *Utopia* [1922a, p. 12] . . . and is supported by . . . Chambers . . . , p. 132" (1956, p. 627n). But cf. Seebohm, pp. 230-31 (above, Prol., n. 7). See also Mackie, pp. 264-65; Caspari, p. 103.

have causes that may lie at some distance from the actual manifestations of the problems, and that these causes can be ascertained
by rational analysis. The lawyer with whom Hythloday argues
has a shallow conception of the problem of theft: he takes it for
granted that the cause lies in the thief's wickedness, and that the
solution of the problem therefore lies in capital punishment,
which eliminates actual thieves and should deter potential ones.
Accordingly, he is surprised that the energetic application of this
policy has not in fact reduced the magnitude of the problem.
Hythloday, on the contrary, finds the immediate cause of theft
in poverty, which places many Englishmen under the "*necessity
. . . of stealing*" (p. 61; my emphasis: "furandi primum, dehinc
pereundi necessitas"). In turn, poverty is the product of a number
of social factors. Wars leave many disabled, and "their disability
prevents them from exercising their own crafts, and their age
from learning a new one" (p. 63). The existence of a great number
of idle rich people produces poverty in two ways. First, these
people support their extravagant lives by reducing others to extreme poverty, whether by extracting as much as possible from
their tenants or by reducing the number of opportunities for
employment through the practice of enclosure. Second, noblemen
retain large numbers of idle men who, when they are turned off,
are disinclined and even unable to support themselves by honest
labor. Finally, another cause of poverty lies in the spread down-
ward through the social scale of the luxurious tastes of the upper
classes:

> Not only the servants of noblemen but the craftsmen and
> almost the clodhoppers themselves, in fact all classes alike,
> are given to . . . sumptuousness of dress and to excessive
> indulgence at table. Do not dives, brothels, and those other
> places as bad as brothels, to wit, taverns,[26] wine shops and
> alehouses—do not all those crooked games of chance, dice,
> cards, backgammon, ball, bowling, and quoits, soon drain

[26] Yale omits "taverns." See Miller 1966, p. 58.

the purses of their votaries and send them off to rob someone? (p. 69)

In short, Hythloday finds the root causes of theft not in the bad
character of individual thieves but in defects in the social system.[27]

The systemic view of the problem of theft implies that in order
to work solutions must also be systemic. By applying a topical
remedy at the point of the symptom, one may be able to block
the manifestation of the causes at that point, but, as Hythloday
later says, such a blockage will only result in the causes producing
another manifestation somewhere else: "while you are intent upon
the cure of one part, you make worse the malady of the other
parts" (pp. 105-7). A real solution of the problem will be achieved
not by applying remedies to its symptoms—the actual thefts—
but to its causes. These true remedies will take the form of legal
and institutional changes designed to eliminate the causes:

> Cast out these ruinous plagues. Make laws that the de-
> stroyers of farmsteads and country villages should either
> restore them or hand them over to people who will restore
> them and who are ready to build. Restrict this right of rich
> individuals to buy up everything and this license to exercise
> a kind of monopoly for themselves. Let fewer be brought
> up in idleness. Let farming be resumed and let cloth-work-
> ing be restored once more that there may be honest jobs to
> employ usefully that idle throng, whether those whom hith-
> erto pauperism has made thieves or those who, now being
> vagrants or lazy servants, in either case are likely to turn
> out thieves. Assuredly, unless you remedy these evils, it is

[27] In this connection, we can see why he deemphasizes war as a cause of
theft: of those reduced to poverty by disabilities incurred in military service
"we shall take no account because wars come sporadically, but let us consider
what happens every day" (p. 63). War, that is, is only an occasional, incidental
cause of poverty and theft rather than a cause that is entailed in the quotidian
functioning of the social system, and it is the latter kind of cause that concerns
Hythloday here.

useless for you to boast of the justice you execute in the punishment of theft. (pp. 69-71)

But theft is not the only systemic problem. We should by this point realize that Hythloday is saying the same kind of thing about counsel to More and Giles as he said about theft to the lawyer at Morton's table. In justification of his refusal to attach himself to a king, Hythloday does not offer a condemnation of individual kings or courts, or even a general condemnation of present-day courts as contrasted to those of a better past time. Instead, he justifies his refusal in terms of claims that, so he thinks, apply to all courts at all times. The problem of counsel, like that of theft, is not traceable to the bad character of individual kings or councilors, and it cannot be solved by sending individual wise men such as Hythloday to court (in fact, Hythloday offers *no* solution), any more than the problem of theft can be solved by hanging individual thieves. Like theft, that is, the problem of counsel is systemic, a product of flaws in the structure of society.

Indeed, More presumably means to suggest the same about serious social problems in general. This presumption in turn allows us to infer some considerations that governed his choice of particular examples. Theft is a good example not only because it is a major current problem in More's England, but also because an analysis of its roots, which extend throughout the social system, provides such a striking illustration of the fact that an elaborate causal network may underlie the actual manifestations of a social malaise. Similarly, counsel is discussed in *Utopia* not merely because of the interest of this topic to a humanist audience or (as Hexter suggests) because More was personally concerned with the problem during these years, but also—something that is more important in understanding the book—because he recognized that counsel is the most serious of all systemic problems. For, as the Morton episode (together with Hythloday's following examples) clearly demonstrates, the malfunctioning of councils nearly precludes the implementation of solutions of other problems.

The fact that the significance of the episode at Morton's table resides largely in its analytic method has occasionally been a theme of recent criticism. Ames says that More offers, in Hythloday's speeches in this episode, "a scientific explanation of the causes of poverty, crime, and injustice," and that this part of the book, "rather than his invention of Utopian society, is More's highest artistic and intellectual achievement":

> He does not find the causes of human misery in the mind or soul, in Fate, in fallible and unchanging "human nature," or in the mental and moral weaknesses of the workers. Instead, More finds the causes of human misery in material conditions. Human beings do wrong under social *compulsion*. (p. 176)

R. P. Adams, taught by McKeon (1935) and Albert Duhamel (1953) to look for the defining achievements of Renaissance culture in methodological advances, follows Ames's lead. In Hythloday's first speech at Morton's table "a historic cape of the mind was turned, one which divides the medieval from the modern world. In it we may see at work that scientific spirit for which More stands pre-eminent among the humanists":

> Not for a moment does Hythlodaye agree that sin is the basic cause of crime. Instead in his analysis such social evils as crime, poverty, and war are all man-made.[28] These are *effects*, which can be traced to their man-made sources, if men will but use their wits rightly. In other words, these causes are within the power of the human mind to discover. Then the social processes by which these causes produce their necessary effects can be studied. Finally, the most practical (or, as we would now say, scientific) way to cure such a social symptom as crime or war, insofar as it is curable, is to take the necessary realistic action required to alleviate or eliminate the ascertained cause. (1962, pp. 125-26)

[28] Why sin does not qualify as "man-made" is not clear.

These assessments call attention to the fact that Hythloday's
early speeches embody the recognition that in order to cure a
social evil one must eliminate its root causes, which may lie at
some distance from their effect. But both treatments are flawed
by the projection of their authors' own secular values onto More
(as well as by vague use of the term "scientific"). Hythloday does
find the root of social evil in the "mind or soul"—specifically,
in the sins of sloth (p. 63), greed (pp. 67, 69), and (as he makes
clear later) pride (pp. 243-45; cf. Hexter, *Ut.*, p. ci). It is
simply that he locates the cause of most theft not in the sins of
the thief but in those of his social and economic superiors, and
accordingly the remedies he proposes are designed either to inhibit the pernicious actions or to improve the character of members of the upper classes.

A much more accurate and precise statement of More's method
and its significance is found in Hexter's several passages on the
subject. The crucial aspects of the method come into focus, Hexter
notes, when we compare the treatment of social problems in
Utopia with that in the works of other northern humanists. Erasmus, for example, is a pungent critic of social abuses, but his
efforts in the formulation of solutions to the problems he identifies
are "invertebrate":

> *The Praise of Folly, The Complaint of Peace*, and the long
> satirical adages are inadequate as social criticism because
> they point to the sickness of early sixteenth century Chris-
> tendom but scarcely ever penetrate inward to discover the
> roots of the disease. Therefore their prescriptions, in the
> rare instances when anything so specific is suggested, are
> mere analgesics and plasters, not radical remedies. (1952,
> p. 64; cf. Caspari, p. 76; Fleisher, p. 8)

Erasmus' observations are "unconnected, particular responses to
social malaises, because he has only a very slight awareness of
the interpenetration of social institutions and social structures"
(*Ut.*, p. c). In particular, Erasmus, like other northern human-

ists, treats the problem of counsel with "bland banality, skipping all the hard parts":

> He says that the prince ought to be uncorrupt and see to it that his whole household is uncorrupt, since the hatred aroused by his followers' vices falls on him. He feels that this part of a prince's task is easy, since it can be accomplished by summoning only good men to the royal service. He further states that councilors should be sagacious and trustworthy; and this is about the sum of the advice that Erasmus has to offer princes on one of the most pressing practical questions that they had to cope with. (1952, pp. 110-11)

Such advice reflects no sense of the fact that the problem of counsel is a function of "the internal structure and management of royal councils[,] . . . that power pressures from without and power tensions from within the conciliar structure prevent it from ever being the totally disinterested symposium of virtuous men of the humanist dream" (p. 111).

By contrast, More's treatment of social problems is characterized by "his capacity to see past the symptoms to the sources of trouble, . . . his grasp of the intricacy and ramification of social structure and social action, . . . his skill at working out expedients to meet particular social problems" (p. 64). He sees "in depth, in perspective, and in mutual relation problems which his contemporaries saw in the flat and as a disjointed series" (*Ut.*, p. ci). *Utopia* embodies the awareness that "in politics, general principles usually operate through specific institutional structures, when they operate at all," and More's recommendations for reform normally take the form of suggestions for institutional changes: "he traces the ills of the realms of Christendom to identifiable institutional defects and proposes institutional remedies for some of them" (1973, pp. 14, 15). These remarks apply, moreover, not just to Hythloday's speeches in the Morton episode but to *Utopia* as a whole.

Hexter's insights embody a great advance in the understanding of *Utopia* and its significance, and I am deeply indebted to them.

Hexter fails, however, to draw one obvious inference from his insights. Like the other humanistic interpreters, he argues that *Utopia* is in effect simply a restatement of Erasmian ideals. But in fact his comparison of *Utopia* with other northern works suggests that More's purpose may be not to restate traditional prescriptions but to explore a particular approach to social analysis and the modification of traditional prescriptions that this approach entails. The accurate observation that More's book is methodologically far more sophisticated than the works of his fellow northern humanists suggests, that is, that one aim of this book directed to humanists is to instruct them in a subject in which they badly needed instruction, the proper method of social study and the substantive consequences of that method. In particular, More would appear to be concerned to show how political facts impose constraints on the possibility of realizing political ideals.

Moreover, the episode at Morton's table makes some other points about method that neither Hexter, Ames, nor Adams notices. The most salient fact about the systemic view of social problems is that it suggests that they are complex, often having a number of causes, some of which may be at considerable distance from the manifestations of the problem. Accordingly, the process of solving them is also likely to be complex, involving not only practical difficulties but also (and this is our present concern) theoretical ones. Since the solution is usually not simply a matter of applying a local remedy to the symptom of the problem but one of effecting legal and institutional changes in diverse parts of the social system, it is as necessary and as difficult to trace the ramifications of proposed solutions as to trace the roots of the problem. And in tracing these ramifications, one does not, as in the case of analyzing a problem, have actual situations to deal with: tracing the ramifications of proposed solutions is a purely mental exercise, where errors are not subject to correction by reference to social fact. There are, however, ways to minimize the risks of theoretical error. These ways constitute the additional methodological points embodied in the Morton episode, points that amount to corollaries of Hythloday's conclusions about the nature of social problems and their solutions.

The first of these corollaries is the proposition that comparative political study is highly instructive in the formulation of solutions. Since problems are complicated, it is a good idea not simply to reason about solutions but also to look for examples of successful solutions of similar problems in other polities. We should recall that Hythloday's unusual capacity for providing such examples, which derives from his great learning and wide experience, constitutes one of Giles's reasons for suggesting that Hythloday attach himself to some king: "I am sure there is none of them to whom you would not be very welcome because you are capable not only of entertaining a king with this learning and experience of men and places but also of furnishing him with examples and of assisting him with counsel" (p. 55). Asked by Cardinal Morton to supplement his criticism of English criminal justice with proposals for an alternative system, Hythloday does not offer a speculative reply but refers instead to solutions of the problem found in other societies:

> Why should we doubt that a good way of punishing crimes is the one which we know long found favor of old with the Romans, the greatest experts in managing the common- wealth? When men were convicted of atrocious crimes they condemned them for life to stone quarries and to digging in metal mines, and kept them constantly in chains.
>
> Yet, as concerns this matter, I can find no better system in any country [nullius institutum gentis magis probo] than that which, in the course of my travels, I observed in Persia among the people commonly called the Polylerites. . . . (p. 75)

The Cardinal's response (p. 81) suggests another important point: such borrowed solutions must be carefully adapted to suit the conditions of one's own country. In England, a precondition for the adoption of the Polylerite system (which does not involve incarceration) would be the limitation of the privilege of sanctuary. Given Morton's reputation and his highly favorable treatment in *Utopia*, anything that he says carries special weight.

The second corollary asserts the utility of carefully controlled experiment in testing solutions. This point is also embodied in the Cardinal's response to Hythloday's suggestion that the Polylerite system be adopted in England. The lawyer whose views Hythloday has been disputing had immediately concluded that the Polylerite system could never "be established in England without involving the commonwealth in a very serious crisis" (p. 81). Morton, however, justly observes that it is impossible, purely on the basis of ratiocination, to decide either that the proposal would not work or that it would. The question can only be resolved empirically: "It is not easy to guess whether it would turn out well or ill inasmuch as absolutely no experiment [*periculum*] has been made." Morton goes on to outline an experimental test, one that includes safeguards based on calculating the ramifications of such a solution. These safeguards—the prior pronouncement (and postponement) of the death sentence for the thieves involved and the limitation of sanctuary—are designed to ensure that the experiment does not result in some criminals escaping punishment:

> If, after pronouncement of the sentence of death, the king were to order the postponement of its execution and, after limitation of the privileges of sanctuary, were to try this system, then, if success proved its usefulness, it would be right to make the system law. In case of failure, then and there to put to death those previously condemned would be no less in the interest of the commonwealth and no more unjust than if execution were done here and now. In the meantime no danger can come of the experiment.[29]

[29] The phrase "in the interest of the commonwealth" replaces Yale's "for the public good." The Latin is "e republica." See Skinner 1967, p. 167.

Like other features of the episode, Morton's proposal testifies to his openmindedness. Lee Cullen Khanna sees "the importance of experimental attitudes . . . [as] the real subject" of *Utopia* (p. 94). It is certainly *one* of the real subjects. See below, pp. 206-7. Brendan Bradshaw calls attention to the fact

The third methodological corollary is not introduced in the direct fashion of the other two. As a result, it easily escapes notice; yet it is the most important of all for understanding More's proceedings in the rest of *Utopia*. We can infer this corollary by considering the nature of the comparative examples that Hythloday offers. The first of these is an actual, historical example: Rome. More could have explored this one at greater length, but he chooses instead to explore that of the Polylerites. And this example is crucially different from the Roman one. For the Polylerite case, though offered by Hythloday as an example from a real contemporary society, is fictitious.

The fiction is, however, of a special kind. Just as Hythloday, the expert in nonsense, says many things that are eminently sensible, so the Polylerites, the "people of much nonsense" (*Ut.*, p. 343n), have a system for the punishment of theft that is worthy of serious consideration. This is the case, first, because the system embodies a sensible view of the legitimate aims of punishment (cf. Fleisher, pp. 21-23, 36), which are, the Polylerites think, to rehabilitate the criminal and to redress the damage done by his crime: "The object of public anger is to destroy the vices but to save the persons and so to treat them that they necessarily become good and that, for the rest of their lives, they repair all the damage done before" (p. 79). This view may reflect Plato's *Laws*, where the Athenian stresses that the purposes of punishment are to deter crime, reform the criminal, and redress the injury to his victim (IX.862C-D). Second, the Polylerite system embodies a series of plausible means for achieving these ends. The Polylerites force thieves to "repay to the owner what they

that More also stresses Hythloday's open-mindedness: "Hythloday . . . embodied this attitude in his qualified approval of the political arrangements which he encountered in the course of his philosophical voyage to Utopia. That we are here concerned with a major polemic of the work is clear from the way in which Hythloday emphasizes the closed and hidebound mentality which he observed everywhere in the west [*Ut.*, pp. 57-81, 107-9], as well as by the fact that Peter Giles . . . drew attention to it in his prefatory verse [*Ut.*, p. 19]" (p. 27).

have taken from him," or, "if the object is lost, the value is made up out of the thieves' goods, and the balance is then paid intact to their wives and children" (p. 77). The thief is sentenced to a life of hard labor, so that "each one, besides earning his own living, brings in something every day to the public treasury." Moreover, "no one is quite without hope of gaining his freedom eventually if he accepts his punishment in a spirit of obedience and resignation and gives evidence of reforming his future life" (p. 79).[30] The Polylerites do not make the mistake of the English, who encourage the thief to add murder to robbery by making the penalty for both crimes the same. In general, their "purpose is never to make it safer to follow out an evil plan than to repent of it."

The Polylerite example, then, differs both from a pure fiction and from a real comparative example. More constructed it by developing a theory of punishment and then imagining and describing a society in which the theory has been implemented; that is, the Polylerite example is a *model* of the theory that informs it.[31] Such a model constitutes a concrete and vivid embodiment of a theory, and it accordingly has as one of its possible functions the *testing* of theory. Strengths or weaknesses that may not be apparent when a theory is presented only through the reasonings

[30] Thomas I. White observes that the treatment of Polylerite (and Utopian) slaves recalls Aristotelian recommendations: the "practices of rewarding them with liberty or an easier servitude and the generally humane treatment of slaves . . . parallel Aristotle's idea that slaves should be treated well and always should have the hope of emancipation" (1976, p. 661n; cf. *Pol.* VII.1330a, and the pseudo-Aristotelian *Economics* I.v). Surtz points out that some of the Polylerite practices reflect those of actual states, especially (as More hints via Hythloday's other example) Rome (*Ut.*, pp. 342-44n).

[31] On models, and the variety of senses in which the term is now employed by social scientists, see Apostel; Kaplan, pp. 258-93; Isaak, pp. 135-54; Golembiewski et al., pp. 427-48. Models are primarily associated with positive theory. The model is usually offered as an isomorph of some system in the real world and its validity measured in terms of its capacity to generate accurate predictions about real-world events. See also Chap. 3, n. 8.

that create it may become obvious when it is realized as a model.[32] A model of the kind presented here, that is, has a function analogous to that of social experiment, and, like the kind of safeguarded experiment suggested by Cardinal Morton, it reflects the awareness that social problems are often so complex that theoretical solutions to them cannot be evaluated simply by ratiocination.

Of course More did not think in terms of theoretical models. But the fact that this twentieth-century term so precisely fits the Polylerite example suggests that it is correct to regard the episode

[32] Cf. Van Dyke, p. 105: "models may . . . have a good deal to do with explanation and prescription. . . . the engineer who makes a model for flood control purposes . . . builds his model on the basis of a theory about the cause of floods, and he can check his theory through tests [on the model]." See also Apostel, p. 11. Discussing the functions of the physical model, Kaplan says that "it allows for experimentation that would otherwise not be feasible. And by varying its construction or operation we can use it to trace out the consequences of alternative sets of assumptions, and so calculate an outcome or assess a theory" (p. 273).

Perhaps it is in this connection that we should note that, despite its attractive features, the Polylerite system hardly seems perfect to modern readers. In particular, this system does not fully embody Hythloday's point that the severity of punishment ought to be proportional to the degree of heinousness of the crime: all thefts of whatever kind or size appear to be punished by perpetual bondage. (This objection does not apply to Utopian criminal justice [*Ut.*, p. 191; see below, p. 204].) Moreover, the Polylerites utilize capital punishment (so forcefully opposed by Hythloday in his condemnation of the English system) for various offenses related to the attempt of a slave to escape. As in the case of the dissonance between Hythloday's claims about councilors and the portrayal of Morton, there are several possible explanations. More may not have noticed the flaws; he may have intended them to undermine Hythloday (see Wooden 1977, pp. 40-41); or (what seems to me most plausible) he may have wanted to make sure that readers would think the Polylerite system preferable to the English (as it certainly is) by substituting for that exceedingly harsh system one only a little less harsh. *We* think the Polylerite punishments shockingly harsh because we are accustomed to milder ones; More's early readers might, for the corresponding reason, have thought lesser punishments than those employed by the Polylerites shockingly mild.

as embodying an anticipation of this powerful methodological concept. Moreover, the notion that one of the purposes of the dialogue of Book I is to illustrate and recommend the use of such models in the assessment of proposed solutions to social problems gains support from a consideration of the nature of Hythloday's paired examples of the meetings of royal councils. These examples in fact model, for the purpose of testing, the theoretical solution of the problem of counsel that is standard in humanist political theory.

The fictional occasion for the introduction of the examples is the exchange between Hythloday and More that follows Hythloday's account of the conversation at Morton's table. This account leaves the character More unconvinced of the justification of Hythloday's refusal to join a council: "I cannot change my mind but must needs think that, if you could persuade yourself not to shun the courts of kings, you could do the greatest good to the public[33] by your advice" (p. 87). Hythloday takes this remark to mean that More espouses the blandly banal approach to the problem of counsel embodied in such works as *The Education of a Christian Prince*. To be precise, he takes it that More espouses the implementation of one half of the theory of counsel found in such works—the half that it is in the power of humanists to implement. In these works, as Hexter says, we read that kings should be uncorrupt and that wise men should go to court to offer disinterested advice. Given that the first of these recommendations is not within the power of humanists to implement, should they nonetheless implement the second? Hythloday assumes that More believes that they should, and he undertakes to refute this view by offering a pair of models in which this half of the theory is applied in the setting of two realistically-described councils. (The irony of the situation—in which Hythloday attributes to the character More a theory that, as Hexter points out, the author More regards as naive—is highly characteristic.)

---

[33] I have substituted "public" for Yale's "common weal." The Latin is "in publicum." See Skinner 1967, p. 167.

These examples are masterpieces, brilliantly conceived and executed. The first offers a meeting of the French privy council, engaged in a discussion of foreign policy. What foreign policy turns out to mean is a collection of stratagems through which the French king can get his hands on as much of other rulers' territory as possible. The extent of his ambition is satirized by means of a tumbling, Rabelaisian catalog of intended gluttonies. Just as Picrochole and his advisers enlarge in imagination his prospective victory over Grangousier to Alexandrian exploits that will carry his victorious armies at least as far as the Euphrates (*Gargantua and Pantagruel* I.xxxiii), so Hythloday's French king and his councilors are

> setting . . . [their] wits to work to consider by what crafty machinations . . . [the king] may keep his hold on Milan and bring back into his power the Naples which has been eluding his grasp; then overwhelm Venice and subjugate the whole of Italy; next bring under his sway Flanders, Brabant, and, finally, the whole of Burgundy—and other nations, too, whose territory he has already conceived the idea of usurping. (p. 87)

The toadying councilors compete with each other in offering nefarious schemes for effecting these ends: treaties meant to be broken; the hiring of German mercenaries; the bribing of the Swiss and of the Emperor; the propitiation of another greedy monarch, the King of Aragon, by ceding him "someone else's kingdom of Navarre"; a prospective marriage alliance to catch the Prince of Castile and the suborning of some of his nobles by pensions; false assurances of friendship to the English, combined with attempts to stir up the Scots and covert sponsorship of a pretender to the English throne (pp. 87-89).

The comedy of the council becomes somewhat chilling when one realizes, as More's intended audience certainly did, that the reconstruction is essentially factual: this model, like that of the Polylerites, is based largely on the contemplation of actual examples. The ambitions attributed to the French king recapitulate

the real ambitions of the monarchs of France in the decades
leading up to the publication of *Utopia*. In summation of his
detailed matching of items in the passage with examples of French
policy, Surtz writes that

> More's portrayal . . . does justice to the territorial ambitions
> of the French kings from 1461 to 1559. Those ambitions
> were not limited by motives of defense, by calculation of
> internal gain, or by patriotic considerations but were the
> expression of greed for glory and for territory curbed only
> by the ready exhaustibility of their military and fiscal re-
> sources and by the resistance of other rulers. (*Ut.*, pp. 353-
> 54n)

Moreover, the stratagems proposed for fulfilling these ambitions
constitute an accurate list of some of those actually pursued by
France in this period. The French really did buy an alliance with
the Emperor Maximilian, cede "someone else's kingdom of Navarre" to the Aragonese, support the Scots in order to diffuse
English military energies, sponsor pretenders to the English
throne, and so on (*Ut.*, pp. 354-57n; Surtz 1957b, pp. 291-
93).[34]

The council on domestic affairs is similar. The sole domestic
concern of the king and councilors of this nameless country is to
determine "by what schemes they may heap up treasure" for the
king (p. 91). Hythloday's claim that kings concern themselves
only with war is not quite true: they are willing to look homeward
if the financial prospects are tempting enough. Again the range
of stratagems offered by the councilors is impressive. It includes
several that ingeniously combine fleecing the citizenry with enhancing the king's reputation for virtue. The value of monies
can be raised or lowered according as the king has money to pay
or to receive; a "make-believe war" can serve as a pretext to raise
money and to raise the king's reputation when later he compas-

[34] It has been pointed out that some of the practices enumerated by Hythloday
also find parallels in the policies of Henry VIII (Ames, pp. 11-12; Surtz 1957b,
p. 292).

sionately decides for peace; "old and moth-eaten laws" can be enforced in order to extort fines while increasing the king's reputation for justice; prohibition of "many things and especially such as it is to the people's advantage not to allow" can be coupled with the sale of dispensations "to those with whose interests the prohibition has interfered"; a corrupted and intimidated judiciary will assure that cases are decided in the king's favor (pp. 91-93). Finally, a blanket justification of the king's extortions can be derived from political theory:

> the king, however much he wishes, can do no wrong; for all that all men possess is his, as they themselves are, and so much is a man's own as the king's kindness has not taken away from him. It is much to the king's interest that the latter be as little as possible, seeing that his safeguard lies in the fact that the people do not grow insolent with wealth and freedom. These things make them less patient to endure harsh and unjust commands, while, on the other hand, poverty and need blunt their spirits, make them patient, and take away from the oppressed the lofty spirit of rebellion. (p. 95)

Philosophy has a role in government after all.[35]

Again the policies recommended correspond in detail to the practices of European monarchs. In particular, as Ames and Surtz show, they are reminiscent of the machinations of Henry VII. Bacon, for example, says that "in his secret intentions . . . [Henry] had no purpose to go through with any war upon France. . . . he did but traffic with that war, to make his return in money" (*The History of the Reign of King Henry VII*, p. 140, quoted *Ut.*, p. 362n). Of Dudley and Empson, Bacon says that "their principal working was upon penal laws, wherein they spared none great nor small; nor considered whether the law were possible or impossible, in use or obsolete, but raked over all old and new statutes, though many of them were made with intention rather

---

[35] For the philosophical positions perverted here, see *Ut.*, p. 365n.

of terror than of rigour" (p. 223, quoted *Ut.*, p. 363n). The
Spanish ambassador to Henry's court reported that "the King
himself said to me, that it is his intention to keep his subjects
low, because riches would only make them haughty" (quoted
Ut., p. 365n).[36]

These councils, then, form persuasive examples of Hythloday's
initial points about kings and councilors. Despite their satiric
quality, they strike any reader as essentially accurate representations: describing governmental councils is, after all, one of
those cases where it is difficult *not* to write satire.

In turn, the verisimilitude of the councils makes them devastatingly effective as theoretical models. In the midst of such
councilors and such counsels, Hythloday imagines himself, an
exemplary humanist moral philosopher, rising to offer a different
kind of advice—deliberative orations pervaded, we note, like
Hythloday's speeches at Morton's table, by the claim that accurate
analysis shows that the expedient is identical to the moral.

In the meeting of the French privy council,

> when so many distinguished persons are vying with each
> other in proposals of a warlike nature, what if an insignif-
> icant fellow like myself were to get up and advise going on
> another tack? Suppose I expressed the opinion that Italy
> should be left alone. Suppose I argued that we should stay
> at home because the single kingdom of France by itself was
> almost too large to be governed well by a single man so that
> the king should not dream of adding other dominions under
> his sway. (p. 89)

He goes on to cite the example of the Achorians, "who live on
the mainland to the south-southeast of the island of Utopia"
(Hythloday's first mention of Utopia). After their king secured
a second realm, it was found that, "being distracted with the
charge of two kingdoms, [he] could not properly attend to either"

[36] For other parallels, see Ames, p. 12, and *Ut.*, pp. 362-65n. Surtz cites
several passages from Erasmus and other humanists that suggest that such
practices were common among European monarchs.

(p. 91). In consequence the Achorians "took counsel together and most courteously offered their king his choice of retaining whichever of the two kingdoms he preferred. He could not keep both because there were too many of them to be ruled by half a king. . . ."³⁷ And Hythloday imagines himself arguing what is of course true, that "all this warmongering, by which so many nations were kept in a turmoil on the French king's account, would, after draining his resources and destroying his people, at length by some mischance end in naught³⁸ and that therefore he had better look after his ancestral kingdom and make it as prosperous and flourishing as possible, love his subjects and be loved by them, live with them and rule them gently, and have no designs upon other kingdoms since what he already possessed was more than enough for him."

Similarly, in the council on domestic policy, Hythloday pictures himself rising to

maintain that these counsels are both dishonorable and dangerous for the king, whose very safety, not merely his honor, rests on the people's resources rather than his own. Suppose I should show that they choose a king for their own sake and not for his—to be plain, that by his labor and effort they may live well and safe from injustice and wrong. For this very reason, it belongs to the king to take more care for the welfare of his people than for his own, just as it is the duty of a shepherd, insofar as he is a shepherd, to feed his sheep rather than himself. (p. 95)

³⁷ The sensible proceedings of the Achorians ("without place" [*Ut.*, p. 358n]), like those of the Polylerites, again underline the inadvisability of assuming that More's joking names signal his disapproval of the ideas associated with them. Contrast Sylvester 1968, p. 298: "The names of these strange lands chart the mental course upon which we are sailing. Beginning with 'much nonsense' (Hythlodaeus' own name and his misreading of his own story), we progress to a countryless people. . . ."

³⁸ Cf. *Ut.*, p. 360n: "The disaster which Hythlodaeus predicted for the French King's conquest struck at Pavia in 1525 when Francis I lost Milan and was taken prisoner by the army of Charles V."

He imagines himself going on to say that "the blunt facts reveal
that they are completely wrong in thinking that the poverty of
the people is the safeguard of peace." Moreover, "to have a single
person enjoy a life of pleasure and self-indulgence amid the groans
and lamentations of all around him is to be the keeper, not of a
kingdom, but of a jail." Finally, he puts before the council "the
law of the Macarians, a people not very far distant from Utopia,"
who force their king to swear "that he will never have at one
time in his coffer more than a thousand pounds of gold or its
equivalent in silver" (p. 97).

If the policies recommended by the other councilors correspond
in detail to the actual practices of European monarchs, the policies
that Hythloday imagines himself espousing are, as Surtz's Commentary makes clear, equally close to the humanist *specula* and
other humanist political writings. Hythloday's advice that the
king "look after his ancestral kingdom and make it as prosperous
and flourishing as possible [ornaret quantum posset, & faceret
quam florentissimum]" (p. 91) seems to echo the proverb "Spar-
tam nactus es, hanc orna," which Erasmus discusses at length in
the 1515 edition of the *Adages*, and which he says in *The Education
of a Christian Prince* "is worthy of being engraved on the devices
of every prince" (pp. 247-48, quoted *Ut.*, p. 360n). Like Hythloday, Erasmus says, in his discussion of this adage, that "the
proper field, and the finest, for the high deeds of princes is within
the frontiers of their own realm" (*Adages*, p. 307). Similar advice
is found in *specula* from Isocrates to Budé (*Ut.*, pp. 360n, 361n).
The idea that the prince should "see to it that he is loved" (*ECP*,
p. 206) had been a commonplace of political thought at least
since Cicero (*Ut.*, pp. 360-61n). Similarly, the sentiment that
the people "choose a king for their own sake and not for his" is,
as Surtz says, immemorial (p. 366n). Erasmus says that the prince
should remember that his children are "born for the state and
are being educated for the state, not for his own fancy" (*ECP*,
p. 142). The idea that an impoverished people is most apt for
revolution finds parallels in several classical sources as well as in
Patrizi and Erasmus (*Ut.*, p. 367n). Hythloday says that a king

who "cannot reform the lives of citizens in any other way than by depriving them of the good things of life must admit that he does not know how to rule free men" (p. 97). Similarly, Erasmus asks: "And who, now, would swell with pride because he rules over men cowed down by fear, like so many cattle?" (*ECP*, p. 178, quoted *Ut.*, pp. 367-68n). Like Hythloday, Erasmus believes that a king should "think himself great in proportion as his people are good; . . . estimate his own happiness by the happiness of those whom he governs; . . . deem himself glorious in proportion as his subjects are free; rich, if the public are rich; and flourishing, if he can but keep the community flourishing, in consequence of uninterrupted peace" (*Complaint of Peace*, p. 46, quoted *Ut.*, p. 369n).[39]

Similar views are also found in More's other writings. Several of the Latin epigrams, for example, provide close parallels to Hythloday's imagined speeches. "De cvpiditate regnandi" says that "Among many kings there will be scarcely one, if there is really one, who is satisfied to have one kingdom. Among many kings there will be scarcely one, if there is really one, who rules a single kingdom well" (*Epigrams*, no. 227). "Popvlvs consentiens regnvm dat et avfert" tells us that "Any one man who has command of many men owes his subjects this: he ought to have command not one instant longer than his subjects wish" (no. 103). "Regem non satellitivm sed virtvs reddit tvtvm" warns that "Fear (accompanied as it is by hatred) does not protect a king from a plundered people, nor do towering palaces and wealth. . . . He will be safe who so rules his subjects that they judge none other more suitable to their interests" (no. 102). The epigram on the coronation of Henry VIII boldly contrasts the good qualities of the new king with the harshness and avarice of his father (no. 1).

[39] Surtz offers a number of additional parallels from antiquity and the Renaissance (*Ut.*, pp. 368-69n). Augustine describes the truly happy ruler in *The City of God* v.24 (and see XIX.19). For an account of the views of northern humanists on all these matters, and the relation of their views to Italian humanist thought, see Skinner 1978, pp. 222-48.

Hythloday's imagined speeches, that is, embody precisely the kind of traditional moral advice that More and his circle thought kings should get and take. Eloquent restatements of this advice, these speeches are convincing and even moving, especially since they contrast so violently with the preceding representations of the kind of scurrilous and, as Hythloday argues, self-deceptive and self-defeating advice that, as every reader knows too well, rulers normally *do* follow. Hythloday (or the author), that is, does not at all mean to mock the traditional wisdom of the *specula*. He means only to drive home its total inapplicability in the existing political context, the absolute futility of enacting this part of the humanist solution to the problem of counsel as long as one is powerless, because of the structure of the institutions of kingship and council, to enact the other part. The point is well made. Even as Hythloday convinces us that such advice *should* be offered and followed, he entirely convinces us that it is folly to offer it in such councils. The model proves, in this case, to be a powerful instrument for the testing of theory.

III

Having analyzed the method that More employs in Book I, we may pause to consider the question of the antecedents of this method. In this way we can begin to clarify the relationship between *Utopia* and the tradition of political theory, and the nature and significance of More's own contribution to it.

We may first consider the views on this question of those few critics who are aware that Book I *has* an important methodological dimension. Ames and R. P. Adams appear to think that More's method has no source but is simply a benefaction of the Spirit of Science. This view of course implies that *Utopia* is a work of the utmost importance, in which "a historic cape of the mind was turned, one which divides the medieval from the modern world" (see above, p. 57). Hexter, too, feels that Book I represents a new departure in political theory, but he sees that More's breakthrough is paralleled in the works of a few of his immediate predecessors and contemporaries: Fortescue, Commynes, Seyssel, Machiavelli, and Guicciardini (1952, pp. 64-65, 111-12; *Ut.*, p. ci). The fact that all these men, including More, "both wrote about politics and actively engaged in the management of affairs of state at a high level" (1952, p. 64) suggests to Hexter that the source of the methodological breakthrough lies in experience rather than learning, in practical politics rather than political philosophy.

We have seen that Hexter supports his point by contrasting the "invertebrate" analysis of humanist political theory with More's holistic approach. Despite the general validity of this contrast, however, it is possible to discern methodological parallels between *Utopia* and earlier works of political theory. Indeed these parallels also obtain in the cases of the other "statesman-writers" cited by Hexter and thus suggest that the method that characterizes these works was in part derived from the tradition of political theory.

As Quentin Skinner has shown, the Renaissance segment of that tradition originated in the independent cities of northern Italy in the thirteenth and fourteenth centuries, in the responses of a number of writers to the external and internal problems of those small polities. These writers are divided into two distinct groups: scholastically-trained legal theorists, and the so-called "pre-humanists," the professional rhetoricians whose attempt to produce a classicized rhetorical culture marks the beginning of Renaissance humanism (Skinner 1978, pp. 27-65).[40] Skinner shows that this dichotomization of political theory persisted through the end of the fifteenth century and that the problems and approaches established by the early theorists provided the conceptual framework of subsequent Italian Renaissance political theory and, with some modification, of northern theory.

Scholastic and humanist theorists agree that the principal danger for the city lies in the pursuit of private or sectional interests in place of the public interest. Most writers in both groups concur

[40] On the origins of humanism, see, in addition to Skinner's brilliant synthesis, Weiss 1947; Kristeller 1961, pp. 12-13, 100-11; 1964, pp. 147-65; Bouwsma 1973, pp. 7-18; Logan, pp. 15-31. Cf. below, pp. 262-63.

in seeing the extreme factiousness of the cities as their greatest weakness. Most humanist writers also find the pursuit of private wealth and the taste for luxury to be dangerous for the city, although "civic humanists," influenced like scholastic theorists by Aristotelian views on this subject, feel that private wealth strengthens civic virtue.[41]

Since the health of the city depends on the citizens' setting aside all private and sectional interests and learning "to equate their own good with the good of their city as a whole" (Skinner 1978, p. 44), the question how to achieve this desired condition becomes the central concern of theory. Humanists and scholastics offer quite different answers. The humanists believe that the key is found in the development of virtue in the citizenry, since only virtuous men can be expected to put the common good before selfish interests. For the scholastics the solution lies in good institutions (p. 45).

As Skinner notes, the viewpoint of the humanists "is reflected in each of the major topics they consider in discussing the practical question of how the common good is to be secured." If the health of the city depends on the virtue of its citizens, the virtue of the leaders is of particular importance, since these men heavily influence the course of the city both directly and through the tendency of other citizens to imitate their leaders. Accordingly, humanist writers treat "with special seriousness the problems of how to promote men of virtue to serve as leaders of the people." A principal part of the answer is that political office must not be restricted to the traditional nobility but be open to men of all classes, a proposition that is developed in conjunction with the idea that the only genuine nobility lies in virtue. "The other major concern of these writers," Skinner says, "is to consider what advice should be given to *podestà* and other magistrates once they have duly been elected and installed in office":

This is the point at which they reveal most clearly their sense that what matters most in good government is not the

[41] On "civic humanism," see (in addition to Skinner) Baron 1938, 1966.

fabric of institutions, but rather the spirit and outlook of the men who run them. They scarcely offer any analysis of the administrative structure of the City Republics; they concentrate all their attention on the question of what attitudes a magistrate must adopt in order to ensure that the common good of his city is constantly pursued. (p. 46)

In general their answer is that the magistrate must exemplify in all his actions the cardinal virtues of classical ethics and the Christian virtues. This is especially the case since, as these writers insist, the politically prudent and the moral are always identical (p. 48). The humanists' conviction of the importance of inculcating virtue in the ruler and the citizenry is also reflected in the attention that they devote, from the turn of the fifteenth century, to the production of works of educational theory.

Scholastic theorists, on the contrary, "tend . . . to devote their main attention to the machinery of government. They present themselves less as moralists than as political analysts, pinning their hopes less on virtuous individuals than on efficient institutions as the best means of promoting the common good and the rule of peace" (p. 60). Since factionalism is the main obstacle to pursuit of the common good, the principal institutional reforms they propose are designed to inhibit the development of factions. Marsiglio of Padua, for example, argues that one encouragement to faction lies in the division of power within the ruling council of a city. Accordingly, he proposes "that magistracy must never be divided. . . . even though the government may consist of 'several men,' it must be 'numerically one government with respect to office,' thus ensuring a 'numerical unity' in 'every action, judgment, sentence or command forthcoming from them' " (p. 61; *Defensor pacis*, p. 81). The most dangerous type of factiousness appears when hostile groups of citizens form rival parties. To avoid this situation, both Marsiglio and Bartolus of Sassoferrato propose that sovereignty should be vested in the people as a whole, "so that no such internecine fighting can in principle arise." To guarantee that delegated authorities do not in fact usurp sovereignty both writers "propose three constraints to be imposed on all rulers and magistrates to prevent them from ignoring the will of the people and so degenerating into tyrants" (p. 63). First, the supreme ruler should be chosen by election rather than hereditary succession. Second, rulers should be allowed the minimum possible discretion in administering the law. Third, "a complex system of checks . . . [should] be imposed on all magistrates and ruling councils to ensure that they remain responsive at all times to the wishes of the citizens who elected them" (p. 64).

It is clear, as Skinner points out (pp. 223-24, 255), that analytic concepts developed in Renaissance political theory underly Hythloday's assessment of the condition of England. The social malaise of which theft is a symptom stems mainly from the circumstance that many members of the propertied classes pursue their private interests rather than the public welfare. These men "are not content . . . to do no good to their country; they must also do it positive harm. . . . Consequently, in order that one insatiable glutton and accursed plague of his native land may join field to field and surround many thousand acres with one fence, tenants are evicted" (*Ut.*, p. 67). "Thus, the unscrupulous greed of a few" (p. 69) is destroying the felicity of England. Hythloday also echoes traditional views when he expatiates on "ill-timed luxury" and its spread through the social order.[42] And

---

[42] Guicciardini laments the fact that the prevailing "style of living" among the Florentine people is "such that everyone wants very much to be rich," and that "this appetite makes men pursue their personal advantage without respect or consideration for the public honor and glory" (*Maxims*, p. 102, quoted Skinner 1978, p. 163). As Skinner notes (ibid.), similar statements are found in Machiavelli's *Discourses*.

Hanson's characterization of English political life in this period confirms Hythloday's analysis:

the absence of a civic frame of reference meant that even the most important political issues were reduced to a merely personal or at best a regional level. Instead of assessing matters in terms of their general implications and thus offering genuine alternatives in the realm of public policy, the barons interpreted them in the framework of personal, familial, and dy-

when, turning to France, Hythloday condemns the use of mercenaries as a "plague" (p. 63) endangering the nation and goes
on to argue the superiority of a citizen army, he is applying
another standard *topos* of the Italian analysis of corruption.[43]

It is also clear that Hythloday's approach to the formulation
of solutions for the problems of England aligns him (and his
creator) with the scholastic theorists, even as, as Hexter points
out, it distinguishes him from earlier humanists. It is in this
connection, as I suggested earlier, that we are to understand the
repeated hints, in the passage immediately preceding the dialogue, to the effect that the primary concern of Hythloday's talk
(and *Utopia* as a whole) is with the bearing of institutional arrangements on the attainment of good government. Hythloday

---

nastic welfare. . . . There was, therefore, not merely an absence of sustained
public policy but a positive antipathy to it among the most influential men
of the realm (p. 134).

[43] More's application of this *topos* sets him apart from other northern theorists
(even as it links him with the Italians), since, as Skinner points out, the relative
merits of citizen and mercenary armies is one of "a number of issues central
to Italian political debate [that] were scarcely accorded any attention in northern
Europe" (1978, p. 244; cf. p. 246). (The moral condemnation of mercenaries
and those who employ them is, however, a frequent topic in Erasmus' writings.
See Surtz 1957b, pp. 297-98.) But Skinner misinterprets More's stand on this
matter. Overlooking Hythloday's comments on mercenaries and citizen-soldiers
in Book I, he deduces More's approval of mercenaries from the fact that the
Utopians utilize them, while doing "everything they can to avoid 'sending their
own citizens' [*Ut.*, pp. 205-7] into battle" (p. 246). But there is good reason
for thinking that More does not approve the Utopian use of mercenaries (see
below, pp. 240-41), and, moreover, the Utopian military establishment epit-
omizes the ideal of the citizen army, a fact that is heavily emphasized. Although
the Utopians loathe war, "nevertheless men and women alike assiduously exercise themselves in military training on fixed days lest they should be unfit for
war when need requires" (p. 201), and "when personal service is inevitable,
they are as courageous in fighting as they were ingenious in avoiding it as long
as they might. . . . Moreover, their expert training in military discipline gives
them confidence" (p. 211). The last thing that Hythloday tells us about the
Utopians is that following the religious ceremony at the end of each month
they pass "the rest of the day . . . in games and in exercises of military training"
(p. 237).

does not suggest that pursuit of the public interest can be assured by exhortations to virtue or by promoting virtuous men to positions of power. Instead, he proposes legal and institutional changes that will *force* men to act in accordance with the public interest (see above, pp. 55-56). The same approach underlies the design of the Polylerite system of criminal justice and the fictitious examples of the Achorians and Macarians in Hythloday's imagined council speeches. The Polylerite system is designed to treat thieves in such a way that "they *necessarily* become good [ut bonos esse necesse sit]" (p. 79; my emphasis). Similarly, the Achorians do not merely entreat their kings to behave with decency. The Achorians' ambitious king was not advised but "*obliged [coactus]* to be content with his own realm" (p. 91; my emphasis). The Macarian law that forbids the king to have more than a thousand pounds of gold in his coffer was "instituted by a very good king, *who cared more for his country's interest than his own wealth*":

> He saw that this treasure would be sufficient for the king to put down rebellion and for his kingdom to meet hostile invasions. It was not large enough, however, to tempt him to encroach on the possessions of others. The *prevention* of the latter was the primary purpose of his legislation. His secondary consideration was that provision was thus made to forestall any shortage of the money needed in the daily business transactions of the citizens. He felt, too, that since the king *had* to pay out whatever came into his treasury beyond the limit prescribed by law, he would not seek occasion to commit injustice. Such a king will be both a terror to the evil and beloved by the good. (p. 97; my emphases)

Hexter is also correct in associating More's approach with that of such writers as Machiavelli and Guicciardini. But he is wrong in suggesting that these writers have no methodological debt to previous political theory. As Skinner makes clear, the brilliant flowering of Italian political theory at the turn of the sixteenth century should be understood primarily in terms of a fusion of the humanist and scholastic strands of earlier Italian theory. This fusion includes, among other things, combinations of the approaches of the humanists and scholastics to securing the pursuit of the public interest.

In his *Tract on the Constitution and Government of the City of Florence* (1498), Savonarola, like earlier theorists in both camps, espouses republican liberty and cites domestic discord and the employment of mercenaries as the prime dangers to this liberty (Skinner 1978, pp. 147-48). To combat these dangers, he "places his entire faith in the efficacy of institutions, arguing in characteristically scholastic style that the only sure solution lies in treating the whole body of the citizens as the supreme authority in all political affairs" (p. 148). Mario Salamonio, in his dialogues on *The Sovereignty of the Roman Patriciate* (c. 1513), finds the cause of Italy's troubles in "a combination of military weakness and enormous wealth" and "accordingly reverts to the old argument . . . that a good civic life must be founded on the virtue of frugality," as well as "the usual attack on 'those who fight with mercenaries' " (pp. 149-50). Considering how the city can be regulated, Salamonio

> begins with a suggestion which is more humanist than scholastic in inspiration, claiming that "the city must concern itself with the *virtus* of its citizens," and that "every ruler must concern himself with *virtus*," offering an example of "all the moral virtues" to his subjects. . . . But his main answer consists of reiterating the same argument which had earlier been developed by Bartolus, Marsiglio and the whole tradition of scholastic legal and political writers in Italy, and which had recently been repeated by Savonarola and his disciples. The key to maintaining a free and happy civic life is said to lie in establishing effective civic institutions, while the key to maintaining these institutions in good order is said to lie in ensuring that the whole body of the citizens retains ultimate sovereignty at all times. (p. 151)

The fusion of humanist and scholastic approaches is carried to its highest point of development in Renaissance Italy in the works of Machiavelli and Guicciardini. Here again the preservation of republican liberty is the supreme value, and again there is said to be an indissoluble link between liberty and the *virtus* (or *virtù*) of the citizens. The use of mercenaries poses a grave danger to liberty, but the principal threat lies in "corruption," which Machiavelli defines as the pursuit of private good instead of the public good (p. 164). The pursuit of private wealth is one instance of this corruption.

Like earlier humanist theorists, Machiavelli and Guicciardini maintain that the principal response to these threats must be the development of civic virtue, which will cause the individual to equate "his own good with that of his city, make him devote his best energies to assuring its freedom and greatness, and in this way cause him to place his courage, his vitality and his general abilities in the service of the entire community" (p. 175). Proper education is one means to develop this *virtù*. These writers, however, also heavily emphasize the development of appropriate laws and institutions as a means of assuring the preservation of liberty and *virtù*. Some ideas of this kind had been incorporated into the civic humanist thought of the early quattrocento. Bruni anticipates Machiavelli in arguing that the main cause of corruption is "the exclusion of the people from playing a sufficiently active role in the business of government" (p. 166), and that it is consequently of great importance that institutional arrangements facilitate the participation of all citizens in the affairs of the city. The later republican theorists were also anticipated by the civic humanists in stressing the importance of mixed constitutions, especially in the cases of Rome and Venice, in preserving liberty (pp. 158, 171). Like Savonarola and Salamonio, however, Machiavelli and Guicciardini accord far more significance to institutional arrangements than the civic humanists. Machiavelli shares with scholastic theorists the insistence that sovereignty should be retained by the populace as a whole (p. 159). He is particularly acute in assessing the effects of Roman institutions and in the process of this assessment goes beyond all earlier theorists and his contemporaries to develop the far-reaching conception of the positive value of internal dissension (p. 181).

According to Machiavelli, factional conflict evinces precisely the active involvement of different classes in government that earlier theorists had advocated. Roman liberty was preserved by means of such conflict, which assured that only laws beneficial to the community as a whole could be passed.

It is clear, then, that More's approach to the analysis and solution of social problems in Book I of *Utopia* finds antecedents and parallels in Italian political theory, particularly in the scholastic branch of this tradition and in the works of those of More's immediate predecessors and contemporaries who were engaged in the attempt to fuse elements of the humanist and scholastic approaches to such problems. But it is not at all obvious where More's specific debts to this tradition lie. Parallels, though clear, are general, and More never in *Utopia* mentions any Renaissance political writer. (It was, of course, a humanist convention to acknowledge indebtedness only to classical writers.) Yet one cannot doubt that More's thinking was shaped to some extent by what he had read or heard of the work of some of these writers. [44]

If the difficulty of determining More's debts to other Renaissance political theorists is attributable partly to the general nature of these debts and to More's reluctance to acknowledge them, it is also and more importantly attributable to the fact that they are small compared with those to ancient authorities. No humanist took the Erasmian "ad fontes" more seriously than More. His way of working is clearly indicated in recent studies of *The History of King Richard III*. This book can only be described as a characteristic product of the tradition of humanist historiography that originated in Italy (cf. Kristeller 1980, p. 7), but no one, as far as I know, has detected a single definite allusion in the *History*

[44] Beginning with Budé in the early sixteenth century, increasingly sophisticated attempts at a similar fusion were undertaken by the French "legal humanists" examined by Donald R. Kelley and George Huppert. It is likely that More knew Budé's *Annotations on the Pandects* (first published 1508), which includes "numerous asides" on ancient and modern institutions (Kelley, p. 76). Budé's commendatory letter on *Utopia* stresses the *mores* and *instituta* of the Utopians.

to any earlier work in this tradition.[45] By contrast, innumerable debts—in form, interpretive concepts, and phraseology—of the *History* to the classical antecedents of this tradition have been cataloged.[46] The same state of affairs obtains in the case of *Utopia*. If no specific debts to Renaissance political theory can be found, there are many clear and heavy ones (especially in Book II) to the body of classical theory that underlies the Renaissance tradition.[47] One may say, indeed, that More's principal debt to

[45] To be sure, this fact may be attributable to the circumstance that not many people have looked for such connections. Until recently, few students of More seem to have been aware of the tradition of Italian humanist historiography and the relation between More's *History* and the biographical monographs in that tradition (but see Fueter, pp. 160-63). Sylvester, for example, does not mention the Italians in the section on "Genesis and Models" of the Introduction to his edition of the *History*. For an attempt to specify more precisely the relation between More and the Italian tradition, see McCullough.

[46] These debts are masterfully summarized in Sylvester's Introduction, pp. lxxx-xcix.

[47] Pace Skinner, who says in his review of the Yale edition of *Utopia* that the similarities between *Utopia* and classical works, including those of Plato, are "usually very slight" (1967, p. 164), and in *Foundations* notes parallels only with some Roman Stoic conceptions (see below, Chap. 3, n. 65, and p. 242). The topic arises in Skinner's discussion of Surtz's treatment of the literary relations of *Utopia*, which is based, as Skinner says, on "the (unexamined) assumption that there has got to be a causal explanation for everything More said—to put it crudely, that he must have got it all from somewhere" (1967, p. 163). Skinner's criticism of Surtz's application of this method (and of the method itself) is generally valid. There is, as he says, "a pervasive gap, . . . throughout Surtz's discussion of the influences on More, between what he claims to show and what he has actually shown" (pp. 163-64). Nevertheless, interspersed among the many insignificant parallels noted by Surtz there are others, particularly between *Utopia* and the political writings of Plato and Aristotle, that can hardly be explained "by invoking nothing more than the contingent fact of . . . [the] similar aims" (p. 163) of these writers, namely, those passages that exhibit not only parallels of subject but also close and sometimes extended parallels of argument and close verbal parallels. Chapter Three includes a detailed study of the relation between More and the Greek theorists and demonstrates, I believe, the fundamental importance, for the interpretation of *Utopia*, of grasping this relation. For More's views on the importance of Greek studies, see *Sel. Let.*, pp. 50-54, 98-101 (*Cor.*, pp. 63-66, 115-18); and n. 4 above.

earlier humanist political thinkers lay in the fact that they called
fresh attention to and provided good texts of the classical theorists.
Moreover, he acknowledges these classical sources, in the indirect
way that his fictional procedure allows. Hythloday is interested
in Greek philosophy, and in Cicero and Seneca among the Latins
(*Ut.*, pp. 49-51). His sailing has been like that of Plato (whose
views he cites on two occasions) (pp. 49, 87, 103). He took with
him to Utopia (among other useful books) "most of Plato's works,
many[48] of Aristotle's, . . . and the works of Plutarch, . . .
Thucydides and Herodotus, as well as Herodian" (pp. 181-83).[49]

In order to understand the nature and significance of More's
engagement with the classical political theorists, it is necessary
to have some sense both of the general relations between Renaissance and classical theory and of the shape of the classical
theoretical tradition. Like other branches of Renaissance thought,
Renaissance political theory is largely a revival and extension of
the corresponding area of classical thought, and like other branches
it proceeds (especially insofar as it is a humanist enterprise) roughly
from the assimilation of Roman achievements to the assimilation
of Greek ones. Moreover, it is clear that the respective approaches
of humanist "moralists" and scholastic "political analysts" (Skinner 1978, p. 60) to the problem of assuring the pursuit of the
common good derive primarily from the respective classical antecedents of the two traditions.

In political theory as elsewhere the thought of the early humanists has its principal sources in the Roman rhetorical tradition,
and especially Cicero and Seneca (the only two Roman philosophers that Hythloday regards as worth reading). Seneca is a Stoic;

[48] Yale has "several." The Latin is "plura." White (1976, p. 637n) argues
for "many," which is also R. M. Adams's translation.
[49] Stapleton says that "amongst the philosophers" More "read especially Plato
and his followers, . . . because he considered their teaching most useful in the
government of the State and the preservation of civic order" (p. 13, quoted
Ut., pp. clvi-clvii). He also observes that More "studied with avidity all the
historical works he could find" (p. 14). In the Letter to Dorp, More says that
Aristotle is a philosopher "whom I love above many" (*Sel. Let.*, p. 52, quoted
White 1976, p. 637; *Cor.*, p. 64).

and though Cicero styles himself a member of the New Academy, his sympathies in ethical and political theory lie mainly with the Stoics, whose views he often rehearses at length. Accordingly, the political ideas of the early humanists are almost exclusively Stoic (see, e.g., F. Gilbert, p. 473; Skinner 1978, pp. 42-48). Moreover, the genres usually employed by the humanists in their political writing—the *speculum* and the history as well as deliberative and demonstrative orations—reflect their dependence on classical rhetoric. The epistolary advice-book is affiliated with the rhetorical tradition from its origin in Isocrates' *To Nicocles*. History, which in the classical world is often regarded as a branch of rhetoric,[50] is a principal vehicle for political theory in antiquity.

It hardly need be said that the leading political ideas of the scholastic theorists derive from Aristotelian theory. The *Politics* (like the *Nicomachean Ethics*) became available in Latin translation in the mid-thirteenth century (Knowles, pp. 191-92). Its impact on Italian scholastic political theory is clearest in the work of the first and greatest member of that tradition, Marsiglio of Padua (c. 1275-1342). Marsiglio regarded his *Defensor pacis* as a supplement to Aristotle's treatment of the causes of civil strife (pp. 4-5; cf. Gewirth, pp. 33-34), and the work is permeated with the concepts of the *Politics*, which is cited at every turn. Skinner observes that the political tracts of Bartolus of Sassoferrato are also "heavily reliant on Aristotle's *Politics* both in doctrine and style of argument" (p. 51). Bartolus "quotes Aristotle repeatedly throughout his political works, in which the main aim— as Bartolus himself indicates—is to deploy an Aristotelian theory of political society in order to diagnose and seek to remedy the internal weaknesses of the Italian City Republics" (pp. 51-52).

Moreover, the basic difference of approach between scholastic and humanist theory—the difference between an institutional and analytic approach and an individual and moralistic one—reflects a parallel dichotomy in classical political theory. This fact will

---

[50] Cicero treats true history, as opposed to annalistic writing, as a branch of the rhetorician's art (*De Or.* II.xi.51-xv.64; cf. *Leg.* I.ii.5, *Or.* XI.37).

become apparent if we trace briefly the development of the dichotomy.

Aristotle's *Politics* is the culminating work in the brief, brilliant tradition that originates in Plato's *Republic*, the theory of the city-state. In this tradition political theory first becomes a branch of speculative philosophy, logically connected with ethics but having its own distinct concerns. The link between ethics and politics is provided by the concept of self-sufficiency (αὐτάρκεια). Ethics has its bases in psychology and physiology, which clarify the nature of man. Given that nature, the central subject of ethics is the determination of the best life for the individual. Ethics leads into politics because, as Plato says, "the individual is not self-sufficient, but has many needs which he can't supply himself" (*Rep.* II.369B). The original subject of political philosophy, then, is the determination of the best form of the polis; that is, of the configuration of men and material resources that will constitute a self-sufficient unit and thus produce for its citizens the happiness that they cannot achieve in isolation from one another.

The principal features of Plato's study of political life are its rationalism and its holism. Plato views the polis as a closed, unified, and organic system of which all the parts are reciprocally affecting and in which the allocation of human and material resources must be governed by a rationally determined and clearly articulated hierarchy of values. The totalitarian nature of his ideal polis reflects this view. Since the philosopher knows precisely what is best for the polis, he is irresponsible if he declines to dictate its every detail: "it would be a sin either for mating or for anything else in our ideal society to take place without regulation" (*Rep.* v.458D-E).

Aristotle's approach to the study of political life is similarly rational and holistic. The treatment of the ideal polis in Books VII and VIII of the *Politics* opens with a discussion, similar to Plato's, of the relation between ethics and politics.[51] These

---

[51] At the end of the *Nicomachean Ethics*, Aristotle offers a different view of

preliminary remarks lead to a discussion of the geographic and demographic requirements of the polis and to the enumeration of the occupational functions that must be performed in it. As in Plato the central conception is that the polis should be a perfectly unified and economical system: the aim is the attainment of a polis of just those components and just that size (in terms of both population and area) that will be self-sufficient (*Pol.* VII. 1323a-1327b). In the other books of the *Politics* Aristotle applies the same sophisticated analytic conceptions to studies of the workings of a number of actual poleis. Since, as Sabine observes, in these books Aristotle treats the "actual apart from the ideal constitution," political philosophy here for the first time moves outside the confines of normative theory into positive theory (p. 108). The departure from normative theory is clearest in the discussion in

---

this relation. The arguments of ethics show what men must do in order to be good. But arguments are not "in themselves enough to make men good" (X. 1179b), for most men "do not by nature obey the sense of shame, but only fear, and do not abstain from bad acts because of their baseness but through fear of punishment. . . . What argument would remould such people?" Thus most men can be made virtuous only by law (1179b-1180a), so that "he who wants to make men . . . better by his care must try to become capable of legislating" (1180b). Hence the philosopher must complement his study of ethics by an examination of the science of legislation, "and in general study the question of the constitution" (1181b). Cf. *Politics* VII. 1333a: "the legislator must labour to ensure that his citizens become good men. He must therefore know what institutions will produce this result, and what is the end or aim to which a good life is directed."

These passages are sources of the institutional approach of scholastic political theory, and there are obvious resonances between them and Hythloday's accounts of various legal and institutional arrangements designed so that men "necessarily become good" (see above, pp. 79-80). The first passage may also be a direct source of Machiavelli's observation that "it is necessary for him who lays out a state and arranges laws for it to presuppose that all men are evil and that they are always going to act according to the wickedness of their spirits whenever they have free scope. . . . men never do anything good except by necessity, but where there is plenty of choice and excessive freedom is possible, everything is at once filled with confusion and disorder. Hence it is said that hunger and poverty make men industrious, and the laws make them good" (*Discourses* I.iii).

Book V of the means by which a tyrant can maintain his position, where the value-free discussion of "political mechanics" (p. 91) makes its first appearance in political theory.

With the *Politics* the first phase of the classical tradition of political theory comes to an end. By the time of Aristotle's death, it was evident, especially from the career of Alexander, that the polis was no longer either actually or potentially a self-sufficient unit. It remained then to think of self-sufficiency as an attribute either of the individual (or the individual and his immediate surroundings) or of a larger political unit that incorporated the polis. Both possibilities are explored in post-Aristotelian thought.

The attempt to locate self-sufficiency in the individual involves not political but ethical theory. And indeed the two principal early philosophical schools associated with this effort—the Epicurean and the Cynic—are only tangentially and negatively concerned with politics. To some extent, this is also the case with Stoicism, which emerged from Cynicism. From the beginning, Stoic writing repeatedly presents the image of the sage who, finding sufficiency in himself, stands apart from a corrupt world. But Stoicism also developed, especially in its Roman phase (see Arnold's rich and durable account; and McIlwain, pp. 105-6), an ethical ideal of the man of action and a political philosophy that became the dominant view of late antiquity.

Stoic ethics has its starting point not in psychology and physiology but in physics and metaphysics. Man's business is to apprehend as much as possible of the plan of nature (the λόγος) and then to conform himself willingly to his part in it.[52] This conformity is virtue, and virtue is the only good.

---

[52] Of course nature (φύσις, as opposed to convention, θέσις) is the standard appealed to by all the ancient schools. I shall not attempt to explain how the Stoics derive their particular injunctions from this source. Indeed, it is difficult to apprehend Stoic doctrine as internally consistent. This fact reflects the endemic paradox, obscurity, and overstatement of Stoic utterances, as well as the long evolutionary history of the school and the circumstance that the ideas of its

Among other things, nature tells us that man is a social being (e.g., Cicero, *Off.* I.xliv.157-xlv.159; Seneca, *Ep.* IX.17); hence one should participate in the life of the community and recognize that its interests take precedence over private ones (Arnold, p. 284; cf. *Off.* I.iv.12, vii.22). The aspirant to virtue will also pursue certain "expedients" (*utilia*: e.g., *Off.* I.iii.10) or "advantages" (*commoda*: e.g., *Off.* II.iii.9; Seneca, *Ep.* LXXIV.17)—such as health, property, and honor—which, though not goods, yet have some degree of worth (Arnold, pp. 288-92). The theory of practical ethics consists in elaborating duties (*officia*), the performance of which constitutes the pursuit of virtue and expediency (*Off.* I.iii.7-10, III.iii.13-15; Arnold, pp. 301ff.; Hunt, pp. 160-62).

Nature also suggests the ideal form of the community. All men are brothers (*Off.* III.vi.28, xvii.69), and this fact implies that the true community is a cosmopolis of which all are citizens and which has the natural law as its constitution (Arnold, pp. 274-75; see also Sabine, pp. 149-50; Reesor; Hammond). This conception, which first appeared in Zeno's polemically-titled *Republic*, bears the same idealizing relation to the realities of the world bequeathed by Alexander as the ideal poleis of Plato and Aristotle bear to the Periclean world. The opposition between these ideals is radical. Whereas the ideal poleis of the city-state theorists are founded on convictions of the intrinsic inequality of different ethnic groups, of different classes of inhabitants of the city, and (to a lesser extent) of the sexes, and are in these and many other ways rigidly traditional and conservative, the Stoic theory of the cosmopolis is based on the explicit denial of the validity of all invidious distinctions of race, caste, and sex, and is characterized by extraordinarily innovative (sometimes fantastic) suggestions (Arnold, pp. 274-79). Money, written laws, law courts, gymnasia, temples and images would not exist in the ideal

---

major early representatives are known only through fragments, through allusions by later philosophers and imaginative writers, and, especially, through Cicero's paraphrases and popularizations.

cosmopolis. The conventions governing sexual relations would be abolished, as would slavery. The bodies of the dead would be disposed of in any convenient way: funeral rites are merely conventional. War, instead of being a natural and honorific activity (as in Plato and Aristotle) is fratricide.

Of course this cosmopolis is only an ideal. Stoic political thought, especially in its connection with the Roman ruling class, developed more practical guides to life in the real cosmopolis. It is symptomatic, for example, that Panaetius, the founder of Roman Stoicism and a member of the inner circle of Scipio Africanus minor, justified slavery by Platonic and Aristotelian arguments that the natural inferiority of some men renders them unable to govern themselves (p. 279). Similar adjustments were made throughout Stoic ethics and politics, particularly by laying greater stress on the "expedients." All the same, Roman Stoic conceptions of ethical and political *officia* are ennobled by the pervasive, as it were haunting, influence of the original vision of the school. Later writers like to say that the ideal cosmopolis actually exists: each man belongs to it, as well as to the particular polity in which he dwells (e.g., Seneca, *De otio* III.4; Epictetus, *Disc.* II.v.26). Ordinary states are to be regarded as "partial realizations" of the ideal (Arnold, pp. 274-75), and the good man should strive to make the realization as complete as possible. Such considerations are reflected in the egalitarian, humanitarian, and anti-militaristic strains that increasingly manifest themselves in Roman philosophical writing, and in literature and law.

Stoic political theory, then, marks a radical departure from city-state theory, one that, since it has so heavily influenced later Western views, it is impossible not to regard as an advance (cf. Carlyle, pp. 8-10; McIlwain, pp. 114-17). But it is important to note that the advance is confined to the area of political ideals. Stoic theory offers only rules of conduct, for individuals and for polities, and a rather amorphous image of the ideal cosmopolis. The sophisticated technical analysis developed in city-state theory finds no parallel in Stoic theory, although there are occasional attempts—notably in

Polybius and Cicero—to adapt to the analysis of the Roman
Republic such conceptions of city-state theory as the sixfold
classification of constitutions and the theory of the mixed constitution.

Such a political philosophy was appropriate and even pre-
dictable in the political situation in which Stoic theory developed. Discussions of the alteration of constitutions or the
foundation of new poleis—colonies—were of practical relevance in the Greece of Plato and Aristotle. But when, in the
later period, thinkers had little reason to imagine that the
design of the polity was or could be in their hands, and when
the polity itself had become such a vast and diverse conglom-
erate that it was impossible to regard it as a closed, organic
system, there was little incentive to cultivate methods for the
design of polities or for the analysis of their rise, maintenance, and decline.

As the natural complement of the world-state, Stoic political theory was viable without major change precisely as long
as the world-state lasted. As Sabine notes, the advent of
Christianity did not entail a discontinuity in political theory.
Paul's ideas of universal brotherhood, natural law, and the
obligation to respect constituted authority are wholly consonant with Stoic thought. Likewise, the political thought of
the Church Fathers is "substantially in agreement with Cicero
and Seneca" (Sabine, p. 181; cf. Arnold, p. 24). Above all,
this is the case with Augustine's *City of God*, which in some
respects, as Sir Ernest Barker observes, represents a culmination of Stoic political thought (Aristotle, *Pol.*, p. lx).

Humanist political theory begins simply as a continuation
of this Christian-Stoic tradition. Early humanist political
writing differs from its medieval antecedents only in its classicized Latinity and the increasing range of its classical references. In addition to the concept of the identity of the moral
and the expedient (above, pp. 51-53), Stoicism contributes
the idea that good government depends on the virtue of the
ruler, especially since his actions will inevitably be imitated by

other citizens (*ECP*, pp. 64, 66). The notion that virtue is
the only true nobility is also Stoic (Arnold, p. 320), and the
idea that wealth is inimical to civic virtue derives primarily from Stoic sources (Baron 1938; Skinner 1978, p.
163). *De officiis* is a source of the belief that the pursuit of
private or factional interests is a great danger to the polity
(I.xxv.85-87, III.vi.26). To be sure, the humanist *specula* in-
herit the Aristotelian classifications that, since Egidio Colon-
na's *De regimine principum*, had provided the organizational
scheme of works in this genre, and they increasingly incorporate *sententiae* and particular attractive-sounding institutional suggestions from Plato and Aristotle. But they are untouched by the central conceptions of city-state theory.

By contrast, Italian scholastic political thought signifies a genuine revival of city-state theory. This revival was initiated by
Aquinas, whose political philosophy incorporates conceptions from the *Politics*, but the full impact of Aristotelian
theory was felt only when the *Politics* was passed on to thinkers such as Marsiglio, whose association with polities similar
in many ways to the Greek city-states enabled them to respond
much more fully to Greek theory. Marsiglio's political thought
is, as Sabine writes, "essentially . . . a recrudescence of the
theory of a city-state" (p. 303):

> The Aristotelian principle which he followed most closely
> was that of the self-sufficing community capable of supply-
> ing both its physical and its moral needs. . . .
>
> Following Aristotle, Marsilio defines the state as a kind
> of "living being" composed of parts which perform the
> functions necessary to its life. Its "health," or peace, consists
> in the orderly working of each of its parts, and strife arises
> when one part does its work badly or interferes with another
> part. (pp. 291-93)

The fusion of the two traditions of early Italian theory—which
we can now understand as in effect the fusion of the two major
strands of classical theory—began when humanists at the turn of

the fifteenth century extended their historical and philological studies to include (and increasingly to focus primarily on) Greek culture in addition to that of Rome. In the area of politics, this new interest is reflected in the production of Latin translations of Greek works of political theory and political history,[53] and in the appearance in humanist writing of conceptions derived from these sources (Baron 1938, pp. 20-34; Kristeller 1965, pp. 45-46; Kohl and Witt, *passim*). The process of assimilation of Greek theory was more or less completed, as we have seen, by Machiavelli and Guicciardini, who fully appreciated the Aristotelian movement from normative toward positive theory. It is at this point—when the classical inheritance has been assimilated and begins to be transcended—that, all observers agree, the modern era of political theory begins. Conformably, northern humanist political theory is a backwater precisely because it is untouched by these developments, remaining purely Stoic and normative in its orientation.

The foregoing sketch provides the context for a fuller understanding of the relation of *Utopia* to the tradition of political theory. For it is clear not only that More, like his great Italian contemporaries, is engaged in an attempt to fuse humanist and scholastic political theory, but also that, like them, he grapples directly with the classical works that underlie these traditions. Indeed we need hardly cite Renaissance theory in order to grasp More's concerns. Whatever in Book I of *Utopia* is parallel to Italian theory is also parallel to its classical antecedents. Above all, More could have derived, and probably did derive, the systemic approach to the analysis of social problems and the formulation of solutions directly from Plato and Aristotle.

Moreover, the first of More's three subsidiary methodological

[53] Bruni translated Aristotle's *Ethics* and *Politics*, as well as other Greek works, including Plato's *Epistles*, speeches of Demosthenes, and a selection of Plutarch's *Lives* (Sandys, p. 46; Pfeiffer, p. 29). A translation of the *Republic* was undertaken by Chrysoloras and completed by Pier Candido Decembrio in the first half of the quattrocento, and the *Laws* was translated by George of Trebizond (Sandys, pp. 20, 221, 63).

points—the value of comparative study—is probably owed to the same sources. Sabine observes that "the Greek was almost forced to think of what would now by called comparative government. Throughout the length and breadth of the Greek world he found a great variety of political institutions, all indeed of the city-state type, but still capable of very great differences" (p. 21). The earliest of the significant writings concerned with politics, Herodotus' *Histories*, is filled with examples of "the strange customs and manners of foreign peoples" (p. 22). (We recall that this is just the kind of information that made Hythloday so interesting to More and Giles.) Plato directed the Academy in the collection of data about historical and contemporary polities, and these data provided the basis for the *Laws*. The Athenian notes that

> Sensible people in several states have framed a good many decent regulations which our Guardians of the Laws should adapt for the state that we are now founding. The Guardians should examine them and touch them up after trying them out in practice, until they think they have licked each single one into shape; then they should finalize them, ratify them as immutable, and render them lifelong obedience. (*Laws* XII. 957A-B)

Aristotle collected 158 Greek constitutions for study, as well as descriptions of the institutions of non-Greek polities. Barker notes that Aristotle "always turned to the observable facts of actual and concrete evidence. . . . The essence of his procedure was observation and registration of all the relevant data; and the object of his study was, in each case, to discover some general theory which, in the Greek phrase, 'saved' . . . the . . . data" (*Pol.*, p. xxviii).[54]

---

[54] Classical rhetorical theory also emphasizes the importance of comparative examples in the treatment of political questions. Aristotle observes in the *Rhetoric* that "it is a useful thing, for the purpose of [oratory on] matters of legislation, not only to seek to understand what constitution is expedient for a state through a study of its past history [the historical method], but also to seek to know the constitutions of other countries and to understand what kinds of constitution are appropriate to what kinds of people [the comparative method]. This explains

It is only when we come to Book II that we realize fully the extent of More's direct and detailed reliance on Greek theory in *Utopia*. In Book I, our present concern, the clearest example is found in Hythloday's analysis of the condition of England. For this analysis not only employs the general method of Greek theory but is also indebted to a particular passage in a Greek text. It is formed, in fact, by More's adaptation of an analytic model from the *Republic*, Plato's description of the oligarchic polis.[55]

For Plato and Aristotle, oligarchy means plutocracy. An oligarchy is "a society where it is wealth that counts . . . , and in which political power is in the hands of the rich and the poor have no share in it" (*Rep.* VIII.550C). In such states, Socrates says, "honour and admiration and office are reserved for the rich, and the poor are despised" (551A). Society is split "into two factions, the rich and the poor, who live in the same state and are always plotting against each other" (551D). Hythloday sees Europe as a plutocracy: every existing polity, as he says at the end of Book II, is "nothing else than a kind of conspiracy of the rich, who are aiming at their own interests under the name and title of the commonwealth" (*Ut.*, p. 241). According to Socrates, the "worst defect" of such a society is that it generates functionless people: "a man can sell all he has to another and live on as a member of society without any real function; he's neither businessman nor craftsman nor soldier, but merely one of the so-called indigent poor" (*Rep.* VIII.552A). The identification of this class as an indicator of social malaise stems from the systemic approach to analysis: society requires the performance of a particular set of functions; the existence of a class that performs none of these functions evinces a social pathology. Hythloday identifies

---

why books of travel are useful aids to legislation, enabling one, as they do, to comprehend the laws of non-Greek peoples. It also explains why the researches of those who write accounts of events are useful aids in political debates. But all this is, strictly speaking, the province of politics, and not of rhetoric" (1.1360a, trans. Barker, *Pol.*, p. 361). Cf. Quintilian III.viii.66.

[55] Surtz (*Ut.*, pp. 317n, 321n) records some of the parallels between the two passages but does not comment on their significance.

two groups of such functionless people: the "huge crowd of idle attendants who have never learned a trade for a livelihood" (*Ut.*, p. 63), and the evicted tenants, who are forced to "sell for a trifle" their household goods (p. 67). Plato discusses the group that corresponds to Hythloday's "idle attendants," and his remarks contributed something to Hythloday's discussion of the nobles who retain these men as well as to his treatment of the retainers themselves:

> When our pauper was rich, did he perform any of the useful social functions we've just mentioned simply by spending his money? Though he may have appeared to belong to the ruling class, surely in fact he was neither ruling, nor serving society in any other way; he was merely a consumer of goods. . . .
>
> Don't you think we can fairly call him a drone? He grows up in his own home to be a plague to the community, just as a drone grows in its cell to be a plague to the hive. (*Rep.* VIII.552B-C; cf. 556B-C)

Hythloday refers to "the great number of noblemen who . . . live idle . . . like drones on the labors of others" (*Ut.*, p. 63), and who not only "do no good to their country . . . [but] must also do it positive harm" (p. 67). The slide of functionless men into poverty is for Plato, as for Hythloday after him, a major cause of both crime and beggary: "all winged drones have been created without stings, but . . . our two-footed ones vary, and some have stings and some not; and . . . the stingless type end their days as beggars, the stinging type as what we call criminals" (*Rep.* VIII.552C). Similarly, in England cast-off retainers "devote all their energies to starving, if they do not to robbing" (*Ut.*, p. 63), and the evicted tenants have no other recourse than "to steal and be hanged . . . or to wander and beg" (p. 67). For Plato as for Hythloday beggary and theft are always found together, because they are consequences of the same social defect: "in any state where there are beggars there are also, hidden away somewhere, thieves and pick-pockets and temple robbers and all

such practitioners of crime" (*Rep.* VIII. 552D). The ultimate cause
of this problem is "lack of education, bad training and a bad
form of government" (552E). Correspondingly, Hythloday's
solution to the problem of theft would involve fundamental changes
in the legal and institutional structure of England, as well as
seeing to it that youths are not "badly brought up" (*Ut.*, p. 71).
In sum, it is evident that More derived his analysis of the condition of England largely from careful consideration and adaptation of Plato's account of the universal characteristics of oligarchies.

A different direct use of a passage in a Greek theoretical work
is found in the second of Hythloday's imaginary council meetings.
Although the particular stratagems proposed by the councilors
reflect the actual practices of European monarchs, the schema
that is fleshed out by these particulars derives from Aristotle's
discussion of the preservation of tyrannies.[56] Tyrannies (one of
the three "wrong" constitutions, "which consider only the personal interest of the rulers" instead of the common interest [*Pol.*
III. 1279a]) can be preserved "in two ways, which are utterly
opposed to one another" (V. 1313a). The first embraces the traditional acts of the tyrant: he will prohibit "everything likely to
produce . . . mutual confidence and a high spirit" in the citizens
(1313b); his "first end and aim is to break the spirit of . . . [his]
subjects," because "a poor-spirited man will never plot against
anybody" (1314a). One of the included policies is that of im-
poverishing the subjects—"partly to prevent them from having
the means for maintaining a civic guard; partly to keep them so
busy in earning a daily pittance that they have no time for plotting" (1313b). The imposition of taxes is one means to this end.
This approach to the preservation of tyrannies underlies the second, collective part of the advice of Hythloday's imagined councilors: "All the councilors agree" that it "is much to the king's
interest" that his subjects be poor,

[56] Surtz (*Ut.*, p. 365n) notes one of the relevant parallels. White notes
another (1976, p. 664), as well as some parallels with the pseudo-Aristotelian
Economics (pp. 664-65).

seeing that his safeguard lies in the fact that the people do
not grow insolent with wealth and freedom. These things
make them less patient to endure harsh and unjust com-
mands, while, on the other hand, poverty and need blunt
their spirits, make them patient, and take away from the
oppressed the lofty spirit of rebellion. (*Ut.*, pp. 93-95)

These considerations, of course, are for private consumption.
The proposals of individual councilors, on the contrary, are all
outwardly respectable, making it appear that the king is devoted
to the common interest. These stratagems reflect Aristotle's second
method for preserving tyrannies: "the tyrant should act, or at
any rate appear to act, in the role of a good player of the part of
King" (*Pol.* v.1314a). He should, for example, "levy taxes, and
require other contributions, in such a way that they can be seen
to be intended for the proper management of public services, or
to be meant for use, in case of need, on military emergencies"
(1314b), and in general he "should appear to his subjects not as
a despot, but as a steward and king of his people" (1315a-b).
These remarks provide the organizing principle that underlies
the grouping of the proposals of individual councilors in Hythloday's meeting. One suggests "a make-believe war under pretext
of which he [the king] would raise money and then, when he
saw fit, make peace with solemn ceremonies to throw dust in his
simple people's eyes because their loving monarch in compassion
would fain avoid human bloodshed" (*Ut.*, pp. 91-93); another
advises him to recall forgotten laws and "exact fines for their
transgression, there being no richer source of profit nor any more
honorable than such as has an outward mask of justice" (p. 93);
and so on.[57]

[57] In an unpublished paper, White calls attention to another passage that
More may have had in mind here: Glaucon's claim, in the *Republic*, that the
supreme injustice is to be unjust while seeming just (II.361A).

Sylvester shows that More also interpreted the character and career of Richard
III in terms of models provided by classical writers: "What Sallust and Tacitus
gave him was a form, a set of techniques and analogues, a literary pattern

In the light of Hythloday's use of conceptions from Greek theory, we see more clearly why More chose to model his fictional speaker so closely on Plato and some of Plato's spokesmen: Hythloday is made to resemble these figures because he, like them, is a city-state theorist. His refusal to enter practical politics forms part of the same pattern. In Epistle VII[58] Plato says that, after considerable observation, "finally, looking at all the States which now exist, I perceived that one and all they are badly governed; for the state of their laws is such as to be almost incurable without some marvellous overhauling and good-luck to boot" (326A). This conclusion undermined his early "ardent desire to engage in public affairs" (325E). If a patient is unwilling to follow medical advice, the doctor is "both manly and a true doctor if he withdraws from advising a patient of that description, and contrariwise unmanly and unskilled if he continues to advise":

> So too with a State, whether it has one ruler or many, if so
> be that it asks for some salutary advice when its government
> is duly proceeding by the right road, then it is the act of a

according to which he could develop his own historical vision. The basic elements in that vision were defined by the sources, oral and perhaps written, which were available to him. More took the raw material that they furnished and shaped it into an historical narrative of compelling power, utilizing, as he proceeded, all that he had learned from the classical authors. The result was a truly humanist history which, combining old forms and new subject matter, often suggested that the present could best be understood when seen in terms of the past" (*The History of King Richard III*, p. xcviii). Baron discusses a similar relation between Bruni's *Laudatio Florentinae urbis* and the *Panathenaicus* of Aelius Aristides and notes the general importance of the use of conceptual models from classical works in Italian humanism. In Aristides' panegyric Bruni "found . . . conceptual patterns which he could use to impose a rational order upon his observations of the world in which he lived. . . . the Greek model served to introduce patterns of thought that accelerated, or even made possible, the intellectual mastery of the humanist's own world. The recognition of this aspect of 'imitation' during the early Quattrocento is one of the lessons we can learn from the study of the *Laudatio*" (1968, pp. 158-59).

[58] Cf. n. 5 above. Hythloday may be alluding to this epistle when he refers to the lesson that Plato learned "from his own experience with Dionysius" (p. 87). But Plato's Sicilian misadventures were known from many sources.

judicious man to give advice to such people. But in the case
of those who altogether exceed the bounds of right government and wholly refuse to proceed in its tracks, and who
warn their counsellor to leave the government alone and not
disturb it, on pain of death if he does disturb it, while
ordering him to advise as to how all that contributes to their
desires and appetites may most easily and quickly be secured
for ever and ever—then, in such a case, I should esteem
unmanly the man who continued to engage in counsels of
this kind, and the man who refused to continue manly.
(330D-331A)

Since *all* polities are badly governed, the case in which the philosopher can give salutary advice to rulers is purely hypothetical.
These passages from Epistle VII are pertinent to Hythloday's
imaginary council meetings, and they put one in mind of the
initial statement of his reasons for declining to join a council:
kings want and will accept advice only on indecent projects;
councils are inherently conservative (*Ut.*, pp. 57-59).

In the *Republic*, Socrates is made to expatiate in similar terms
on the justified withdrawal of the philosopher from politics. Philosophers come to understand "that political life has virtually
nothing sound about it, and that they'll find no ally to save them
in the fight for justice," and so "they live quietly and keep to
themselves" (VI.496C-D). Since, that is, "there's no existing
form of society good enough for the philosophic nature" (497B),
philosophers "can reasonably refuse to take part in the hard work
of politics" (VII.520B).[59]

[59] Cf. Bradshaw, p. 22; and see n. 77 below. The philosopher *will* enter
politics "in the society where he really belongs; but not, I think, in the society
where he's born, unless something very extraordinary happens":

"I see what you mean," he said. "You mean that he will do so in the
society which we have been describing and which we have theoretically
founded; but I doubt if it will ever exist on earth."

"Perhaps," I said, "it is laid up as a pattern in heaven, where those
who wish can see it and found it in their own hearts. But it doesn't matter

What the philosopher should do instead of entering practical
politics is, presumably, what Socrates and Plato did: instruct
receptive men about the best state of the commonwealth. Hythloday says that the desire to provide such instruction was the only
reason for his return from Utopia (which he regards as the best
commonwealth [p. 237]): "I lived there more than five years
and would never have wished to leave except to make known that
new world" (p. 107).[60]

Similar justifications of the philosopher's refusal to enter practical politics are found in Roman Stoic thought, despite its characteristic emphasis on the duty of political participation. Cicero
ranks such participation higher than philosophic contemplation
in the scale of *officia* (*Off.* i.xliii.153-55), but he insists that
"scholars, whose whole life and interests have been devoted to
the pursuit of knowledge, have not, after all, failed to contribute
to the advantages and blessings of mankind. For they have trained
many to be better citizens and to render larger service to their
country. . . . And not only while present in the flesh do they
teach and train those who are desirous of learning, but by the

---

whether it exists or ever will exist; it's the only state in whose politics he
can take part." (*Rep.* ix.592A-B)

In Utopia, all the highest political and religious officers are selected from the
"company of scholars" (p. 133: "ex . . . literatorum ordine"). Cf. More's letter
to Erasmus of 31 October 1516, where he says he is anxious to find out whether
Utopia meets with the approval of Tunstal, Busleyden, and Jean le Sauvage:

but their approval is more than I could wish for, since they are so fortunate
as to be top-ranking officials in their own governments, although they
might be won over by the fact that in this commonwealth of mine the
ruling class would be completely made up of such men as are distinguished
for learning and virtue. No matter how powerful those men are in their
present governments—and, true, they are very powerful—still they have
some high and mighty clowns as their equals, if not their superiors, in
authority and influence. (*Sel. Let.*, p. 80; *EE*, 2:372)

[60] In view of this remark, we can perhaps clear Hythloday of the obscure
but sinister involvement in the international capitalist conspiracy suggested by
Kinney: "we must ask why Hythlodaeus is in Antwerp, then headquarters of
international commerce and banking; we are tempted also to ask why he left
Utopia" (1976, p. 430).

written memorials of their learning they continue the same service after they are dead" (i.xliv. 155-56). Moreover, many thoughtful men have withdrawn from *negotium* into *otium* because they "could not endure the conduct of either the people or their leaders" (i.xx.69). Seneca writes that "if the state is too corrupt to be helped, if it is wholly dominated by evils, the wise man will not struggle to no purpose, nor spend himself when nothing is to be gained" (*De otio* iii.3). And in fact there is not "a single . . . [state] which could tolerate the wise man or which the wise man could tolerate" (viii.3). "It is of course required of a man that he should benefit his fellow-men," but we must

> grasp the idea that there are two commonwealths—the one, a vast and truly common state, which embraces alike gods and men, in which we look neither to this corner of earth nor to that, but measure the bounds of our citizenship by the path of the sun; the other, the one to which we have been assigned by the accident of birth. . . . [The] greater commonwealth we are able to serve even in leisure—nay, I am inclined to think, even better in leisure. . . . Our school at any rate is ready to say that both Zeno and Chrysippus accomplished greater things than if they had led armies, held public office, and framed laws. The laws they framed were not for one state only, but for the whole human race. Why, therefore, should such leisure as this not be fitting for the good man, who by means of it may govern the ages to come, and speak, not to the ears of the few, but to the ears of all men of all nations, both those who now are and those who shall be? (iii.5-iv.2, vi.4; cf. *De tranquillitate animi* iii-iv, *Ep.* viii.1-2, xiv.12-13)

The existence of such eminently respectable and obviously relevant precedents for Hythloday's position seriously undermines the currently fashionable view that More means us to regard Hythloday's refusal to join a council as a dereliction of duty and as one of a number of circumstances designed to suggest to us that Hythloday's views in general are to be regarded with suspicion (cf. note 9 above). Hythloday is in fact suspect for several reasons, but this refusal is not one of them.

In answer to the question of the relation between the method of Book I of *Utopia* and previous political theory, then, we must conclude that More's originality in this area is somewhat less than Ames, Adams, and Hexter imagine. For the most part, he is simply a practitioner of the analytic techniques developed in Greek theory and revived in the Italian Renaissance. More has, however, extended this method in two important ways. If the systemic approach itself, and the heavy reliance on comparative study that attends it, are not original with him, his emphasis on the value of carefully controlled experiment and of theoretical models as ways of evaluating proposed solutions to social problems is, as far as I know, unprecedented.[61]

Both More's innovations evince an imperfect confidence in the power of ratiocination to serve as an adequate guide to the solution

----

[61] As I noted above (p. 95), Plato's Athenian says that the Guardians of the Laws should "examine and touch up" laws adopted from other polities "after trying them out in practice" (*Laws* III.957B). But this review on the basis of experience is fundamentally different from Morton's proposal for a safeguarded, tentative implementation of the Polylerite system of criminal justice.

There would have been some sort of precedent for More's use of models to test solutions if Plato had completed the trilogy proposed in the *Timaeus*. In that dialogue, which is a sequel to the *Republic*, Socrates says that he would gladly "listen to anyone who should depict in words our State [i.e., the Republic] contending against others in those struggles which States wage" (19C) and opines that Critias and Hermocrates "could show our State engaged in a suitable war and exhibiting all the qualities which belong to it" (20B). Critias claims that ancient Athens was such a polity and promises that he and Hermocrates will describe it in detail: "the city with its citizens which you described to us yesterday, as it were in a fable, we will now transport hither into the realm of fact; for we will assume that the city is that ancient city of ours, and declare that the citizens you conceived are in truth those actual progenitors of ours" (26D-E). But the *Critias* breaks off after brief accounts of the geography and the social and political structure of ancient Athens and its rival Atlantis (cf. Chap. 3, n. 100), and Hermocrates' discourse was evidently never begun. We may wonder whether this unfinished project was suggestive to More. Cf. the Manuels, pp. 120-21.

of human problems. *The Praise of Folly* exhibits similar skepticism, and indeed such positions are common in humanism, a fact
that reflects (in addition to the practical experience of such humanists as More) the connection of humanism with the rhetorical
tradition, which had always opposed the pure rationalism of philosophy. Neither Plato nor Aristotle (despite the empiricism of
the latter) feels that any preliminary test of theories is necessary,
since each assumes that theoretical conclusions are bound to be
valid if only the reasonings that lead to them are. The same
difference between More and his philosophical predecessors is
reflected in their attitudes toward social change. Hythloday stresses
before and after his account of Utopia that the Utopians, though
highly satisfied with their constitution, are receptive to ideas for
its improvement (pp. 109, 237; cf. n. 29 above). Plato and
Aristotle regard the constitutions of their ideal commonwealths
as essentially immutable (since perfect), although Plato does make
allowance for the possibility of improvements in the constitution
of the "second-best" polis described in the *Laws*, an allowance
embodied in the institution of the Nocturnal Council (XII.951A-
953D, 960B-962E; see below, pp. 206-7).

In fact, although More's method (especially the parts of it
identified by previous commentators) cannot be explained or adequately characterized by allusion to the "scientific spirit," aspects
of this method are in a strict sense scientific. More's realization
that theoretical results can be, in effect, no more than hypotheses,
and the complementary realization that these results need to be
verified by tests, links him with the most advanced scientific
thinkers of the age, who were just beginning to develop the
conceptions of hypothesis and hypothesis-testing by experiment
(see Copleston, 3:281-82). These conceptions are what distinguishes the scientific method from a merely empirical one, and
the fact that More grasped and utilized them gives him perhaps
a better claim to be called the creator of political science than
Machiavelli, who is often accorded that title but is innocent of
such conceptions.

Finally, if the basic elements of More's method in Book I are a legacy of city-state theory, one of the purposes for which he employs that method distinguishes him sharply from earlier practitioners. In Hythloday's first speech at Morton's table and in his second imaginary council meeting, Greek theory provides, as we have seen, conceptual frameworks for analysis of aspects of contemporary society. In both these passages, and indeed in all the examples that Hythloday offers in the part of the book we have examined, a central purpose is to establish that, in a true view, a particular policy or set of policies that appears to be expedient (and can be justified only in terms of expediency) is in fact inexpedient, and that, conversely, policies that are consistent with traditional morality are truly expedient.

City-state theory, however, had normally led its practitioners in the opposite direction. Plato, to be sure, claims in the *Republic* and the *Laws* that he is devising poleis that combine perfect justice with perfect expediency, but his Greek notion of justice is so different from later Western conceptions that the claim has little force. Platonic justice is compatible with gross social and economic inequities between different classes of citizens, and with the support of the citizens by a slave population that has no rights at all (cf. pp. 176-77 below). Aristotle's ideal constitution includes similar inequities, and he frankly acknowledges that the good life that it provides is not for all inhabitants of the polis: "some may share in it fully, but others can only share in it partially or cannot even share at all" (*Pol.* VII.1328a). Moreover, Aristotle's investigations lead him to the important conclusion that the virtue of the good citizen is not identical to that of the good man. This conclusion follows from the fact that "the excellence of the citizen must be an excellence relative to the constitution":

> It follows on this that if there are several different kinds of constitution there cannot be a single absolute excellence of the good citizen. But the good man is a man so called in virtue of a single absolute excellence.
>
> It is thus clear that it is possible to be a good citizen

without possessing the excellence which is the quality of the good man.[62] (III.1276b)

These considerations of Aristotle, together with the clinical discussion of political mechanics in the *Politics*, constitute a major source of medieval and Renaissance ideas of a political morality different from private morality and the attendant notion that political necessity or *ragione di stato* sometimes dictates policies that conflict with traditional morality (see Post, pp. 253, 290-309). Aquinas notes Aristotle's demonstration that "it is not the same without qualification to be a good man and a good citizen" and reluctantly acknowledges that political morality may differ from private (*In libros politicorum*, lib. 5, lect. 3, trans. A. H. Gilbert, p. 83n). Stoic theorists, of course, insist that *honestas* is perfectly consistent with *utilitas*, in both private and public matters, and the early humanist *specula*, works in the Stoic tradition, faithfully repeat this claim. But as the lessons of the *Politics* (supplemented, no doubt, by the lessons of politics) begin to be more fully assimilated in the fifteenth century, the other possibility begins to be explored in humanist writing. In later fifteenth-century *specula*, the notion that political and private morality differ appears in the form of the widely-shared agreement that the virtues of the prince are not identical to those of the ordinary man. To be sure, this statement usually means little more than that the prince has the opportunity to practice certain virtues, and the obligation to assume a certain hauteur, not open to private individuals (Skinner 1978, pp. 125-27).[63] Felix Gilbert points out that the authors of these *specula* regard *magnificentia* and

[62] For man as a private individual, as distinguished from man as a citizen, Aristotle thinks that the prudent is wholly compatible with the moral: "Practical wisdom . . . is linked to virtue of character, and this to practical wisdom, since the principles of practical wisdom are in accordance with the moral virtues and rightness in morals is in accordance with practical wisdom" (*Eth. Nic.* X.1178a). Of course Aristotle's conception of the moral life is rather different from the Christian conception.

[63] This idea also derives from Aristotle. See *Eth. Nic.* I.1099a, IV.1122b-1125a, X.1178a; *Pol.* III.1277a-1278b.

maiestas as among the most important princely virtues, so that
they place great emphasis on "hunts, tourneys, and games," and
on "everything which contributed to making an outward impression of princely power" (p. 465; cf. A. H. Gilbert, pp. 91-92,
and *passim*). Like earlier humanists, these writers agree that "no
one can be accounted a man of true *virtus* unless he displays all
the leading Christian virtues as well as the 'cardinal' virtues
singled out by the moralists of antiquity" (Skinner 1978, p. 126).
But the prince is occasionally allowed to deviate from this ideal
standard. Patrizi acknowledges in *De regno et regis institutione* (c.
1475) that in certain circumstances it is proper for the prince
"that by simulating and dissimulating he should often show the
contrary of the truth" (7.10, trans. A. H. Gilbert, p. 126).[64]
In *Principis diatuposis* (c. 1470), Platina asks whether anyone "is
ignorant that he has greater obligation to his native land, to his
relatives, his children, his neighbors, to the citizens of the same
nation and language than to aliens and foreigners? . . . The law
of nations is to be kept, faith is to be kept, I do not say with
robbers, or pirates, who are the common enemies of all, not with
those with whom one is at war" (2.4, 5, trans. A. H. Gilbert,
p. 124). And Machiavelli is quite clear that the good prince is
not always a good man, that the prudent is often wildly different
from the moral (e.g., *Prince*, Chap. 15, *Discourses* III.xli). Sabine
observes that "the closest analogue to Machiavelli's separation of
political expedience from morality is probably to be found in
some parts of Aristotle's *Politics*" (p. 340), and indeed Machiavelli's list of the specifically princely or political virtues largely
derives (directly or indirectly) from Aristotle's account of the
machinations of the tyrant (*Prince*, Chaps. 15-21; *Pol.* v.1313a-
1315b).[65] (This is the account that Hythloday employs for a very

[64] See Sydney Anglo's discussion (pp. 175-79) of this and other passages
quoted in this paragraph. And see F. Gilbert, esp. pp. 463-69.

[65] Cf. *Il Principe*, ed. Burd, p. 289n; A. H. Gilbert, pp. 92, 107, 127,
152-54.

To the true Christian-Stoic theorist, on the contrary, such notions are unacceptable. In *The Education of a Christian Prince*, Erasmus says that if the

different purpose.) The fact that the prince may on occasion disregard moral imperatives implies, moreover, that other citizens, acting in his service, may do likewise. In the passage quoted above, Platina goes on to say that to the enemies of the polity "your citizens should not render a price agreed on for a life; they commit no fraud even if the citizens having sworn do not carry out their agreement." Pontano declares in *De obedientia* (1490) that

---

prince finds he "cannot defend . . . [his] realm without violating justice, without wanton loss of human life, [and] without great loss to religion," he should "give up and yield to the importunities of the age. . . . It is far better to be a just man than an unjust prince" (p. 155; cf. Hythloday's second imaginary council speech, *Ut.*, p. 95.26-30). In *De officiis*, Cicero says that "there are some acts either so repulsive or so wicked, that a wise man would not commit them, even to save his country" (I.xlv.159). At the same time, it is clear that the idea that public morality differs from private found some encouragement in Cicero's treatments of conflicting *officia* and of apparent conflicts between *honestas* and *utilitas*. "In choosing between conflicting duties," Cicero says, "that class takes precedence which is demanded by the interests of human society" (I.xlv.160). Apparent conflicts between *honestas* and *utilitas* are resolved by arguments designed to show how "it often happens, owing to exceptional circumstances, that what is accustomed under ordinary circumstances to be considered morally wrong is found not to be morally wrong" (III.iv.19; cf. vii.33; and cf. Quintilian XII.i.36-44). It is permissible, for example, to kill a tyrant, because "we have no ties of fellowship with a tyrant. . . . as certain members are amputated, if they show signs themselves of being bloodless and virtually lifeless and thus jeopardize the health of the other parts of the body, so those fierce and savage monsters in human form should be cut off from what may be called the common body of humanity" (III.vi.32; cf. xxv.95, xxix.107-8). The influence of these conceptions, and of Cicero's particular applications of them, is apparent, for example, in the relation between the passage from Platina quoted above and *Off.* III.v.22, xxix.107, and in that between *Off.* III.iv.19 and the statement of Castiglione's messer Federico that "when serving one's masters it is sometimes permitted to kill not just one man but ten thousand men, and do many other things that might seem evil to a man who did not look upon them as one ought, and yet are not evil" (*Courtier*, p. 117). Speaking as a rhetorician, Cicero at one point treats conflicts between *honestas* and *utilitas* as both real and frequent: "circumstances . . . very often bring it about that utility is at variance with moral value [ut utilitas cum honestate certet]" (*Part. Or.* xxv.89).

It is the act of a wise man, when two ills are put before him, always to choose the smaller one. Hence it is permissible, for the sake of the state and of a king who is father of his people, sometimes to tell falsehoods; though when time and circumstances require silence about the truth, especially when the safety of the king, the kingdom, and the fatherland is in question, he who prudently keeps still certainly does not seem to be a liar. Or if he uses deception he does not seem straightway to be a liar, since he acts like a prudent man who balances utility and necessity with the true and the false [cum prudentis hoc sit et utilitatem necessitatemque cum vero falsoque pensitantis]. (4.12, trans. A. H. Gilbert, p. 127; cf. n. 25 above)

City-state theory, that is, normally helped to lead those who practiced or admired it toward the conclusion that in politics the prudent and the moral are often quite diverse. But Hythloday argues the opposite, and—what is important here—he argues this position by using the method of city-state theory to support a central conclusion of Stoic—and traditional humanist—theory. In Book I, moreover, he supports this position well. Every reader is convinced that the supposedly expedient English criminal justice is in fact as ineffective as it is immoral, and that the cynical policies advocated in Hythloday's imaginary council meetings do, as Hythloday claims in the Stoic speeches that he imagines himself delivering in these councils, lead to disaster.

Book I of *Utopia* contains, then, another innovation in addition to its purely methodological advances. If attempts to fuse humanist and scholastic theory characterize the most creative and advanced political theorists of the early sixteenth century, then More (far from languishing in the backwater of the traditional *speculum*) belongs with this group, for this is precisely the kind of work in which he is engaged. Alone among the northern humanists of his time, he apprehends the power of the analytic method of city-state theory and grapples with the disturbing substantive results associated with that method. Given the chro-

nology, his work is presumably independent of the corresponding
Italian achievements.[66] It is, moreover, quite different in thrust
from them. In the cases of More's great Italian contemporaries,
the fusion of the two traditions of theory involves abandonment
of the normative perspective of Stoic theory; for More, on the
contrary, this fusion appears to involve an attempt to bring the
method of city-state theory to bear in an effort to establish the
prescriptions of the Stoic tradition on a firmer basis, to reinforce
the Ciceronian argument that these prescriptions are imperative
not only for moral but also for practical reasons. Correspondingly, More's application of this method undermines some major
substantive conclusions of city-state theory, in both its Greek and
Italian forms. One recalls Chambers's remark that *Utopia*, like
The History of King Richard III, "is an attack on the non-moral
statecraft of the early Sixteenth Century" (p. 117): "Parts of
Utopia read like a commentary on parts of *The Prince*. . . . before
The Prince was written, ideas used in *The Prince* had been gaining
ground. They were the 'progressive' ideas, and we may regard
Utopia as a 'reaction' against them" (p. 132; cf. above, n. 25).
This is, I believe, a fair statement of one of the purposes of the
book; and we are now able to understand more clearly how More
goes about the accomplishment of this purpose. All the same, we
should not forget that the views advanced in the part of *Utopia*
we have examined so far are Hythloday's, and that they are
therefore not necessarily identical to More's own. Nor have we
yet heard all that Hythloday has to say.

IV

Hythloday's second conciliar example ends with a question:
"Summing up the whole thing, don't you suppose if I set ideas
like these before men strongly inclined to the contrary, they would

[66] Writing in 1515-16, More could have known Savonarola's *Tract on the
Constitution and Government of Florence* (1498) and, just conceivably, Salamonio's *Sovereignty of the Roman Patriciate* (c. 1513), but certainly not the
work of Machiavelli or Guicciardini.

turn deaf ears to me?" (*Ut.*, p. 97).[67] This question, like that at the end of the preceding example ("What reception from my listeners, my dear More, do you think this speech of mine would find?" [p. 91]), seems designed not to elicit the views of his auditors but to elicit applause and agreement.

More does agree, but in an unanticipated tone. At the conclusion of Hythloday's account of the conversation at Morton's table, More had responded with approbation and courtesy: " 'To be sure, my dear Raphael,' I commented, 'you have given me great pleasure, for everything you have said has been both wise and witty' " (pp. 85-87: "Profecto mi Raphäel inquam magna me affecisti uoluptate, ita sunt abs te dicta prudenter simul & lepide omnia"). The present reply, on the contrary, is blunt and vehement, evincing irritation, even anger:

> "Deaf indeed, without doubt," I agreed, "and, by heaven, I am not surprised. Neither, to tell the truth, do I think that such ideas should be thrust on people, or such advice given, as you are positive will never be listened to. What good could such novel ideas do, or how could they enter the minds of individuals who are already taken up and possessed by the opposite conviction? In the private conversation of close friends this academic philosophy is not without its charm, but in the councils of kings, where great matters are debated with great authority, there is no room for these notions."[68] (pp. 97-99)

What motivates this anger? The primary answer would seem to be that More (the character) has been insulted. The theory of counsel just modeled with such devastating results is, after all,

---

[67] The translation is from R. M. Adams's edition. Yale turns the interrogative into an exclamation.

[68] More's relative optimism about the possibility of a philosopher's accomplishing anything by joining a council evidently stems in part from a view of what goes on in councils rather different from that entertained by Hythloday. Hythloday's representation of councils (at which More does not demur) could scarcely be summarized as "great matters . . . debated with great authority."

one that Hythloday attributes to him. But the inefficacy of drop-
ping Stoic pearls among courtly swine is not a point that is difficult
to grasp. Erasmus, not notably sophisticated about such matters,
observes in *The Education of a Christian Prince* that "he is called
a 'traitor' . . . who by his frank advice recalls the prince to a
better course when he has swerved to those interests which are
neither becoming nor safe for himself nor beneficial to the state"
(p. 233, quoted *Ut.*, p. 366n). More immediately dissociates
himself from the theory: "Neither . . . do I think that such ideas
should be thrust on people . . . as you are positive will never be
listened to."

Even before this episode Hythloday has made it clear that he
does not regard More as his intellectual equal. Since More had
said that Hythloday's account of the conversation at Morton's
table was both "wise and witty," Hythloday could have inferred
that More did not fundamentally disagree with the view of the
nature of councils that the account illustrates. If, therefore, after
this account More still disagrees with him on the question whether
a philosopher should join a council, the source of this disagreement must be somewhere farther up the line of argument. But,
evidently not listening very closely to what More says, Hythloday
simply assumes that More is a bit thickheaded—another English
lawyer, like the one Hythloday had demolished so easily at Morton's table. (Later he approvingly recounts the fact that the Utopians "absolutely banish from their country all lawyers" [p. 195]).
Accordingly, without further attempt to understand More's views,
Hythloday launches into examples that make again the points
about councilors and councils that he had already made.

More may also be irritated by what seems to him the unfairness
and obtuseness of Hythloday's models of the philosopher at court.
Hythloday appears to be unable to imagine that the philosopher
in this setting could do anything other than offer routine pon-
tifications. To More, this use of learning would obviously fail
to satisfy the criterion of utility (see above, pp. 41-42): "What
good could such novel ideas do" ("Quid enim prodesse possit")?
Hythloday's models embody a conception of philosophy associated

with the despised scholastics: "In the private conversation of close friends this academic philosophy [*philosophia scholastica*] is not without its charm." Even the characteristic use of litotes[69]—"non insuauis"—is damning, evoking as it does the contrast between an employment of the intellect that is at best not unpleasant and one that is genuinely useful.

More's anger provokes anger on Hythloday's part—especially since More has come close to calling him a scholastic philosopher, the worst insult that a humanist can offer or be offered. If More in anger becomes heated, Hythloday becomes icy. Up to this point Hythloday's manner has been at least ostensibly polite. His speeches are prefaced by "mi More" (pp. 56, 84, 90), and his style is gracious and expansive. Now, however, and for the next several pages, he becomes cold and curt: " 'That is just what I meant,' he rejoined, 'by saying there is no room for philosophy with rulers' " (p. 99: "Hoc est, inquit ille, quod dicebam non esse apud principes locum philosophiae"). Suddenly, then, we have a real dialogue (before we had a monologue with occasional interruptions), and an angry one.

Recognizing that More *chose* to create anger between his fictional characters at this point, we should ask why he did so. One part of the answer, having to do with rhetorical strategy, is clear. The change in the emotional temperature of the work acts as an intensifier, making the passage more vivid and thus more effective and memorable. This is an appropriate place for intensification, since what follows is one of the crucial passages of the book. Hythloday becomes fervent in two other places in *Utopia*: in his account of the appalling injustices of English society, and in the peroration of Book II. These passages, together with the present one, are surely the most impressive and memorable parts of the book, and this fact, though attributable primarily to their substance, is also partly owing to the highly-charged nature of the writing in them.

What is not clear is why More chose to create the anger in a

_____

[69] On More's subtle use of this figure, see McCutcheon 1971.

way that is bound to qualify our initial, highly favorable, impression of Hythloday. In fact, all the exchanges between Hythloday and More in Book I have this effect. Like the ironic undercutting of the Letter to Giles, the joking names scattered throughout, and the attribution of most of the ideas of the book to a character other than More, the revelation of unattractive traits in Hythloday—and traits that cast some doubt on the precision and objectivity of his mental functioning—serves to distance and dissociate the author from the views presented in his book. This fact can, for now, only puzzle the reader and, as I suggested earlier, make him more cautious in his responses.

Hythloday's first brief reply to More's criticism has suggested that he can conceive of no other morally acceptable role for the philosopher at court than the one modeled in his imagined council meetings, and More now proceeds to describe an alternative role, one that takes into account Hythloday's valid analysis of the systemic defects of councils. He begins by repeating the charge that Hythloday's model of the philosopher in council embodies a futile scholasticism. It is true that there is "no room for philosophy with rulers"—not, that is, "for this academic philosophy [*non huic scholasticae*] which thinks that everything is suitable to every place" (p. 99). What is "scholastic" about the philosophy employed by Hythloday in the imagined councils? *Not* its substance, which is the Stoic wisdom of the humanist *specula*. What More means is that Hythloday's remarks share with scholasticism a failure to consider context, to suit utterances to the nature of the audience: this philosophy "thinks that everything is suitable to every place."[70]

Complaints that scholastics fail to consider context—whether

---

[70] The style of Hythloday's narratives of the council meetings may also be intended to illustrate his insensitivity to his audience. Miller (1965-66, p. 305) notes the curious fact that these accounts are embodied almost entirely in two gargantuan sentences—the first of 464 words (pp. 86.31-90.22) and the second of 924 (pp. 90.22-96.31). These "syntactical extravaganza[s]" contrast sharply with the "curt, lucid sentences" of More's replies—in which he makes the point "that the manner of advice is as important as the matter."

in the interpretation of literary works or in their mistaken notions
about style and rhetorical strategy—constitute a main theme of
humanist attacks on scholasticism.[71] This fact reflects not only
the affiliation of humanism with the rhetorical tradition (and the
ancient rivalry between rhetorician and philosopher) but also the
permeation of humanism with the sense of history, the essence
of which is the realization that context affects significance (see
Panofsky, pp. 82-113; Burke; Logan). Indeed, the systemic approach to social problems constitutes a response to the same realization: particular laws and institutions can be evaluated only
in the context of the entire system that includes them as parts.
Hythloday, then, might be accused of failing to apply his own
insights here.[72]

The philosopher can do some good at court, More says, if he
exemplifies an "alia philosophia ciuilior," one that is responsive
to context. This philosophy "knows its stage, adapts itself to the
play in hand, and performs its role neatly and appropriately [cum
decoro]."[73] A man needn't always say all that he knows. It is
necessary to accommodate oneself to the ambient clownage:

[71] See, for example, More's Letter to Dorp, Sel. Let., pp. 29-32 (Cor., pp.
45-48), and The Praise of Folly, pp. 84-85, 89-93, 109-14.

[72] Although Hythloday's argument is scholastic in this respect, it is absurd
to claim, as Wooden does, that Hythloday is "an exaggerated type of the
humanists' scholastic adversaries" (1977, p. 42), and that he is thus "the focus
of a pervasive secondary level of attack in the Utopia, . . . [t]he targets of
. . . [which] are . . . the scholastic theologians and schoolmen" (p. 30). On
Hythloday as a humanist moral philosopher, see above, pp. 33-35, 42-44.
Later Hythloday mocks scholastic dialectic (Ut., p. 159)—a passage that Wooden
handles by the stunning assertion that "there is no evidence of conscious irony
in these remarks; rather this passage represents an example of the naiveté toward
all things Utopian which is a consistent feature of Hythloday's characterization"
(p. 34).

[73] White (1978, pp. 149-50n) points out that the use of the term decorum
and the theatrical imagery of the speech suggest that More has in mind Cicero's
lengthy discussion of decorum in De officiis (I.xxvii.93-xlii.151). The most
clearly relevant passage is that in which Cicero observes that we "work to the
best advantage in that rôle to which we are best adapted. But if at some time
stress of circumstances shall thrust us aside into some uncongenial part, we

Otherwise we have the situation in which a comedy of Plautus is being performed and the household slaves are making trivial jokes at one another and then you come on the stage in a philosopher's attire and recite the passage from the *Octavia* where Seneca is disputing with Nero. Would it not have been preferable to take a part without words than by reciting something inappropriate to make a hodgepodge of comedy and tragedy? You would have spoiled and upset the actual play by bringing in irrelevant matter—even if your contribution would have been superior in itself. . . .

So it is in the commonwealth. So it is in the deliberations of monarchs. If you cannot pluck up wrongheaded opinions by the roots, if you cannot cure according to your heart's desire vices of long standing, yet you must not on that account desert the commonwealth. You must not abandon the ship in a storm because you cannot control the winds.[74]

On the other hand, you must not force upon people new and strange ideas which you realize will carry no weight with persons of opposite conviction. On the contrary, by the indirect approach you must seek and strive to the best of your power to handle matters tactfully. What you cannot turn to good you must at least[75] make as little bad as you can. (pp. 99-101)

It is interesting how closely this passage resembles the analysis of "true prudence" by Erasmus' Folly (cf. Dean 1946, p. 25). Arguing that "nothing is more foolish than wisdom out of place,

---

must devote to it all possible thought, practice, and pains, that we may be able to perform it, if not with propriety [*si non decore*], at least with as little impropriety as possible [*quam minime indecore*]" (I.xxxi.114; White compares *Ut.*, p. 100.1-2).

[74] Bradshaw observes that More gives to the metaphor of the ship of state the opposite thrust to that given it by Plato: "What good can the skilled navigator do, asked Plato, if the crew will not acknowledge the need for his expertise but struggle to gain control of the helm themselves in order to pillage the cargo?" (p. 23; *Rep.* VI.488A-489D).

[75] "At least" ("saltem") is, as Miller notes (1966, p. 58), omitted in Yale.

. . . [and] nothing . . . more imprudent than unseasonable
prudence" (*Praise of Folly*, p. 38), Folly also employs a theatrical
metaphor:

> If a person were to try stripping the disguises from actors
> as they play a scene upon the stage, showing to the audience
> their real looks and the faces they were born with, would
> not such a one spoil the whole play? . . . Destroy the illusion
> and any play is ruined. It is the paint and trappings that
> take the eyes of spectators. Now what else is the whole life
> of mortals but a sort of comedy, in which the various actors,
> disguised by various costumes and masks, walk on and play
> each one his part, until the manager waves them off the
> stage? (p. 37)

True prudence involves accommodating oneself to "things as they
are":

> The part of a truly prudent man . . . is (since we are mortal)
> not to aspire to wisdom beyond his station, and either, along
> with the rest of the crowd, pretend not to notice anything,
> or affably and companionably be deceived. But that, they
> tell us, is folly. Indeed, I shall not deny it; only let them,
> on their side, allow that it is also to play out the comedy of
> life.[76] (p. 38)

Hythloday has a less pleasant name for More's "philosophia
ciuilior." To him it is folly indeed, and worse. If More comes

[76] On this passage, a source in Lucian, and an analogue in More's *Richard
III*, see Dean 1943, pp. 320-22. In *De libero arbitrio*, Erasmus says that St.
Paul "knew the difference between what things are lawful and what are expedient. It is lawful to speak the truth; it is not expedient to speak the truth to
everybody at every time and in every way" (pp. 40-41). Tinkler observes that
this is a Paul "who, like Erasmus, has been studying under Cicero and Quintilian" (unpubl. paper). The approach to counsel advocated by Erasmus and
the character More, that is, is one sanctioned by the rhetorical tradition, even
as Hythloday's position has affinities with the philosophical tradition—facts that
reinforce one's sense that the perennial dispute between rhetorician and philosopher importantly underlies the debate of Book I.

close to calling Hythloday a scholastic philosopher, Hythloday comes precisely as close to calling More a liar: "To speak falsehoods, for all I know, may be the part of a philosopher, but it is certainly not for me" (*Ut.*, p. 101). He now begins, that is, to arrogate to himself moral superiority to More, in addition to the intellectual superiority that he has assumed all along. (We may think that More's threat to the latter provokes the assertion of the former.)

More important, he argues that More's theory of counsel is, like the naive theory of the *specula*, invalid. It is not the case, he claims, that he has overlooked the need for adjusting remarks to their context:

> Although that speech of mine might perhaps be unwelcome and disagreeable to those councilors, yet I cannot see why it should seem odd even to the point of folly. What if I told them the kind of things which Plato creates in his republic or which the Utopians actually put in practice in theirs? Though such institutions were superior (as, to be sure, they are), yet they might appear odd because here individuals have the right of private property, there all things are common. (p. 101)

The problem is that such accommodation simply doesn't work: "By this approach . . . I should accomplish nothing else than to share the madness of others as I tried to cure their lunacy" (p. 101):[77]

---

[77] It is not then the case, as Wooden says, that Hythloday "hardly understands and does not deny the accusation" that his approach in the council meetings is scholastic (1977, p. 39).

Socrates says that the small company of philosophers, having "seen the frenzy of the masses," realize that "if they're not prepared to join in the general wickedness, and yet are unable to fight it single-handed, they are likely to perish like a man thrown among wild beasts, without profit to themselves or others, before they can do any good to their friends or society" (*Rep.* VI.496C-D). There is a direct allusion to the simile in the same Platonic passage later in Hythloday's speech:

As to that indirect approach of yours, I cannot see its rel-
evancy. . . . At court there is no room for dissembling,
nor may one shut one's eyes to things. One must openly
approve the worst counsels and subscribe to the most ruinous
decrees. He would be counted a spy and almost a traitor,
who gives only faint praise to evil counsels.

Moreover, there is no chance for you to do any good
because you are brought among colleagues who would easily
corrupt even the best of men before being reformed themselves. By their evil companionship, either you will be se-
duced yourself or, keeping your own integrity and inno-
cence, you will be made a screen for the wickedness and
folly of others. (p. 103)

In fact, according to Hythloday More's indirect approach is,
like the English policy of hanging thieves and the royal policies
of Hythloday's paired conciliar examples, not only ineffective
but also morally and religiously unacceptable. A Christian is
simply not allowed to temporize in the way More advises:

People who have made up their minds to rush headlong
down the opposite road are never pleased with the man who
calls them back and tells them they are headed the wrong
way. But, apart from that, what did I say that could not
and should not be said anywhere and everywhere? If we
dismiss as out of the question and absurd everything which
the perverse customs of men have made to seem unusual,
we shall have to set aside most of the commandments of

Plato by a very fine comparison shows why philosophers are right in
abstaining from administration of the commonwealth. They observe the
people rushing out into the streets and being soaked by constant showers
and cannot induce them to go indoors and escape the rain. They know
that, if they go out, they can do no good but will only get wet with the
rest. Therefore, being content if they themselves at least are safe, they
keep at home, since they cannot remedy the folly of others. (*Ut.*, p. 103)
We may think, though, that Hythloday's dismissal of More's proposed solution
to the problem of counsel violates the principle that, wherever possible, proposals should be tested empirically.

Christ even in a community of Christians. Yet he forbade us to dissemble them, and even ordered that what he had whispered to his disciples should be preached openly from the housetops. . . . But preachers, like the crafty fellows they are, have found that men would rather not change their lives to conform to Christ's rule, and so, just as you suggest, they have accommodated his teaching to the way men live, as if it were a leaden yardstick. At least in that way they can get the two things to correspond on one level or another. The only real thing they accomplish that I can see is to make men feel a little more secure in their consciences about doing evil.[78] (p. 101)

Once more, that is, Hythloday argues that a morally dubious expedient is, in a true view, inexpedient. This rule applies even in the present case, where More espouses the use of an imperfectly moral means to an end that is morally impeccable.

The real disagreement between Hythloday and More, then, is not (as Hythloday had thought) about the nature of the problem of counsel but on the question whether, given that nature, the philosopher can realistically hope to make things even a little less bad by joining a council. And this disagreement amounts to a disagreement on the fundamental political question whether the virtue of a good citizen is identical to that of a good man—whether, on the political level, *utilitas* is ever inconsistent with *honestas*. Hythloday appears to believe that there are *no* such cases, that there is never a difference between the truly prudent and the perfectly moral. The character More, though not disputing Hythloday's analyses of other cases, claims that in at least this one case there *is* a difference; that is, that however regrettable the fact may be, political and private morality are not always identical.

What is the author's own position on the question of the validity

[78] I quote from R. M. Adams's translation (pp. 29-30). On several problems in the Yale version, see Prévost 1964, pp. 95-96; Miller 1966, pp. 57, 63.

of the "indirect approach"? As Hexter says, it is impossible to tell. More's speech is "unique in *Utopia*":

> It is full, it is carefully argued, it is highly coherent, it is vehement and tinged with a strong moral conviction. Up to this point all the coherence, vehemence, and moral conviction have been on Hythloday's side. And after this point, in the scant five pages remaining before More wrote finis to . . . [Book I], the scales are again weighted in Hythloday's favor. Set any of the other arguments that More ascribes to himself against those he ascribes to Hythloday, and the disparity in their quality . . . is unmistakable. Set this one argument against all that Hythloday says in opposition to the involvement of the intellectual in a bureaucracy, and although the positions maintained are irreconcilable, they are so evenly matched that it is impossible to tell on the face of them which represented More's own belief. . . . For once, and only for once, Hythloday gets paid back in coin as good as he gave. (1952, pp. 131-32)

Nor is the dispute resolved later in *Utopia*: the question is dropped at this point and is never taken up again. Except in cases where the proper resolution is clearly implied, unresolved disagreement in philosophical dialogues may be taken to signal uncertainty on the author's part.[79] This rule presumably applies in the present instance. But since the dialogue of Book I functions in part as an introduction to Book II, we should anticipate that the larger questions embodied in the dispute (and in the dialogue

[79] See Bevington. Correspondingly, as Bevington says, "whenever we find an agreement between the . . . principals, we are surely safe in assuming the author's concurrence" (p. 500). On the interpretation of *Utopia* and other philosophical dialogues, see also Kristeller 1980, pp. 7-8. Baker-Smith observes that "More's handling of the dialogue form is much closer to Cicero's than to Plato's—after all they were both lawyers. While Socrates' companions do little more than gasp or naively set up the situations for his dialectic to exploit Cicero's speakers all have equal rights. For him as for More dialogue is exploratory and reader inclusive; we are not compelled to passive assent but provided with differing views and left to judge for ourselves" (p. 12). Cicero is not always as evenhanded as Baker-Smith suggests, but the comparison is still valid.

as a whole)—those of the general solution of the problem of counsel, the possible means of effecting reforms, and the relation between the politically prudent and the moral—will be among the concerns implicit in the Utopian construct.

In the meantime, we note that the anger More has created in this passage has, in addition to its function as an intensifier, another purpose: to make it plausible that Hythloday should now proceed to divulge the full extent of his radicalism. Addressing an emissary of the King of England and a leading citizen of Antwerp, neither of whom he has known long, Hythloday might well be reluctant to reveal his communism. This was a shocking confession then as now, though perhaps less then, since, as Lewis observes (pp. 167-68), a communist revolution could hardly be perceived, in the early sixteenth century, as a real threat to the existing order. Stung by More's attack, perhaps feeling that he has lost the initiative (for Hythloday is certainly one who "talks for victory"), even perhaps exhilarated to discover that More is worthy of the full truth, Hythloday decides in the intensity of the moment to play his trump card. The access of confidence that this decision entails is evident in the return to polite address: "Yet surely, my dear More, to tell you candidly my heart's sentiments, it appears to me that wherever you have private property and all men measure all things by cash values, there it is scarcely possible for a commonwealth to have justice or prosperity" (*Ut.*, p. 103).[80]

More needed to render this turn in the dialogue dramatically plausible because it is dialectically necessary. Having introduced the systemic approach to the study of social problems, and having revealed through it the depth and complexity of such problems as crime, poverty, and counsel, he is now ready for a discussion of some questions raised by this approach. Two of these questions—whether, given the nature of the problem of counsel, a philosopher should nevertheless go to court, and the related ques-

[80] Hythloday's communism is foreshadowed on p. 101, where he refers to "the kind of things which Plato creates in his republic or which the Utopians actually put in practice in theirs. . . . Though such institutions were superior (as, to be sure, they are) . . ."

tion of the extent of the harmony of the expedient and the moral—
have been aired in the vehement exchange between Hythloday
and More. Another of them is whether the systemic approach
does not imply that justice can be attained only through economic
communism. Systemic analysis reveals that greed for possessions,
on the part of rulers and others, underlies both the problem of
poverty and theft and that of counsel.[81] Is it therefore the case
that the only way to eradicate these and other social malaises is
to abolish the institution of private property and thus preclude
the invidious economic and social distinctions that this institution
entails? That the systemic approach prompts this question is clear
from the prototypal works of systemic theory. In the *Republic*,
Plato concludes that the attainment of justice in the commonwealth
requires that the Guardians, at least, hold all things in common;
in the *Politics*, Aristotle disputes this conclusion, both in his
critique of the *Republic* and in his own plan of a perfect commonwealth, where private property is retained.[82] (We may surmise that it was More's consideration—presumably in conversation with Giles—of this question and that of the relation between
the expedient and the moral that led to the writing of the ur-
Utopia; on second thought, he decided it was advisable to provide
his readers with an introduction to the issues and methods embodied in the Utopian construct.)

On the question of communism, Hythloday represents the
Platonic position—though it is immediately evident that, unlike
Plato, he believes that justice can be attained only if society as a
whole, and not just its ruling class, is communized. In his fervor,
indeed, Hythloday misrepresents Plato, who hardly claimed that

[81] Fleisher observes that Book I suggests that "private property . . . is not
only bad in itself, it is the relentless corruptor of all the other social institutions"
(p. 40).

[82] *Rep.* III.416C-417B, and *passim*; *Pol.* II.1260b-1264b, VII.1329b-1330a.
See below, 208-9.

Hexter is wrong, then, in claiming that Hythloday "suddenly takes off at
an angle from the course he had set in his previous remarks" and "abruptly
launches . . . into a eulogy of the community of all things as practiced in
Utopia" (1952, pp. 22, 24; see above, p. 15). The passage does not, that is,
support the view that *Utopia* is a disunified work.

"the one and only road to the general welfare lies in placing everyone on an equal footing" (p. 105; cf. p. lxxxvii).[83]

We can now see why Hythloday has not offered a solution to the problem of counsel: its solution would involve the kind of thorough systemic reordering that he has up to this point declined to discuss. (We find in Book II that the problem has disappeared with the reordering of Utopian society.) Similarly, in the perspective Hythloday now offers, his earlier proposals for the solution of the problem of theft and poverty are seen as only partial, stopgap measures. While private property lasts,

> there will always remain a heavy and inescapable burden of poverty and misfortunes for by far the greatest and by far the best part of mankind.
>
> I admit that this burden can be lightened to some extent, but I contend that it cannot be removed entirely. A statute might be made that no person should hold more than a certain amount of land and that no person should have a monetary income beyond that permitted by law. Special legislation might be passed to prevent the monarch from being overmighty and the people overweening; likewise, that public offices should not be solicited,[84] nor be put up for sale, nor require lavish personal expenditures. (p. 105; cf. pp. 69-71)

More had earlier introduced a pair of metaphors to characterize true solutions to social problems: "If you cannot pluck up wrong-headed opinions by the root, if you cannot cure according to your heart's desire vices of long standing . . ." (p. 99: "Si radicitus euelli non possint opiniones prauae, nec receptis usu uitijs mederi queas . . ."; cf. pp. 95.39-97.4). Now, in this crucial thematic

---

[83] "Placing everyone on an equal footing" is Miller's correction (1966, pp. 61-62) for Yale's "the maintenance of equality in all respects." The Latin is "rerum . . . aequalitas." Miller observes that the context would also justify rendering the phrase, more narrowly, as "equal allocation of goods." On Hythloday's misrepresentation of Plato, see also p. 210 below.

[84] I omit Yale's "with gifts," which, as Miller points out (1966, p. 58), is not warranted by the Latin.

passage, which constitutes More's most explicit and general statement about the nature of social problems and the implication of
that nature for the design of solutions to them, Hythloday offers
an elaborate development of the metaphor of disease—to be exact,
of systemic infection, which cannot be cured by topical applications. By measures such as those he has just enumerated, "as
sick bodies which are past cure can be kept up by repeated medical
treatments, so these evils, too, can be alleviated and made less
acute." More precisely, one set of symptoms of the systemic
defects can be alleviated at the cost of having these defects produce
other symptoms at other points:

> There is no hope, however, of a cure and a return to a
> healthy condition as long as each individual is master of his
> own property. Nay, while you are intent upon the cure of
> one part, you make worse the malady of the other parts.
> . . . the healing of the one member reciprocally breeds the
> disease of the other as long as nothing can so be added to
> one as not to be taken away from another.[85] (pp. 105-7)

Plato repeatedly employs the metaphor of disease in much the
same way,[86] and Hythloday's remarks seem to echo a passage in
the *Republic* about men who "spend their whole time making and
correcting detailed regulations . . . , under the illusion that they
are reforming society": "And a fine time they have of it! For all
their cures and medicines have no effect—except to make their
ailments still more complicated—yet they live in hope that every
new medicine they are recommended will cure them" (IV.425E-
426A). In fact, however, this kind of operation is "about as
hopeful as cutting off a Hydra's head" (426E).

If Hythloday meant to regain the conversational initiative by

[85] On medical metaphors in *Utopia* and their appropriateness to Hythloday,
see McCutcheon 1969, esp. pp. 23, 31-32. Hythloday's given name links him
with the archangel Raphael, whose name means "the healing of God" and who
was regarded as "a symbolic physician who cures souls as well as bodies and
illuminates darkened minds" (p. 23).

[86] E.g., *Rep.* II.372E, VIII.564B-C; *Statesman* 297E-298E; Epistle VII 330C-
331A. And cf. Plutarch, "Lycurgus" V.2.

the shocking revelation of his communism, his stratagem certainly succeeds. More, who does not dispute the systemic view of problems but who disagrees with the claim that it implies the need for communism, seems stunned. In contrast to the impassioned eloquence with which he defended his position on counsel, he now manages only a brief and routine recapitulation of the traditional objections to communism:

> "But," I ventured, "I am of the contrary opinion. Life cannot be satisfactory where all things are common. How can there be a sufficient supply of goods when each withdraws himself from the labor of production? For the individual does not have the motive of personal gain and he is rendered slothful by trusting to the industry of others. Moreover, when people are goaded by want and yet the individual cannot legally keep as his own what he has gained, must there not be trouble from continual bloodshed and riot? This holds true especially since the authority of magistrates and respect for their office have been eliminated, for how there can be any place for these among men who are all on the same level I cannot even conceive." (p. 107)

And after similarly ineffectual objection by Giles to the claim that "a better-ordered people is to be found in that new world than in the one known to us," Hythloday is invited to speak about Utopia and speaks for the entire remainder of *Utopia*, no one venturing to interrupt him again.

If More's presentation of the arguments against communism is feeble, the arguments themselves are not. Moreover, their source makes them eminently respectable: as has been pointed out, they derive from Aristotle's critique of the *Republic* (see *Ut.*, p. 382n; White 1976, p. 671; and see below, pp. 208-9). Since they also embody firmly-held beliefs of almost all More's contemporaries, they do not demand eloquent presentation.[87]

More, then, for the purposes of his dialogue, allots himself

---

[87] Bradshaw (p. 16) points out that Aristotle's arguments against communism had been adapted by Aquinas. In *De officiis*, Cicero doubts that a "more ruinous policy" than equal distribution of property could be conceived (II.xxi.73).

the Aristotelian position on the question whether the systemic approach implies the necessity for communism. This question, like those raised in the debate on counsel, is not resolved in Book I, and again (more clearly in this case) the discussion of it functions to introduce Book II by bringing into the reader's mind a central theoretical issue that is implicit in the Utopian construct.[88]

Hythloday's remarks in these final pages of Book I also suggest that there is a link between the question of the relation between the expedient and the moral and that of the relation between justice and the nature of the economic order. Where there is private property, "it is scarcely possible for a commonwealth to have justice or prosperity" (p. 103); "I am fully persuaded that no just and even distribution of goods can be made and that no happiness can be found in human affairs unless private property is utterly abolished" (p. 105). Justice, that is, demands an "even distribution of goods," and such a distribution is also the key to the prosperity and happiness of the commonwealth. Here too, then, the morally correct and the politically prudent will be found to be identical. Correspondingly, More, from the Aristotelian position he takes, denies that the prosperity and happiness of the state are compatible with communism. The objections to communism that More recapitulates are, as H. S. Herbrüggen points

[88] Cf. Hexter's shrewd remarks on the function of the recapitulation of Aristotle's objections:

> More's argument serves to set the theme and provide the springboard for Hythloday's description of the Utopian commonwealth, and by the time he has finished describing it, he has not merely defended the community of property in general; he has specifically met all More's objections to it point by point. And this strongly suggests that More made the argument simply that it might be met point by point. . . . Yet even this does not do full justice to the artfulness of More's procedure when we call to mind that the Discourse which met the objections was written before the Dialogue in which they are raised. Thus he did not tailor the answers to fit the objections. . . . he tailored the objections to fit the answers he already had given. (1952, p. 42)

More precisely, the objections are tailored to suggest to the reader some of the concerns that were in More's mind when he undertook the design of the Utopian construct, and that accordingly should be in the reader's mind when he examines it.

out, *realpolitisch* objections (p. 258). More does not deny that absolute equality is *right* but that it is *practical*: as in the matter of counsel, political necessity dictates some deviation from the morally ideal.[89]

According to Hythloday, all More's arguments would be overthrown if he could visit Utopia: "you should have been with me in Utopia and personally seen their manners and customs as I did. . . . In that case you unabashedly would admit that you had never seen a well-ordered people anywhere but there" (*Ut.*, p. 107). Surtz notes that this response embodies the principle that "no line of argumentation is valid against an actual fact" (1957a, p. 183). Since the institutions of the Utopians are at once most wise and most holy—"prudentissima atque sanctissima" (*Ut.*, p. 102)—their commonwealth presumably demonstrates the harmony not only of the prudent and the moral but also, what is considerably more, of the prudent and the Christian. At the same time, the perfect justice of this uniquely "well-ordered" commonwealth, where "affairs are ordered so aptly that virtue has its reward, and yet, with equality of distribution, all men have abundance of all things," validates his claim that communism provides the way to social justice. Thus the example of Utopia, if More could only visit that country, would resolve both the great questions that the book inherits from Greek theory.

No one, however, had really visited Utopia. In More's time, there were no places remotely like that commonwealth,[90] although nowadays instructive examples of essentially the Utopian type lie ready to the theorist's hand. More, then, did not have comparative examples against which to test the conclusions of theory. Nor was experiment feasible for testing them (even if More had been in a position of power), since they involve the entire structure of

[89] Fleisher notes that Hythloday's claim that "the general welfare lies in placing everyone on an equal footing" implicitly questions the Aristotelian argument that "proportionate, not equal, justice is necessary in order to encourage and reward civic virtue and promote the common good" (p. 41; cf. *Pol.* III.1280a-1281a).

[90] Pace Arthur E. Morgan, who argues at length that the description of Utopia is a factual account of the Incan empire.

society rather than some more or less isolable corner of it. Failing
these avenues for the testing of theory, the best course is to create
an imaginative model.

More had already hinted that his book is superior to previous
works of political theory because it employs this technique: Hythloday refers to "the kind of things which Plato creates in his
republic or which the Utopians actually put in practice in theirs"
(p. 101). But the Utopians don't practice anything in their republic, which doesn't exist. Reading back from fiction to fact, we
see that the point of the comparison is to call attention to what
More regards as a methodological advance over Plato. Unlike
the *Republic*, which presents its conclusions simply in the form
of argument, *Utopia* offers an actual model, so that it tests results—provides an opportunity to glimpse how they might work
out in practice—even as it states them.[91]

Hythloday, to be sure, avers that Utopia confirms the validity
of his own theoretical views, and this is why he offers his account
of it.[92] But given the distance that the author has established
between himself and Hythloday, we may suspect that the description of Utopia will suggest conclusions not entirely identical
to those that Hythloday draws from it.

[91] We should recall in this connection Giles's praises of the methodological
advances embodied in *Utopia*, as well as the seeming hints in the Letter to
Giles about More's pride in the method of his book (above, pp. 26-28).

Aristotle says that "it would shed a great deal of light on the value of Plato's
ideas, if we could watch the actual construction of a constitution such as he
proposes" (*Pol.* II. 1264a). Plutarch maintains that Lycurgus is superior to Plato
in that he "produced not writings and words, but an actual polity which was
beyond imitation" ("Lycurgus" XXXI. 2).

[92] If Book I has affinities with deliberative oratory, Book II is, from Hythloday's point of view, a demonstrative oration in praise of Utopia. Quintilian
observes that the demonstrative form, which normally has the praise (or dis-
praise) of an individual as its subject, can also be employed in the praise of a
city (III.vii.26). This application is represented in such works as Bruni's *Laudatio Florentinae urbis* and its model, Aristides' *Panathenaicus*. See above, n.
57.

Chapter
Three
❦
Utopia

I

To examine the theoretical questions advanced at the end of Book I of *Utopia*, More employed the original and central exercise of Greek political philosophy, the determination of the best form of the commonwealth.[1] This exercise, which has its ancestry in the inveterate Greek practice of comparing polities, and its literary antecedents in such passages as the debate among spokesmen for monarchy, aristocracy, and democracy in Herodotus' *Histories* (III.80-82), entered political philosophy in Plato's *Republic*. In their attempt to specify the nature of the perfectly just man, Socrates and his companions are led into discussion of the perfectly just polis. The resulting exchanges delineate in effect the Idea of the polis. "Perhaps," Socrates suggests, the Republic "is laid up as a pattern in heaven, where those who wish can see it and found it in their own hearts" (IX.592B).[2] Although there is small chance that this polis will ever actually exist, the determination of its form has practical value. Like the image of the just man, the Republic provides a model to guide action: "By looking at these perfect patterns and the measure of happiness . . . they would

[1] To preclude misunderstanding, let me say at once that this statement does not imply that Utopia must be More's ideal commonwealth. The exercise can, as we shall see, be undertaken for reasons other than elaborating one's own ideal.

[2] See Chap. 2, n. 59. Plato says that the Republic is "nowhere on earth" (IX.592B: "γῆς γε οὐδαμοῦ"). In view of the close connection between the *Republic* and *Utopia*, the phrase may, as Nagel (p. 173) and Kristeller (1980, pp. 9-10) surmise, have given More the suggestion for the title of his book.

enjoy, we force ourselves to admit that the nearer we approximate to them the more nearly we share their lot" (v.472C-D; cf. Bradshaw, pp. 19-20).

In the *Republic*, Plato's earliest political work, speculative development is untrammeled by practical considerations. In particular, Plato does not acknowledge that the recalcitrance of human nature imposes constraints on the realization of political ideals. The most important reflection of this fact is found in the circumstance that the Republic is a government of men—the philosopher-rulers—rather than of law. Indeed, Plato always regarded government by wise men as preferable to even the best government by law. In the *Laws*, however, a late work, he takes account of the fact that it is in practice extremely difficult to assure a supply of wise men and elaborates the optimal pattern for a polis governed by law—his "second-best state" (*Laws* v.739A, IX.874E-875D). It is this work rather than the *Republic* that provided, as Sabine says, the "point of departure" (p. 68) for the third and last of the great best-commonwealth exercises of Greek theory, the discussion of the ideal polis in the seventh and unfinished eighth books of Aristotle's *Politics*. For Aristotle is acutely aware of the constraints that empirical fact places upon theory. According to Aristotle, Plato erred in the *Republic* by not considering "the teaching of actual experience" (*Pol.* II.1264a). Even in discussing a nonexistent, ideal polis "it cannot be right to make any assumption which is plainly impossible" (1265a), since in order for a pattern of an ideal polis to be useful, the ideal conditions "must be capable of fulfilment as well as being ideal" (VII.1325b).

It is crucial to understand that the best-commonwealth exercise is not, for Plato and Aristotle, simply a matter of piling together seemingly ideal features of a polis. As the quintessential manifestation of the rationalistic and holistic character of Greek political theory, the exercise has at its core the conception of the polis as a system of reciprocally-affecting parts. Since the polis aims at self-sufficiency, its ideal form is a structure of just those elements that will constitute a self-sufficient unit. Plato's pro-

nouncement that "society originates . . . because the individual
is not self-sufficient" (*Rep.* II.369B; p. 87 above) leads immediately to the specification of the human needs—food, shelter,
clothing—that must be supplied within the polis, and this list,
in turn, leads to the development of a list of essential occupations
(370C-371E). Superfluity in any component of the polis is as
harmful as deficiency. One manifestation of social pathology is
"a multitude of occupations none of which is concerned with
necessaries" (373B; cf. IV.399E). The provision of the luxuries
produced by these professions means that "the territory which
was formerly enough to support us will now be too small," a
circumstance that fosters aggression: "If we are to have enough
for pasture and plough, we shall have to cut a slice off our
neighbours' territory. And if they too are no longer confining
themselves to necessities and have embarked on the pursuit of
unlimited material possessions, they will want a slice of ours too"
(373D). By contrast, in the ideal polis "the land must be extensive
enough to support a given number of people in modest comfort,
and not a foot more is needed" (*Laws* V.737D; cf. *Rep.* IV.423B).

The method of Aristotle's best-commonwealth exercise is essentially the same as that of the *Republic* and *Laws*, but Aristotle
characteristically articulates the principles of this method in a
much more explicit and systematic fashion. Book VII of the
Politics opens, as I pointed out earlier, with a statement of the
relation between ethics and politics: "Before we can undertake
properly the investigation of our next theme—the nature of an
ideal constitution—it is necessary for us first to determine the
nature of the most desirable way of life [for the individual]. As
long as that is obscure, the nature of the ideal constitution must
also remain obscure" (1323a). There follows a recapitulation of
Aristotle's views on the best life. Axiomatically, the end of life
is happiness. The constituent elements of the best life, then, are
"external goods; goods of the body; and goods of the soul," for
"no one would call a man happy" who was seriously deficient in
respect of any of these classes of goods. But "differences begin
to arise when we ask, 'How much of each good should men have?

And what is the relative superiority of one good over another?' "
The truth is that external goods and goods of the body are merely
instrumental. Thus, "like all other instruments, [they] have a
necessary limit of size": "any excessive amount of such things
must either cause its possessor some injury or, at any rate, bring
him no benefit" (1323b). On the contrary, "the greater the amount
of each of the goods of the soul, the greater is its utility."

It is evident that the goal of the polis is to facilitate the achievement of happiness by its citizens: "There is one thing clear about
the best constitution: it must be a political organization which
will enable all sorts of men to be at their best and live happily"
(1324a).[3] There follows an argument against the idea that the
happiness of the polis lies in war and conquest, which concludes
with a restatement of the view that the goal of the polis is to
secure the good life for its citizens:

---

[3] Cf. *Pol.* I.1252b: the polis exists "for the sake of a good life." Similar
statements are found in *Pol.* III.1278b, 1279a, 1280b-1281a, 1282b, IV.1295a.
Likewise, Plato says at one point that the goal of the polis is "to promote the
happiness . . . , so far as possible, of the whole community" (*Rep.* IV.420C;
cf. VII.519E; *Laws* I.631B, V.743C).

Both Plato's and Aristotle's conceptions of the political goal, however, sometimes exhibit a curious distortion produced by taking literally the anthropo-
morphic metaphor for the polis. Between Aristotle's discussion of the best life
of the individual and the sensible statement of the goal of the polis quoted in
the text there intervenes a brief and, to the modern reader, perplexing treatment
of the question "whether the felicity of the state is the same as that of the
individual, or different":

> The answer is clear: *all* are agreed that they are the same. The men who
> believe that the well-being of the individual consists in his wealth, will
> also believe that the state as a whole is happy when it is wealthy. The men
> who rank the life of a tyrant higher than any other, will also rank the
> state which possesses the largest empire as being the happiest state. The
> man who grades [the felicity of] individuals by their goodness, will also
> regard the felicity of states as proportionate to their goodness. (1324a;
> Barker's interpolation)

The same strange reasoning—in which the polis is regarded as a kind of
gigantic man, whose ends are the same as those of other men, rather than as
an instrument for the fulfillment of the aims of its citizens—appears several

if military pursuits are . . . to be counted good, they are
good in a qualified sense. They are not the chief end of
man, transcending all other ends: they are means to his chief
end. The true end which good law-givers should keep in
view, for any state or stock or society with which they may
be concerned, is the enjoyment of partnership in a good life
and the felicity thereby attainable. (1325a)

The formulation of the goal of the polis leads in turn to discussion of the physical and institutional components necessary to
secure the attainment of this goal. It is made clear early in the
discussion that the governing principle is, as in Plato, self-sufficiency (1326b; cf. I.1252b),[4] which implies certain demographic and geographic requirements and the fulfillment of a
specific list of occupational functions. The polis requires "such
an initial amount of population as will be self-sufficient for the
purpose of achieving a good way of life in the shape and form
of a political association" (1326b; cf. III.1275b). Population may
exceed this number, but not by so much that the citizens are
unable to "know one another's characters," something that is
necessary "both in order to give decisions in matters of disputed
rights, and to distribute the offices of government according to
the merit of candidates." Thus the "optimum standard of population . . . is, in a word, 'the greatest surveyable number
required for achieving a life of self-sufficiency.' " Similarly, the
territory of the polis must be such as to ensure "the maximum
of self-sufficiency":

and as that consists in having everything, and needing nothing, such a territory must be one which produces all kinds
of crops. In point of *extent* and size, the territory should be
large enough to enable its inhabitants to live a life of leisure
which combines liberality with temperance. . . . What was
said above of the population—that it should be such as to

---

other times in the *Politics* (1323a, 1323b, 1334a), and also in the *Republic*
(IV.435E, VIII.544D-E). See below, pp. 187-88.

[4] See also the discussion of self-sufficiency in *Eth. Nic.* I.1097a-b.

be surveyable—is equally true of the territory. (1326b-1327a)

In addition to having an appropriate population and territory, the polis must provide six "services": food, the required arts and crafts, arms, "a certain supply of property, alike for domestic use and for military purposes," "an establishment for the service of the gods," and "a method of deciding what is demanded by the public interest and what is just in men's private dealings" (1328b). Thus the polis must include specific occupational groups: "a body of farmers to produce the necessary food; craftsmen; a military force; a propertied class; priests; and a body for deciding necessary issues and determining what is the public interest." Discussion of the best arrangements for fulfilling and maintaining these requirements (including a long discussion of the proper education of citizens) occupies the remainder of Aristotle's treatment of the ideal polis.

The best-commonwealth exercise, then, is made up of four sequential steps, which underlie the design of the *Republic* and *Laws* and are clearly articulated in the *Politics*. On the basis of a conception of man's nature (both Plato and Aristotle devote some space to this topic, which properly belongs to psychology and physiology), one first determines the best life of the individual (the principal subject of ethics and the starting point of politics). The second step involves the determination, given these conclusions about the individual, of the overall goal of the commonwealth and of the contributory goals the joint attainment of which will result in the attainment of the overall goal. The third step constitutes the elaboration of the required components of a self-sufficient polis. Finally, the theorist must determine the particular form that each of these components should be given in order to assure that, collectively, they will constitute the best polis, that truly self-sufficient entity that achieves all the contributory goals, and thus the overall goal, of the polis.

It has always been recognized that *Utopia* is related to Plato's and Aristotle's accounts of the ideal polis. But treatments of the relation, when they have gone beyond general statements that More was inspired by these works, have usually been restricted to the enumeration of particular geographic, demographic, and institutional parallels between Utopia and the ideal poleis of Greek theory (especially that of the *Republic*).[5] More is thought, that is, simply to have appropriated a selection of desirable-sounding features from the Greek works, a view of the relation that fits comfortably with the common notion that the Utopian construct is a collection of randomly-chosen and whimsically-ordered features that seemed (for the most part) ideal to More.[6] Surtz, for example, writes that More goes to the *Republic* "for the broad bases of the *Utopia*, e.g. the search for justice . . . [and] the

---

[5] More penetrating views of the relation are found in recent studies by White (1976, and a study of Plato and *Utopia* forthcoming in the *Journal of the History of Philosophy*) and Bradshaw, pp. 14-26.

[6] Schoeck, for example, writes that

The implied framework of values in *Utopia* . . . is an ordered sense of the concepts and ideals of Christian faith; yet it is only implied, and the bond of understanding between written work and reader is as nebulous but as strong as this linkage with a commonly accepted framework. Within this implied framework More felt completely free to try on "points of view without any responsibility for rejection or adoption"; he regarded the views presented "with almost every possible degree of approbation and shade of assent." (1956, p. 280, quoting Sir James Mackintosh from *Utopia*, ed. Lupton, p. xli)

Similarly, André Prévost says that "on a souvent l'impression, dans la deuxième partie surtout, que l'auteur nous livre des notes de réflexions ou de lectures hâtivement rassemblées par un fil ténu" (1964, p. 97). Cf. J. W. Allen, quoted above, p. 24. This view is encouraged by the superficial resemblances between the Utopian construct and the wishful and fantastic accounts of a Golden Age or perfect society that have always formed part of imaginative literature and have sometimes affected political theory. This tradition, which More could hardly not have had in mind, contributed something to the fictional setting of his construct. Moreover, some fanciful details near the beginning of the account of Utopia—the name Abraxa (p. 113; cf. p. 386n), the transformation of Abraxa-Utopia from peninsula into island, the Utopian method of hatching eggs (p. 115)—probably mock the tradition, in the manner of Lucian's *True History*. But it is (as I hope to make clear) a fatal error to be led by these resemblances to imagine that Utopia is a whimsical potpourri.

introduction of communism into the best state," while "for many
of his details he turns to the more realistic and practical *Laws*"
(*Ut.*, p. clvii). The *Politics* "may be the ultimate, though remote,
source for such items as the following: condemnation of wars of
conquest and dedication to peacetime pursuits, . . . the end of
government as the good of the citizens, . . . the objections to
communism, the traditional case for democracy, and education
as the foundation of the state because of the importance of early
impressions" (p. clxiii). In his Commentary, Surtz annotates
numerous specific parallels (and differences) between More and
Plato, as well as a good many between More and Aristotle.

Among his annotations of Aristotelian parallels, however, is a
scattered series of notes (pp. 389, 397, 401, 495, 514) that
suggests that the choice of topics in the account of Utopia reflects,
and follows roughly the order of, Aristotle's list of the six necessary services of the polis—a fact that should have made Surtz
wonder whether Utopia might owe an underlying constructional
schema, as well as some materials that flesh it out, to Greek
theory. And indeed White has recently shown not only that More's
debts to the *Politics* are direct and extensive but also that many
of them reflect the fact that the design of the Utopian construct
is fundamentally informed by the concept of self-sufficiency:

> Self-sufficiency is not an explicitly avowed goal of Utopia,
> but it should be clear that simply because of Utopia's avowedly
> ideal, or at least superior, nature, self-sufficiency is a nec-
> essary aim of the society. That is, it seeks both the end (full
> human development) and the means (self-reliance and a
> static culture) implied by αὐτάρκεια. More has at least
> implicitly and quite possibly consciously adopted Aristotle's
> idea[7] as the basis of Utopia. And there are a number of
> similarities between specific institutions or practices de-
> scribed by these two thinkers which demonstrate their gen-
> eral agreement on self-sufficiency as the fundamental goal
> of the state. (1976, p. 642)

---

[7] Self-sufficiency is also the aim of Plato's ideal polis (above, pp. 132-33).

One can in fact go a good deal further and say simply that More's Utopian construct embodies the results of a best-commonwealth exercise performed in strict accordance with the Greek rules. The construct includes all the parts of the exercise, and it includes nothing of substance that is not either a part of it or of More's comments on his results. This fact, which provides the quietus for the view of the account of Utopia as whimsical mélange, would be obvious were it not that More decided to present his best-commonwealth exercise in a form that doubly disguised it. First, unlike Plato and Aristotle, he offers not dialectics but a model that embodies the end-product of dialectics.[8] Second, the model is presented as a fictional travelogue. The choice of this mode of presentation entailed suppressing or disguising the

[8] Since Hythloday describes not only the Utopian system as it was at the time of his arrival but also the response of the system to the new secular and religious knowledge brought by the Europeans (*Ut.*, pp. 181-85, 217-19), and since the particular nature of the response is clearly determined by the nature of the Utopian system, the Utopian construct is a kind of crude *simulation* model. Richard E. Dawson explains that "simulation, as a social science research technique, refers to the construction and manipulation of an *operating* model, that model being a physical or symbolic representation of all or some aspects of a social or psychological process" (p. 3; cf. Coplin, pp. 1-2; Hermann, p. 274). It is pleasant to note in this connection the study of Carlos Domingo and Oscar Varsavsky, who have created a mathematical simulation model of (More's) Utopia.

Two other parallels to the kind of enterprise undertaken by More in the Utopian construct are suggested by remarks in Ursula K. Le Guin's introduction to *The Left Hand of Darkness*:

This book is not extrapolative. If you like you can read it, and a lot of other science fiction, as a thought-experiment. Let's say (says Mary Shelley) that a young doctor creates a human being in his laboratory; let's say (says Philip K. Dick) that the Allies lost the second world war; let's say this or that is such and so, and see what happens. . . . In a story so conceived, . . . thought and intuition can move freely within bounds set only by the terms of the experiment, which may be very large indeed.

The purpose of a thought-experiment, as the term was used by Schrödinger and other physicists, is not to predict the future—indeed Schrödinger's most famous thought-experiment goes to show that the "future," on the quantum level, *cannot* be predicted—but to describe reality, the present world.

various components of the dialectical substructure of the model—
its generative postulates and the arguments involved in the four
steps of the best-commonwealth exercise—and a partial abandonment of the logical order of topics in the exercise for the
rather different order (or disorder) of the traveler's tale—geography, and then any number of topics in any associative order.[9]
The crucial arguments deducing the best life of the individual
from human nature are presented out of their logical place and
attributed not to the author (nor to Hythloday, who is only
recording what he saw and heard) but to the Utopian moral
philosophers, and they are offered not as a step in the generation
of the Utopian construct but simply as supposedly interesting
incidental information about Utopian philosophy. The conclusion
about the goal of the commonwealth that follows from this view
of the best life of the individual is presented in one sentence at
the end of the account of Utopian occupations: "the constitution
of their commonwealth looks in the first place to this sole object:
that for all the citizens, as far as the public needs permit, as
much time as possible should be withdrawn from the service of
the body and devoted to the freedom and culture of the mind"
(p. 135). The contributory goals of the commonwealth, and the
arguments about the array of features calculated to facilitate the
attainment and maintenance of these goals, can for the most part
be inferred only by examining the individual features of Utopia
and their interrelations.

It is clear that the best-commonwealth exercise offered a perfect
way of exploring the questions raised in Book I. The question
whether social justice necessitates communism had been the most
conspicuous concern of the original best-commonwealth exercises.
Moreover, the degree of compatibility between the politically
expedient and the imperatives of morality and religion can be
precisely determined by examining the institutions and policies

[9] The Manuels point out that the particular order chosen by More in turn
influenced the form of subsequent travel narratives: "the schema of Book II
. . . was adopted in scores of genuine, as well as imaginary, travel accounts,
and became an accepted framework for circumstantial reporting on newly discovered lands" (p. 23).

of an ideal commonwealth constructed according to Greek principles, since by definition such a commonwealth is characterized
by perfect expediency: the best-commonwealth exercise is designed to generate the constitution of a polis that acts with perfect
rationality to assure that its citizens individually and collectively
pursue their real interests.

These considerations suggest the solution to the much-discussed
problem of why More made Utopia non-Christian.[10] More and
all his contemporaries—including Machiavelli and Guicciar-

[10] This problem is insoluble as long as we assume, like the humanistic
interpreters, that the purpose of the Utopian construct is to offer a mirror of
a perfectly reformed Europe. Attempts to reconcile this view of More's intention
with the non-Christian character of Utopia rely on one of two arguments: either
that More was constrained to make his islanders non-Christian because their
island was in the New World (Hexter 1952, p. 50), or that he wished to
instruct and/or shame Europe by showing that a commonwealth effectively
more Christian than any European one could be built by reason alone, without
benefit of revelation (e.g., Chambers, pp. 127-28; Surtz 1957a, pp. 6, 199;
1957b, p. 7; Manuel and Manuel, p. 123; Bradshaw, pp. 8-14). The first of
these arguments is absurd. If More had wanted to represent a perfect commonwealth in Utopia, it would have been little trouble for him to have made
his Utopians Christian: if this island has been visited in the distant past by a
stray boatload of Romans and Egyptians (*Ut.*, p. 109), it might just as plausibly
(or implausibly) have been visited by a boatload of missionary Christians (as
in fact it was, at last). Cf. R. P. Adams 1962, p. 132. In any case, More
never feels bound by known facts about the New World. Surtz points out that
"the inhuman cruelty and the passionate lust of the savage Indians, which fill
many a page of early accounts, are the antithesis of the humane kindness and
reasonable conduct of the Utopians" (1957a, p. 23). The second argument,
though it calls attention to an important aspect of *Utopia* (its pervasive allusions
to the relation between reason and revelation), is also problematic. If More
truncated a presentation of his ideal commonwealth in order to lesson Christian
Europeans in the way this argument suggests, he was giving up a good deal
(the opportunity to present a perfect mirror) for a small return. The general
harmony of reason and revelation had been widely accepted by European in-
tellectuals for centuries. It had been influentially reasserted by Ficino and Pico
(Kristeller 1943, pp. 27-29, 320-23; 1979, pp. 204-5) and, as Surtz points
out, had been affirmed by the Fifth Council of the Lateran in 1513 (1952, p.
166.) Moreover, it seems unlikely that More would devote energy to shaming
those Europeans who needed it in a book directed primarily to a select group
of Europeans (humanists) who did not.

dini—knew that moral, and Christian, behavior is advisable on suprarational, religious grounds. The liveliest question in early (pre-Reformation) sixteenth-century political thought, however, is that raised in Book I of *Utopia*: how far, in political life, is this kind of behavior advisable, or unadvisable, on purely prudential grounds? More realized that this question could be answered by seeing what a society pursuing perfect expediency through perfectly rational calculations would be like. This realization was doubtless prompted by the fact that, as I noted above, the political works of Plato and Aristotle in which the best-commonwealth exercise originates also provide the most authoritative bases for the claim that the expedient sometimes differs from the moral. If one wànts to refute or modify these conclusions, then, a most effective way is to show that the best-commonwealth exercise, if performed more correctly, does not in fact lead to them.

It is also clear why More chose to present his results as a fictionalized model. He presents them as a model because he feels, as he indicates in Book I, that this form of presentation represents an important methodological advance in the systemic approach to social analysis (see above, pp. 64-66, 130). He disguises the model as a fiction for the same reason that *Utopia* as a whole is presented as a fiction. Fictional dialogue is conventional in humanist philosophical writing; underlying this convention is the valid observation that the appeal, hence the utility, of a learned work is enhanced if its lessons are dressed in the sugar-coat of fiction. Sidney's later description of the poet's calculations applies to the humanist tradition as a whole:

> he doth not only show the way, but giveth so sweet a prospect
> into the way, as will entice any man to enter into it. . . .
> He beginneth not with obscure definitions, which must blur
> the margent with interpretations and load the memory with
> doubtfulness; but . . . with a tale forsooth he cometh unto
> you. . . . And, pretending no more, doth intend the winning
> of the mind from wickedness to virtue. . . . For even those

hard-hearted evil men who think virtue a school name, and know no other good but *indulgere genio*, and therefore despise the austere admonitions of the philosopher, . . . yet will be content to be delighted—which is all the good-fellow poet seemeth to promise—and so steal to see the form of goodness (which seen they cannot but love) ere themselves be aware, as if they took a medicine of cherries. (*An Apology for Poetry*, pp. 113-14)

In his second letter to Giles More acknowledges that such considerations underlie the mode of presentation of the Utopian construct: "I do not pretend that if I had determined to write about the commonwealth and had thought of[11] such a story as I have recounted, I should have perhaps shrunk from a fiction [*fictio*] whereby the truth, as if smeared with honey, might a little more pleasantly slide into men's minds" (*Ut.*, p. 251).

But if More's decision to present his results in fictional form was taken for clear reasons, it is not at all clear why he scrupulously dissociates himself from the account of Utopia (see above, pp. 31, 114-15). What are we to make of the fact that he takes great pains (as he hints in the prefatory Letter to Giles) to construct a model that embodies the results of a best-commonwealth exercise and then holds the model wryly at arm's length? If it were only that he dissociates himself from the *secularity* of Utopia, there would be no problem. But, as we discover at the end of Book II, he claims to be repelled by a number of aspects of his construct: "When Raphael had finished his story, many things came to my mind which seemed very absurdly established in the customs and laws of the people described—not only in their method of waging war, their ceremonies and religion, as well as their other institutions, but most of all in . . . their common life and subsistence—without any exchange of money" (p. 245). The explanation of this dissociation, as well as of other points about

---

[11] Yale has "remembered." The Latin is "ac mihi tamen venisset in mentem talis fabulae."

Utopia, requires a detailed examination of More's best-commonwealth exercise.

II

The cornerstone of the Utopian edifice is the lengthy passage on Utopian moral philosophy (pp. 161-79). This passage also constitutes the only substantial fossil, as it were, of the dialectics that underlay the construction of Utopia. Introduced as incidental information (and often treated as such by critics of *Utopia*), the passage contains the crucial first step of the best-commonwealth exercise, the determination of the best life of the individual. Since the conclusions of this step differ in some highly significant ways from those of the Greek theorists, and since all important aspects of the Utopian construct follow more or less inevitably from these conclusions, More evidently thought it necessary to include (in a way that would not violate the decorum of his fictionalized model) a detailed account of the reasonings that lead to them.

If the full importance of the passage has not been recognized, this circumstance is attributable not only to unawareness of the precise nature of the relation between *Utopia* and the Greek treatments of the ideal polis but also to the extraordinarily convoluted and difficult development of the passage itself. Craig R. Thompson justly remarks that its logic "is not always clear and not always convincing even when clear" (1965, p. 537). Surtz, who has contributed more to its understanding than any other scholar, makes similar concessions (1957a, pp. 18, 61). He also suggests the primary explanation for the confusing development of the passage, which is that it was entailed in More's decision to construct it as a sort of paradoxical *declamatio*.

The *declamatio* was a standard rhetorical exercise, one in which, according to Erasmus, More took special pleasure (*EE*, 4:21; trans. Flower, p. 238; Thompson 1974, pp. xxxiv-xxxv). In one of its forms, the speaker assumes the character of some historical or mythical figure (Thompson 1974, p. xxxii). Lucian demonstrated the witty possibilities inherent in such *prosopopoeiae* (especially in "Phalaris"), as well as in the mock-encomium (especially "The Fly"). Erasmus acknowledges these precedents in *The Praise of Folly* (pp. 2, 9), a brilliant *declamatio* that is also a mock-encomium. The premise of this work is paradoxical: folly will be "praised . . . in a way not wholly foolish" (p. 3). Erasmus can manage this feat because his definition of folly includes much more than its usual meaning. Surtz rightly says that More's passage on Utopian moral philosophy, which purports to summarize the views of the Utopian philosophers and is thus a sort of *declamatio*, involves a similarly paradoxical praise of *voluptas* effected through the same kind of enlargement of definition (1957a, pp. 9-11).[12]

This word is introduced very near the beginning of the passage:

> They discuss virtue and pleasure [De uirtute disserunt, ac uoluptate], but their principal and chief debate is in what thing or things, one or more, they are to hold that happiness consists. In this matter they seem to lean more than they should to the school that espouses pleasure [in factionem uoluptatis assertricem] as the object by which to define either the whole or the chief part of human happiness. (*Ut.*, p. 161)

Voluptas is closely associated with the hedonism of Epicurus, who is sometimes referred to as "voluptatis assertor" (*Ut.*, p. 442n). It normally means bodily pleasure (though, to be sure, Epicurus also stressed mental pleasures). Thus the account of Utopian moral philosophy is introduced as if it were to be a defense of the view that the best life is that of sensual indulgence. In fact it turns out that the Utopians define *voluptas* as "every movement and state of body or mind in which, under the guidance of nature, man delights to dwell" (p. 167), that they regard mental pleasure as preferable to bodily pleasure, and that they regard the principal mental pleasures as arising from the practice of traditional virtues

---

[12] Hexter (1973, p. 135n) notes that *voluptas* occurs seventy-two times in *Utopia*, "as often as *homo*, more often than any other noun but *res*." Sixty-nine of these occurrences are in the account of Utopia.

(p. 175). But this information is, as Surtz points out, deliberately withheld for several pages, so that the suggestion that the Utopians defend sensuality as the key to happiness can have maximum effect.

The paradoxical praise of *voluptas*, and of Epicurus, had an important precedent in Valla's *De vero falsoque bono*, which in its original version was called *De voluptate*.[13] Valla's work furthers, in his controversialistic fashion, the gradual humanist rehabilitation of Epicurus that began with Petrarch and Boccaccio and in which (after Valla) Ficino, Pico, and others played a part (D. C. Allen; Wind, pp. 48-71). Like the Utopian moral philosophers, Valla makes *voluptas* carry more than its usual meaning: *voluptas* "is a good, from whatever source, located in a sense of delight felt by the soul and the body. This is approximately what Epicurus meant, and what the Greeks called edonén" (I.xv.1).[14] Considering the importance of Valla to humanists in general and particularly to Erasmus, as well as the resemblances between Valla's argument and that of the Utopians (some of which will be discussed below), it seems certain that More's passage is indebted to *De vero falsoque bono*.[15]

Since the rehabilitation of Epicurus and *voluptas* was not, by

[13] On the principal redactions of this work and their dates—1431, 1433, and 1444-49—see Valla, ed. Lorch, pp. xxx-liii; ed. Hieatt and Lorch, pp. 8-9, 16-26, 350.

[14] I quote from the translation of Hieatt and Lorch. This definition is, as Valla's speaker notes, derived from that of Cicero's spokesman for Epicureanism, Torquatus (*Fin.* II.iv.13).

[15] Erasmus surely knew *De vero falsoque bono* when he wrote the colloquy "The Epicurean" (publ. 1533). He may have known it as early as the period of *De contemptu mundi* (written c. 1488). See Hyma, pp. 159-60, 186-87; Tracy, pp. 36, 66, 75; *De contemptv mvndi*, pp. 29-30. For early expressions of his admiration for Valla, see *Cor.*, 1:31, 45-48, 53-54 (*EE*, 1:99, 113-15, 119-20). Valla's dialogue appears on two lists of books at Oxford in 1483 (Weiss 1967, p. 175); that is, about ten years before More arrived there. Wind shows how, "on the authority of Plotinus, sustained in this instance by Epicurus, a noble *voluptas* was introduced as the *summum bonum* of [Florentine] Neoplatonists" (p. 69). This circumstance undoubtedly contributed to Erasmus' and More's interest in the paradoxes of *voluptas*.

More's time, a new topic, More's intended readers presumably were able to understand the passage (if not its bearing on the structure of the Utopian commonwealth) and to appreciate its paradoxicality and deliberate disorderliness as aspects of the *festivitas* that helps the teachings of *Utopia* slide more pleasantly into men's minds. For the modern reader, however, it is a great help to have the parts of the argument restored to their logical sequence, and I shall effect such a restoration in the following analysis.

The Utopian concerns in moral philosophy are the same as those of European philosophers. They debate the nature of the good: does it (as European Aristotelians claim) include the goods "of the soul and of the body and of external gifts" (*Ut.*, p. 161; cf. *Pol.* VII. 1323a), or is it the case (as Stoics insist) that the only true goods are "the endowments of the soul"?[16] And they discuss "virtue and pleasure," presumably debating which of these is the *supreme* good. These questions are crucial parts of the central topic of moral philosophy, the nature of the best life: "their principal and chief debate is in what thing or things, one or more, they are to hold that happiness consists." A note in Surtz's Commentary clarifies the argument here: "All disputants agree that all men seek happiness. The point at issue is: what constitutes the object of this happiness? The four traditional schools of philosophy give varying answers. . . . The Utopians have narrowed the battle to two: the virtue of the Stoics and the pleasure of the Epicureans" (p. 442).[17] In fact, as Hythloday next informs us,

[16] The prevailing Utopian view on this question becomes clear in the following pages. The highest bodily pleasure, health, is regarded as a good (pp. 173-75), as are "beauty, strength, and nimbleness" (p. 177). The pleasures of "eating and drinking, and anything that gives the same sort of enjoyment, they think desirable, but only for the sake of health"; that is, these things are conditions of goods rather than goods in themselves. The same is true of external goods (such as riches) since the Utopians value them only insomuch as they are necessary for personal development.

[17] These are also the contenders in Valla's *De vero falsoque bono*, where Stoicism and Epicureanism are called "the two noblest of all the philosophical schools" (III. vii. 1). In this dialogue the Stoic position, presented first, is refuted

the Utopians have decided that "pleasure . . . [is] the object by which to define either the whole or the chief part of human happiness."

The Utopians base their view, as any conclusion about the best life should be based, on a particular conception of the nature of man.[18] For them, the first and most obvious fact about that nature is that man is completely self-interested. This assumption is implicit in the strategy of their argument, which establishes the advisability of virtuous behavior not on the ground that virtue is worth pursuing for its own sake, or on any appeal to altruism, but solely on the ground that such behavior is dictated by considerations of self-interest:[19] "To pursue hard and painful virtue and not only to banish the sweetness of life but even voluntarily to suffer pain from which you expect no profit . . . they declare to be the extreme of madness" (p. 163). Indeed the view of man as exclusively self-interested clearly underlies both books of *Utopia*, which everywhere embodies a concept of human nature identical to that implied in the passage on Utopian moral philosophy. In his peroration, Hythloday says that outside Utopia men "look after their private interests only" (p. 239). This claim is certainly justified by the examples of European behavior that Hythloday cites in Book I. If in Utopia men "seriously concern themselves with public affairs," the difference does not imply that Utopians

by spokesmen for classical and Christian Epicureanism. Valla thus alters the order of exposition (and the thrust) of *De finibus*, where the views of Cicero's Epicurean spokesman are refuted by Cicero himself and followed by expositions and critiques of Stoic and Academic ethics.

The Utopians attribute to religion the idea that the end of life is happiness (pp. 161.38-163.1)—i.e., this principle is, as in the Greek best-commonwealth exercises, axiomatic.

[18] Augustine (*CG* XIX.3) approvingly cites Varro's procedure for determining the best life: "To begin with, since the Ultimate Good sought for in philosophy is not the good of a tree, or a beast, or of God, but of man, he concludes that we must first ask: What is man?"

[19] This is the appropriate starting point for More's exploration of the degree of compatibility between the expedient and the moral and Christian. See pp. 140-41 above.

are less self-interested than Europeans but is a consequence of the fact that in Utopia "nothing is private," so that public interest is identical with self-interest—or, as Hythloday puts it at the end of Book I, in Utopia "affairs are ordered so aptly that virtue has its reward" (p. 103). Moreover, since the conditions of nurture are so radically opposed in Europe and Utopia, it is fair to conclude, as More probably means us to realize, that human characteristics common to both cultures constitute the unalterable core of human nature.

What this self-interested creature strives for is of course his own pleasure. The Utopians "maintain, having carefully considered and weighed the matter, that all our actions, and even the very virtues exercised in them, look at last to pleasure as their end and happiness" (p. 167).[20] Since the self that the individual strives to gratify is partly rational and partly animal, he seeks both spiritual and physical pleasures: pleasure includes "every movement and state of body or mind in which, under the guidance of nature, man delights to dwell." The strength of the drive for mental pleasures is not very apparent in Europe, where bad nurture and the pressures of work preclude the full manifestation or satisfaction of this drive. The Utopians, however, are unwearied "in their devotion to mental study" (p. 181). Their leisure hours "are commonly devoted to intellectual pursuits" (p. 129; cf. p. 159). Many of them voluntarily attend the pre-dawn lectures, going "some to one and some to another, according to their natural inclination."

Man's reason is not only a seat of pleasure but also a guide to it. "Right reason," like the senses, "aim[s] at whatever is pleasant by nature" (p. 167). Utopian moral philosophy is itself an example of this fact, since its object is the determination of the strategy for maximizing pleasure. *Utopia* as a whole suggests that this is the normal function of reason, and that men generally act in accordance with what they rationally determine to be their

[20] Epicurus says that "we choose the virtues too on account of pleasure and not for their own sake" (Diog. Laer. x.138, quoted Surtz 1957a, p. 32). Cf. Cicero, *Fin.* I.xvi.54.

self-interest. If the Utopians concern themselves with the public welfare while Europeans seek only their private welfare, "assuredly in both cases they act reasonably" (p. 239).

There is, however, enormous variation in the rational capacity of individuals. Even in Utopia, where institutional arrangements maximize the opportunity for intellectual development, "many minds . . . do not reach the level for any of the higher . . . disciplines" (p. 129). Nor can ordinary citizens be counted on to assimilate even the more obvious conclusions of the intellectual disciplines. Despite the arguments of the Utopian philosophers that demonstrate the worthlessness (at least in Utopia) of gold and silver (pp. 169-71), "if in Utopia these metals were kept locked up in a tower, it might be suspected that the governor and the senate—for such is the foolish imagination of the common folk—were deceiving the people by the scheme and they themselves were deriving some benefit therefrom" (p. 151).[21]

Despite the ineradicable tincture of folly in man, and despite large individual differences in rational capacity, the individual's •nature can be improved or debased by his nurture. Just as by participation in the slaughter of animals "mercy, the finest feeling of our human nature [clementiam humanissimum naturae nostrae], is gradually killed off" (p. 139; cf. p. 171), so native courage in the Utopians is enhanced by "their good and sound opinions, in which they have been trained from childhood" (p.

[21] It is not, then, necessary to agree with Ames, who writes that in such passages "we leave Utopia almost completely and go to England. The chief magistrates of Utopia could have little use for gold and the people could have little reason to fear them. But how foolish would the English people be to imagine that Henry VII or Henry VIII sought profit for themselves! Such irony the London citizen would understand" (pp. 173-74). More knew that even in the rational commonwealth reason could not always control baseless fear. The most striking example lies in the fact that religious superstition would long since have died out in Utopia had not "whatever untoward event that happened to anyone when he was deliberating on a change of religion been construed by fear as not having happened by chance but as having been sent from heaven" (*Ut.*, p. 217). (I have corrected Yale here as suggested by Miller 1966, p. 61.)

211). Given full scope for development, rationality becomes an enormously strong force. The Utopians know that, rationally, one should not grieve at the death of good men—and so in fact "no one mourns for them" (p. 223). Many passages on the effects of Utopian education suggest that early training is especially important in the improvement or debasement of the individual's nature:

> They take the greatest pains from the very first to instill into children's minds, while still tender and pliable, good opinions which are also useful for the preservation of their commonwealth. When once they are firmly implanted in children, they accompany them all through their adult lives and are of great help in watching over the condition of the commonwealth. (p. 229)

Charles Boewe remarks that such details as the observation that a child put to a wet nurse "looks on his nurse as his natural mother" (p. 143) and even the parallel behavior of Utopian chickens (p. 115) express "More's profound conviction of the power of early training" or early association (p. 308). Europe, as Hythloday points out, provides melancholy examples of the same phenomenon: "When you allow your youths to be badly brought up and their characters, even from early years, to become more and more corrupt" (*Ut.*, p. 71), how can you be surprised that they become criminals? Similarly, kings cannot be expected to approve good advice "because they have been from their youth saturated and infected with wrong ideas" (p. 87).[22]

The view of human nature that underlies Utopian ethical the-

---

[22] More's letter to Gonell provides external confirmation of his belief in the crucial importance of early training: "the more do I see the difficulty of getting rid of this pest of pride, the more do I see the necessity of getting to work at it from childhood. For I find no other reason why this inescapable evil so clings to our hearts, than that almost as soon as we are born, it is sown in the tender minds of children by their nurses, it is cultivated by their teachers, it is nourished and brought to maturity by their parents; while no one teaches anything, even the good, without bidding them always to expect praise as the recompense and prize of virtue" (*Sel. Let.*, p. 106; *Cor.*, p. 123).

ory is, as we should expect, close to that of Epicurus, who also believed that man is a self-interested seeker after pleasure (Surtz 1957a, pp. 28-33). But in fact the assessment in *Utopia* would hardly be disputed by any relatively objective observer of human behavior. Charles Trinkaus notes that "the Pauline, Augustinian and the Lutheran positions all regarded man in his natural state . . . as inescapably egocentric, an egocentricism that could be transcended only through an influx of divine love" (p. 133). Here at least Machiavelli, whose "estimate of human nature is as low as any theologian could have wished" (Anglo, p. 183), is at one with his religious brethren. Later in the sixteenth century we find in Montaigne a formulation of the pleasure principle close to that of the Utopians: "Whatever they say, in virtue itself the ultimate goal we aim at is voluptuousness [*volupté*]" (*Essays* I.20, trans. Frame, p. 56; cf. *Ut.*, p. 167).

What is most to the point, however, is that the Utopian view of human nature differs in no essential respect from the views of the Greek best-commonwealth theorists. In the *Republic*, Glaucon maintains that "self-interest . . . [is] the motive which all men naturally follow if they are not forcibly restrained by the law and made to respect each other's claims" (II.359C), and Plato lets him illustrate this point with the story of Gyges' ring. Later, Socrates explains that the human soul is divided into three elements, each of which "has its own pleasures, its own desires, and its own governing principles": "one element in a man gives him understanding, another spirit and enterprise, while the third [, which] shows itself in too many forms for us to be able to describe it in a single word [, may be] called . . . after its most salient characteristics, 'desire,' because of the violence of the desires for food and drink and sex and the like, or 'acquisitiveness,' because wealth is the means of satisfying desires of this kind" (IX.580D-E; cf. 588A-590A). In the *Laws*, the view of man as a pleasure-seeker is given heavy emphasis: "Human nature involves, above all, pleasures, pains, and desires, and no mortal animal can help being hung up dangling in the air (so to speak) in total dependence on these powerful influences. . . . what we all seek . . . [is] a predominance of pleasure over pain throughout our lives" (v.732E-733A). This view is based on "observation," which

tells me that all human actions are motivated by a set of three needs and desires. Give a man a correct education, and these instincts will lead him to virtue, but educate him badly and he'll end up at the other extreme. From the moment of their birth men have a desire for food and drink. Every living creature has an instinctive love of satisfying this desire whenever it occurs, and the craving to do so can fill a man's whole being, so that he remains quite unmoved by the plea that he should do anything except satisfy his lust for the pleasures of the body, so as to make himself immune to all discomfort. Our third and greatest need, the longing we feel most keenly, is . . . the flame of the imperious lust to procreate, which kindles the fires of passion in mankind. (vi.782D-783A)

The view of man's nature in Aristotle's *Politics* is similarly unflattering: "Man, when perfected, is the best of animals; but if he be isolated from law and justice he is the worst of all. . . . if he be without virtue, he is a most unholy and savage being, and worse than all others in the indulgence of lust and gluttony" (i.1253a). Indeed "the naughtiness of men is a cup that can never be filled. . . . It is the nature of desire to be infinite; and the mass of men live for the satisfaction of desire" (ii.1267b). Correspondingly, we find that, although "some crimes . . . are due to lack of necessities[,] . . . want is not the only cause of crimes. Men also commit them simply for the pleasure it gives them, and just to get rid of an unsatisfied desire" (1267a).

If there is little substantive difference between the views of human nature in *Utopia* and the Greek theorists, there also appears, at first, to be little difference between the conceptions of the best life of the individual that are based on these views. The Utopian moral philosophers maintain that pleasure is the object of happiness, but they find that the most pleasurable life is the life of virtue. Plato and Aristotle, employing some arguments that anticipate the Utopians', also find that the pleasure-seeker man discovers his greatest pleasure in the life of virtue. Thus, although Plato and Aristotle conclude that the object of happiness is virtue rather than pleasure, the distinction between their conclusion and that of the Utopians is (in this respect) slight.

The Utopian argument that the most pleasurable life is the life of virtue has its starting point in the fact that man is a creature partly spiritual and partly physical. Both these components seek pleasure; hence "the pleasures which . . . [the Utopians] admit as genuine they divide into various classes, some pleasures being attributed to the soul and others to the body" (*Ut.*, p. 173). In both categories, it is vital to distinguish between true and false pleasures. False pleasures include "whatever things mortals imagine by a futile consensus to be sweet to them in spite of being against nature (as though they had the power to change the nature of things as they do their names)" (p. 167). In reality these things "are all so far from making for happiness that they are even a great hindrance to it." They may be distinguished from true pleasures by the application of three criteria: true pleasures comprise "whatever is pleasant by nature—whatever is not striven after through wrong-doing nor involves the loss of something more pleasant nor is followed by pain." Presumably on the basis of these criteria, the Utopians determine that the class of false pleasures includes pride based on the possession of superfluous goods or of "empty and unprofitable honors" (p. 169), as well as the titillations of gambling and hunting.

The argument here is highly confusing, partly because of its elliptical nature and partly because it includes logical errors. The second and third criteria for distinguishing true and false pleasures are drawn from Epicurus' rules for choosing between competing pleasures. These rules, which More could have encountered in a number of places (Surtz 1957a, pp. 29-30; Trinkaus, p. 157), find perhaps their most influential statement in Cicero's *De finibus.* "The wise man," Torquatus says, "always holds . . . to this principle of selection: he rejects pleasures to secure other greater pleasures, or else he endures pains to avoid worse pains"

(*Fin.* I.x.33, quoted *Ut.*, p. 445n; cf. I.x.36). Diogenes Laertius quotes a letter of Epicurus that includes a formulation of the second principle that is closer to the Utopian version: "since pleasure is our first and native good, for that reason we do not choose every pleasure whatsoever, but ofttimes pass over many pleasures when a greater annoyance ensues from them" (x.129, quoted *Ut.*, p. 453n). But these criteria are not, as the Utopians imagine, applicable to making qualitative distinctions among pleasures—to distinguishing those that are "pleasant by nature" from those that are not—but only to choosing pleasures so as to maximize the individual's total of pleasure, where all pleasures are regarded (as by Epicurus) as qualitatively equal. To confuse matters further, the Utopians add a third criterion: what is pleasant by nature includes "whatever is not striven after through wrong-doing." It is not evident how they conclude that true pleasure must satisfy this condition.[23]

Further confusion arises from the circumstance that the three criteria are not in fact employed in the determination that the pleasures of pride, gambling, and hunting are false. This determination is effected by direct application of the conception that

[23] Two other statements of the principles of selection (pp. 163, 177) include only the two Epicurean principles. If we grant that wrongdoing always involves injury to others, then the third criterion follows from the arguments of the preceding passage, which claims to show that "nature . . . bids you take constant care not so to further your own advantages as to cause disadvantages to your fellows" (p. 165).

The latter notion is Stoic (see p. 90 above, and cf. *Off.* III.v.22, quoted below, n. 94), as are other conceptions of natural injunctions in the section on moral philosophy. In particular, there is the Utopian definition of virtue as "living according to nature since to this end we were created by God" (p. 163: the marginal gloss says coyly "Hoc iuxta Stoicos"; cf. *Off.* III.iii.13; Sen., *Ep.* v.4), and the attendant notion that "that individual . . . is following the guidance of nature who, in desiring one thing and avoiding another, obeys the dictates of reason." Cf. *Off.* III.v.23, where Cicero speaks of "the Reason which is in Nature, which is the law of gods and men." All "will hearken to that voice . . . who wish to live in accord with Nature's laws." Indeed, the contamination of Utopian Epicureanism by Stoicism accounts for many of the difficulties of the section.

true pleasures are "pleasant by nature" and false pleasures correspondingly unnatural. Men who take pride in fine coats imagine that it is "by nature and not by their own mistake" that such possessions are important (p. 167). The same error convinces men that "empty and unprofitable honors" are pleasant: "What natural and true pleasure can another's bared head or bent knees afford you? Will this behavior cure the pain in your own knees or relieve the lunacy in your own head?" (p. 169). Likewise, how can there be pleasure "in shooting dice upon a table? You have shot them so often that, even if some pleasure had been in it, weariness by now could have arisen from the habitual practice. Or what sweetness can there be, and not rather disgust, in hearing the barking and howling of dogs?" (p. 171). In general, "although the mob of mortals regards these and all similar pursuits—and they are countless—as pleasures, yet the Utopians positively hold them to have nothing to do with true pleasure since there is nothing sweet in them by nature. . . . The enjoyment does not arise from the nature of the thing itself but from their own perverse habit" (pp. 171-73).

These arguments, as Surtz writes, violate the axiom that no line of argument is valid against a fact (1957a, p. 56): whether or not they should, many men find intense and lasting pleasure in such activities. The arguments are also unnecessary, since equivalent results could have been obtained much more plausibly by applying the Epicurean criteria and thus avoiding the problematic qualitative distinctions of the passage. There is, however, no reason to doubt that More regarded the Utopian arguments as valid. As Surtz shows, the arguments and the conclusions drawn from them closely resemble passages in others of More's works, and in those of Erasmus (pp. 36-77).

It is clear, moreover, why More is concerned to establish that unaided reason suggests qualitative distinctions among pleasures. Without such distinctions, he evidently believed (see pp. 165-66 below), it is impossible to show that purely prudential—rational—considerations dictate a moral life for the individual, and thus in turn impossible to argue that there is a degree of harmony between the prudent and the moral on the collective, political level. The theory that the politically prudent and the moral are identical is Hythloday's, not More's, and we cannot tell from the argument of Book I exactly how far the author of *Utopia* thought the harmony between them extended. It is, however, certain that he *wished* it to extend very far. And he was perhaps especially interested in demonstrating that prudential considerations alone dictate a life close to Stoic and Christian norms because Valla had so forcefully argued the opposite position, thus providing an influential sanction for ethical (and, by implication, political) views of which More clearly disapproved.

In Books I and II of *De vero falsoque bono*, Valla investigates precisely the question treated in the section on Utopian moral philosophy: what conclusions can be derived by unaided human reason about the best life for the individual?[24] To determine the answer, Valla allows one of his speakers, Maffeo Vegio, to adopt— "playfully[,] . . . in the manner of Socrates, whom the Greeks called eiróna" (III.vii.3; cf. 5)—a rationalistic, Epicurean position. From this position, Vegio crushingly refutes the position of the first speaker, Catone Sacco, the representative of classical Stoicism and its humanist admirers. Vegio argues that there is no rational sanction for the Stoic pursuit of virtue for its own sake. Man is clearly a pleasure-seeker by nature, and, since reason affords him no cause to believe in God or the afterlife, there is no justification for following any other course than that of maximum pleasure, a course in which he can be guided by the hedonic calculus of Epicurus. To be sure, he may sometimes choose virtuous action, because the virtues can be means toward mental pleasures. But there are no qualitative distinctions among pleasures. In particular, the pleasure of philosophic contemplation is linked to and in no way superior to sensual pleasure:

> Who doubts that the pleasures of the body are generated
> with the aid of the soul, and the pleasures of the soul with

---

[24] The following remarks are indebted to Trinkaus's detailed explication (pp. 105-50) of *De vero falsoque bono*.

the compliance of the body? Isn't what we conceive with the
mind almost corporeal, that is, dependent on what we see
or hear or perceive by one of the other senses? It is from
this that contemplation takes its origin. . . . Therefore you
must, if you please, stop exalting this "contemplation" with
lofty words.

The philosophers' rationale in contemplating . . . the
heavens, the earth, and the seas, is the same as that of boys
and girls when they look at the stores around the Forum and
admire and compare the ornaments of the jewelers. . . . your
pleasure in contemplating the sky and the stars is no greater
than mine when I gaze at a lovely face. . . . (II.xxviii.5-8)

Reason tells us that we are like the animals "in almost everything":

They eat, we eat; they drink, we drink; they sleep, and so
do we. They engender, conceive, give birth, and nourish
their young in no way different from ours. They possess
some part of reason and memory, some more than others,
and we a little more than they. . . . finally, they die and
we die—both of us completely. (II.xxxi.6)

When unaided reason is the guide to life, then, "man has no
choice but to accept his animal nature and live by the pleasure
principle" (Trinkaus, p. 125). Epicureanism is to Valla "the
natural life of the ordinary man, and . . . without the Christian
revelation this must be considered a good and desirable life,
however egocentric and to whatever 'immoral' means it may
resort. For it cannot be condemned as 'immoral' from a natural,
pre-Christian standpoint" (p. 135).

It is only when empirical data are supplemented by the truths
of revelation that reason can legitimately derive the conclusion
that the best life is the life of virtue. These corrected arguments,
voiced by Antonio Raudense, Valla's "Christian-Epicurean"
spokesman in Book III of *De vero falsoque bono*, begin, like
Vegio's, from the empirically-based view of man as an egocentric
pleasure-seeker, but, since they incorporate additional premises

from revelation, they result in a different strategy for the maximization of pleasure. Antonio concedes that, as Trinkaus puts it, "even a naturalistic and material conception of egocentric good carries within it elements of altruism—not simply because it brings advantage to the self to wish well to others, but because seeing the good of others brings a spontaneous pleasure" (pp. 131-32).[25] But, in general,

> virtue is not to be desired for itself, as something severe, harsh, and arduous, nor is it to be desired for the sake of earthly profit [propter utilitates que terrene sunt]; it is to be desired as a step toward that perfect happiness which the spirit or soul, freed from its mortal portion, will enjoy with the Father of all things, from whom it came.
>
> Who would hesitate to call this happiness "pleasure," or who could give it a better name? . . . From all of which it is to be understood that not virtue but pleasure must be desired for itself by those who wish to experience joy, both in this life and in the life to come. (III.ix.2-3)

Moreover, in the present life the life of virtue, though hard, entails one keen pleasure: "Indeed a kind of probable pleasure is not lacking in this life, and the greatest such comes from the hope of future happiness, when the mind, which is aware of right action, and the spirit, which unceasingly contemplates divine things, consider themselves a kind of candidate for the heavenly, represent to themselves the promised honors, and in a way make them present" (III.x.2). Only the Christian, then, can legitimately conclude that some pleasures are qualitatively superior to others and that happiness demands virtue.[26] To Valla, "there can be no

[25] According to Plutarch, Epicurus concluded that altruism provides the highest pleasure: "Epicurus, who places happiness in the deepest quiet, as in a sheltered and landlocked harbour, says that it is not only nobler, but also pleasanter, to confer than to receive benefits. 'For chiefest joy doth gracious kindness give' " ("That a Philosopher ought to converse especially with Men in Power," 778C, quoted Surtz 1957a, p. 32).

[26] St. Augustine had come to the same conclusion: "in my judgment, Epicurus

serious alternative to his conception of Christian morality, no
possible compromise or partial natural morality. It is either the
morality of Revelation or none at all" (Trinkaus, p. 119).

It is important to note, however, that for Valla, as for Augustine, Christian revelation does not imply the need to devalue
or disallow man's nonrational part. Valla follows Augustine "in
fully accepting man's passions as a natural and good part of man's
nature" (p. 156). In *De vero falsoque bono* as in the later *Repas-
tinatio dialecticae et philosophiae*, Valla "holds that the affects and
passions are the central force of man's nature, so that virtue lies
not in curbing, tempering, or compensating them, but in their
full and forceful expression directed towards those objectives
which contain the greatest good for the individual" (p. 157).
This position, which is of crucial importance in humanist moral
thought, is often rightly associated with the implied psychology
and ethics of the rhetorical tradition (where Augustine's primary
intellectual affiliation lay).[27] But it should be remembered that
this position, while antithetical to the Stoic view, is largely compatible with the views of Plato and Aristotle, who, as we have
seen, though insisting that man should be ruled by reason, do
not deny the independence and legitimacy of the claims of his
other components.[28]

The closeness of the relationship between Valla's arguments

---

would have carried off the palm if I had not believed what Epicurus would
not believe: that after death there remains a life for the soul, and places of
recompense" (*Confessions* VI.xvi, quoted Surtz 1957a, p. 27).

[27] See, in addition to Trinkaus, Struever; Baron 1971; Bouwsma 1973, pp.
9-17; 1975; 1976, pp. 422-27; and see below, p. 264.

[28] It should also be remembered that one influential Stoic—Seneca—allows
the claims of the body:

it is quite contrary to nature to torture the body, to hate unlaboured
elegance, to be dirty on purpose, to eat food that is not only plain, but
disgusting and forbidding. Just as it is a sign of luxury to seek out dainties,
so it is madness to avoid that which is customary and can be purchased at
no great price. Philosophy calls for plain living, but not for penance; and
we may perfectly well be plain and neat at the same time. (*Ep.* V.4-5)

This passage may be a source of the similar reasonings in *Ut.*, pp. 177-79.

and those of the Utopians is obvious, both where the Utopians' conclusions agree with his and where they do not. Sharing with Valla the belief that it is man's nature to seek his own pleasure, the Utopians agree that without knowledge of God and immortality there is no rational sanction for the life of virtue. If there were no reason to anticipate an afterlife of reward for virtues and punishment for crimes,

> the Utopians have no hesitation in maintaining that a person would be stupid if he did not realize that he ought to seek pleasure by fair means or foul, but that he should only take care not to let a lesser pleasure interfere with a greater nor to follow after a pleasure which would bring pain in retaliation. To pursue hard and painful virtue and not only to banish the sweetness of life but even voluntarily to suffer pain from which you expect no profit (for what profit can there be if after death you gain nothing for having passed the whole present life unpleasantly, that is wretchedly?)— this policy they declare to be the extreme of madness.[29] (*Ut.*, p. 163)

At the same time, the Utopians also agree with Valla that even men with no knowledge of religious truths would sometimes act altruistically for the sake of the mental pleasure that such acts provide:

> to take away something from yourself and to give it to others is a duty of humanity and kindness which never takes away as much advantage as it brings back. Not only is it compensated by the return of benefits, but also the actual con-

[29] "If he did not realize that he ought" is Miller's correction (1966, p. 58) of Yale, which reads simply "would be stupid not to seek . . ."

Hythloday commends the fact that the Utopians in their religious services "carefully see to it that everywhere the younger are placed in the company of the elder. If children were trusted to children, they might spend in childish foolery the time in which they ought to be conceiving a religious fear towards the gods, the greatest and almost the only stimulus to the practice of virtues" (*Ut.*, p. 235).

sciousness of the good deed and the remembrance of the
love and good will of those whom you have benefited give
the mind a greater amount of pleasure than the bodily pleasure which you have forgone would have afforded.[30] (pp.
165-67; cf. n. 25 above)

According to Valla, unaided reason can go no further in providing sanctions for virtuous behavior. And reason is all the
Utopians have. At the end of his account of the Utopians' "view
of virtue and pleasure," Hythloday tells us that "they believe that
human reason can attain to no truer view, unless a heaven-sent
religion inspire man with something more holy" (p. 179). But
of course the Utopians have been able to advance far beyond the
limits that Valla sets for reason, so that in fact their views are
very close to the Christian-Epicurean position developed in Book
III of *De vero falsoque bono.*

They have been able to effect this advance because they have
derived by unaided reason precisely those truths that Valla says
are necessary premises for the rationalization of the life of virtue
and that he says can be obtained only from revelation. For the
Utopians never "discuss happiness[31] without uniting certain principles taken from religion as well as from philosophy, which uses
rational arguments" (p. 161). Like Valla, they agree that "without
these principles . . . reason [is] insufficient and weak by itself
for the investigation of true happiness." The crucial principles
are that "the soul is immortal and by the goodness of God born
for happiness," and that "after this life rewards are appointed
for our virtues and good deeds, punishment for our crimes" (pp.
161-63). And "though these principles belong to religion, yet
they hold that reason leads men to believe and to admit them"
(p. 163).

[30] I have altered the translation in Yale according to Miller's corrections
(1966, p. 63).

[31] "Discuss happiness" is Skinner's correction (1967, p. 159) for Yale's
"discussion of philosophy." The Latin is "Neque enim de felicitate disceptant
unquam."

As in *De vero falsoque bono*, the addition of these "religious" premises does not alter the fact that man seeks—and *should* seek—his own pleasure, nor does it invalidate the Epicurean hedonic calculus as the means for choosing between competing pleasures. Man should still "take care not to let a lesser pleasure interfere with a greater nor to follow after a pleasure which would bring pain in retaliation"—as we hear twice more in the section (pp. 167, 177)—but, given the religious premises, the Utopians conclude that "happiness rests not in every kind of pleasure but only in good and decent pleasure" (p. 163). In particular, acts of self-sacrificing generosity become infinitely more advantageous, since to the mental pleasure that comes even to the nonbeliever from such acts will be added the rewards of the afterlife: "Finally—and religion easily brings this home to a mind which readily assents—God repays, in place of a brief and tiny pleasure, immense and never-ending gladness" (p. 167).

It seems certain that More is consciously revising Valla's arguments, and it is easy to see why he wanted to revise them in these particular ways. What is not so easy to see is why he thought that the arguments by which he reached his desired conclusions were persuasive. To a modern reader, the claim that the Utopians were led to their religious principles by reason, and the arguments for the qualitative distinctions among pleasures, are likely to seem dialectically the weakest points in *Utopia*. Moreover, since the reader doubts that the religious principles really can be derived by reason, their insertion appears to be a violation of the rules of the best-commonwealth exercise, and, given the significance of the consequences that derive from this insertion, a violation that largely invalidates this step and the following steps of More's exercise. These objections cannot be countered with entire success, but one can show both that More had excellent precedents for his view, and that, moreover, he could have arrived at similar conclusions by less dubious arguments.

The claim that natural reason can lead to certain key religious doctrines is a standard theme of medieval and Renaissance theology and philosophy. As Surtz points out, Aquinas maintains

that "man, without supernatural grace, can come to the knowledge
. . . of moral and religious truths, such as the existence and
perfections of God, the immortality and spirituality of the soul,
the duties of man toward his Creator, and the punishments and
rewards of the future life" (1952, p. 163; cf. Gilson, pp. 69-
84; Copleston, 2:312-23).[32] Ficino says that "the whole of natural
religion is for man a most firm foundation for immortality"
(*Commentaria in Plotinum*, p. 1754, trans. *Ut.*, p. 445n). Kristeller notes that Ficino's *Theologia Platonica* "served as an arsenal
of arguments for those who were interested in defending immortality on philosophical or theological grounds" (1979, p.
191). Some years before More wrote *Utopia*, Colet had claimed,
in his *Exposition of Romans*, that the "philosopher man . . . could
easily, through the things that are made, see God, omnipotent
and eternal" (pp. 65-66, quoted Surtz 1957b, p. 25). More's
sympathy with such views is clear from a passage in *A Treatise
upon the Passion* endorsing the opinion of Nicholas de Lyra:

> vnto the Paynims and Gentils, to whom the law was not
> gyuen, nor neuer had heard of Christ, it was sufficient
> [according to de Lyra] for their saluacion to belieue those
> two pointes onelye which saynt Paule here reherseth [He-
> brews 6:6], that is to wit, that there is one God, and that
> he wyl reward them that seke him. And those two pointes
> be such, as euery man may attayne by natural reason, holpen
> forth wyth suche grace as God keepeth fro no man, but

[32] Surtz adds that "More was an ardent admirer and constant defender of
the Angelic Doctor." In the *Responsio ad Lutherum*, for example, More praises
"that most learned and also most holy man, Saint Thomas Aquinas" (p. 355,
quoted Surtz 1957a, p. 108).

The Nominalists, however (whose reputation is notoriously poor among
humanists), deny, for the most part, that such rational proofs are possible. See
Surtz 1957b, p. 22; Gilson, pp. 85-87; Copleston, 2:518-34; 3:80-88, 96-
101. Chambers (p. 135) points out that Pomponazzi's "On the Immortality
of the Soul" (publ. 1516) also denies that unaided reason can lead to knowledge
of the immortality of the soul. "Therefore More's *Utopia*, among other things,
is a contribution to this current controversy" (pp. 135-36). Cf. Kristeller 1979,
pp. 192-95.

from him that by his own defaute, eyther wyl not receyue
it or deserueth to haue it wythdrawen. (p. 43, quoted *Ut.*,
p. 523n; cf. p. 525n)

Moreover, the inclusion of such principles in the purely rationalistic best-commonwealth exercise is sanctioned by the fact
that, as More says in the *Dialogue Concerning Heresies*, "all the
hole nomber of the olde phylosophers . . . founde out by nature
and reason that there was a god eyther maker or gouernour or
bothe of all this hole engyne of the worlde" (p. 69, quoted Surtz
1957b, p. 27). The Epicureans, to be sure, stopped at this point,
holding that, though the gods exist, they are indifferent to human
affairs and that man's soul is mortal (*Ut.*, p. 444n).[33] But in the
prototypal best-commonwealth exercise, Socrates claims that "our
soul is immortal" (*Rep.* x.608D) and that "the prizes and rewards
which the just man receives from gods and men while he is still
alive . . . are nothing in number and quality when compared to
the things that await the just man and unjust man after death"
(613E-614A; cf. *Phaedo*, esp. 77A-81E; Kristeller 1979, p. 184).

More could, of course, have argued plausibly that purely
mundane considerations dictate a life of virtue. This is the position
of Epicurus, who maintains that "the consciousness of right and
the fear of detection" (*Ut.*, p. 445n) constitute sufficient incite-
ments to virtue, and who determines on the basis of mundane
calculations that "we cannot lead a life of pleasure which is not
also a life of prudence, honour, and justice. . . . For the virtues
have grown into one with a pleasant life, and a pleasant life is
inseparable from them" (Diog. Laer. x.132, quoted Surtz 1957a,
p. 32). In More's time, as Surtz observes, Pomponazzi was
teaching that virtue is independent of the belief in immortality
and is most genuine when practiced without hope of reward or
fear of punishment (1957a, p. 18; Pomponazzi, "On the Immortality of the Soul," pp. 360-65, 373-75). Later in the sixteenth century, Montaigne offered an admirable statement of

---

[33] Cf. Kristeller 1979, p. 185, and, on other classical views on immortality,
pp. 184-85.

what the Utopians could have concluded about nonreligious sanctions for virtue:

> What I like is the virtue that laws and religions do not make but perfect and authorize, that feels in itself enough to sustain itself without help, born in us from its own roots, from the seed of universal reason that is implanted in every man who is not denatured. This reason, which straightens Socrates from his inclination to vice, makes him obedient to the men and gods who command in his city, courageous in death not because his soul is immortal but because he is mortal. (*Essays* III.12, trans. Frame, p. 811)

But the Utopians explicitly reject the claim that there are sufficient mundane incentives to the life of virtue, both in the section on moral philosophy and in that on Utopian religion, where we read that they do not doubt that a man who thinks that "souls likewise perish with the body or that the world is the mere sport of chance . . . will strive either to evade by craft the public laws of his country or to break them by violence in order to serve his own private desires" (*Ut.*, pp. 221-23). More was probably influenced in his denial of the sufficiency of mundane sanctions by Valla. Plato, too, while acknowledging that an atheist "may have a naturally just character . . . and because of his loathing of injustice . . . not [be] tempted to commit it" (*Laws* X.908B, quoted Surtz 1957b, p. 51) stresses, as Surtz notes, that "a correct view of the existence, providence, and nature of God . . . [is] the foundation of morality" (e.g., *Laws* X.885B-C).[34]

There are also sanctions in pagan philosophy for the idea that certain pleasures are false and others true "by nature." Indeed, for this part of Utopian moral philosophy More relies heavily on ethical works of Plato and Aristotle. The *Philebus* includes a detailed discussion of the distinction between true and false pleas-

---

[34] Similarly, Cicero writes that "in all probability the disappearance of piety towards the gods will entail the disappearance of loyalty and social union among men as well, and of justice itself" (*De natura deorum* I.ii.4, quoted Surtz, *Ut.*, p. 526n).

ures (36C-52B), and More was certainly indebted to this treatment.[35] In the *Nicomachean Ethics*, Aristotle writes that "some
things are pleasant by nature . . . ; while others are not pleasant
by nature, but some of them become so by reason of injuries to
the system, . . . by reason of acquired habits, . . . [or] by reason
of originally bad natures" (VII.1148b, quoted White 1976, p.
651). White notes that Aristotle anticipates the Utopians not only
in distinguishing between natural and unnatural pleasures but
also in identifying "disease and habit as factors which explain
why the latter are perceived as being pleasurable." Indeed, the
close correspondence of language between the *Ethics* and a passage
in *Utopia* strongly suggests that Aristotle is a direct source for
the Utopian arguments. The Utopians maintain that men's enjoyment of false pleasure arises not "from the nature of the thing
itself but from their own perverse habit. The latter failing makes
them take what is bitter for sweet, just as pregnant women by
their vitiated taste suppose pitch and tallow sweeter than honey.[36]
Yet it is impossible for any man's judgment, depraved either by
disease or by habit, to change the nature of pleasure any more
than that of anything else" (*Ut.*, p. 173, quoted White 1976,
pp. 650-51).[37]

---

[35] The dependence of Utopian ethical theory on the *Philebus* was pointed out
long ago by Cassirer (p. 110). Following his lead, Jones has examined the
matter in detail (1971). Many of the parallels adduced in the following pages
are noted by her.

The distinction between true and false pleasures is also a subject of interest
to Ficino and Pico (Wind, pp. 49-51), as More presumably knew.

[36] Cf. *Eth. Nic.* x.1173b: "if things are pleasant to people of vicious constitution, we must not suppose that they are also pleasant to others than these,
just as we do not reason so about the things that are wholesome or sweet or
bitter to sick people." See also 1176a.

[37] The ideas and the imagery of this passage reappear in *The Four Last Things*:
"like as a sick man feleth no swetenes in suger, & some women with child
haue such fond lust that thei had leuer eate terre than tryacle, & rather pitch
than marmelade, . . . so we grosse carnal people hauing our tast infected, by
the sicknes of sin & filthy custom of fleshly lust, fynd so gret liking in the vile
& stinking delectacion of fleshly delite, that we list not once proue, what maner

The Utopian conclusions about *true* pleasures, and thus about the best life, are also reminiscent of Plato and Aristotle. With them the Utopians share, first, the division of pleasures "into various classes, some pleasures being attributed to the soul and others to the body." For this division they have especially the precedent of the *Philebus*. There Protarchus defends pleasure as the supreme good, and it at first appears that Socrates will oppose the claim of wisdom to that of pleasure. But in fact he develops the position that the best life combines the mental pleasures with a variety of bodily pleasures. In the *Nicomachean Ethics* Aristotle also distinguishes between the pleasures of thought and those of the senses (x. 1175a-b), and like Plato he thinks that both kinds of pleasure are necessary to the good life: "all innocent pleasures," as he says in the *Politics*, "help us to achieve our end [i.e., happiness]" (VIII. 1339b). The Utopians, of course, share this view.

Within the two classes of pleasures, the Utopian subdivisions also follow Plato and Aristotle. The Utopians distinguish four types of mental pleasure: "To the soul they ascribe intelligence and the sweetness which is bred of contemplation of truth. To these two are joined the pleasant recollection of a well-spent life and the sure hope of happiness to come." The first pair corresponds to Plato's "unalloyed knowledge," which "has to do with the things which are eternally the same without change or mixture" (*Phlb.* 59C; cf. 61D-E); as Jones points out (1971, p. 64), the sentence describing the second pair recalls Plato's description of the pleasures and pains of anticipation: "the sweet and cheering hope of pleasant things to come, the fearful and woful expectation of painful things to come" (32C).[38]

---

of swetenes good and vertuous folke fele & parcieue in spiritual pleasure" (p. 74, quoted Surtz 1957a, p. 42).

According to Diogenes Laertius, Epicurus also maintained that desires that are "neither natural nor necessary . . . are due to illusory opinion." Examples, according to a scholium, are "desires for crowns and the erection of statues in one's honour" (x. 149, quoted Surtz 1957a, p. 210n).

[38] Surtz (1957a, p. 62) notes that More's sentence also echoes his earlier passage on the satisfaction derived from self-sacrifice (*Ut.*, pp. 165-67, quoted

The classification of bodily pleasures is also close to Plato. The Utopians divide these into two kinds. The first, further divided into two,

> is that which fills the sense with clearly perceptible sweetness. Sometimes it comes from the renewal of those organs which have been weakened by our natural heat. These organs are then restored by food and drink. Sometimes it comes from the elimination of things which overload the body. . . . Now and then, however, pleasure arises, not in process of restoring anything that our members lack, nor in process of eliminating anything that causes distress, but from something that tickles and affects our senses with a secret but remarkable moving force and so draws them to itself. Such is that pleasure which is engendered by music.

In the same fashion, Plato distinguishes between the bodily pleasures that occur "when things are restored to their natural condition" (42D) and "those the want of which is unfelt and painless, whereas the satisfaction furnished by them is felt by the senses, pleasant, and unmixed with pain" (51B).[39] But the Utopians differ from Plato in claiming as "the second kind of bodily pleasure . . . that which consists in a calm and harmonious state of the body"; that is, health. In the *Philebus* Plato several times denies that the mere absence of pain can be regarded as a pleasure, on the ground that pleasure must involve motion (32E-33B; 42C-44B; 51A; 54A-55A; cf. *Rep.* IX.583C-585A). Clearly More has these passages in mind when he tells us that the Utopians

---

above, pp. 161-62). Epicureans also stress the pleasures of recollection (e.g., Cicero, *Fin.* I.xvii.57).

[39] Aristotle, however, contests the view that "pain is the lack of that which is according to nature, and pleasure is replenishment":

> these experiences are bodily. If then pleasure is replenishment with that which is according to nature, that which feels pleasure will be that in which the replenishment takes place, i.e., the body; but that is not thought to be the case; therefore the replenishment is not pleasure, though one would be pleased when replenishment was taking place, just as one would be pained if one was being operated on. (*Eth. Nic.* X.1173b)

"long ago rejected the position of those who held that a state of stable and tranquil health . . . was not to be counted as a pleasure because its presence, they said, could not be felt except through some motion from without" (*Ut.*, p. 175). (To be sure, "the absence of pain without the presence of health they regard as insensibility rather than pleasure.")[40]

Finally, More derives from Plato and Aristotle the important idea that the various pleasures can be ranked; and the particular hierarchy that the Utopians propound is close to those of the Greek thinkers. The Utopians "cling above all to mental pleasures, which they value as the first and foremost of all pleasures." In the *Philebus* Plato also urges the superiority of the mental pleasures. It is noteworthy, however, that whereas for Plato the pure philosophic contemplation of truth is the supreme pleasure (52A-B; 57A-59D; 61D-E), the Utopians hold that "the principal part . . . [of mental pleasure] arise[s] from the practice of the virtues and the consciousness of a good life."[41]

---

[40] The idea that freedom from pain is a pleasure is a key doctrine of Epicurus (e.g., Diog. Laer. X.131), and More's classification of bodily pleasures may owe something to Cicero, *Fin.* II.iii.9-10, where the Epicurean Torquatus defends a distinction between "static" pleasure (i.e., freedom from pain) and "kinetic" pleasure. In the dialogue Cicero himself refuses to grant that freedom from pain is a pleasure.

[41] This characterization of the highest mental pleasures is not entirely consistent with the list of mental pleasures on p. 173 (quoted above). Cf. White 1976, p. 651n: "The first passage emphasizes the contemplative life in a way that the second one does not. More probably regards the active life of virtue as the ultimate source of pleasure because the recollection of a good life, hope of eternal reward, and the consciousness of a good life presume the practice of virtues."

More's own view of the highest pleasure is recorded in "Twelve Weapons," published five years before *Utopia*: "Thou shalt no pleasure comparable finde / To thinwarde gladnes of a vertuous minde" (p. 27, quoted Surtz 1957a, p. 63). Fleisher notes that the Utopian hierarchy of mental pleasures "is quite consistent with the omission of speculative reason from More's psychology, his hostility to speculative philosophy and theology, the priority given to doing over knowing, the public over the private, and the importance assigned to industry and study" (p. 57). Distrust of speculative thought and correspondingly high val-

As for bodily pleasures, the Utopians disagree with Plato in that "they give the palm to health" (p. 177). Indeed they regard health as in a sense the foremost pleasure. Although mental pleasures are superior to those of the body, health is highly desirable both in itself and as a precondition of the mental (and the other bodily) pleasures:

> many hold it to be the greatest of pleasures [*uoluptatum maximam*]. Almost all the Utopians regard it as great and as practically the foundation and basis of all pleasures. Even by itself it can make the state of life peaceful and desirable, whereas without it absolutely no place is left for any pleasure. (pp. 173-75)

The Utopians are closer to Plato in their attitude toward the pleasures of restoration:

> The delight of eating and drinking, and anything that gives the same sort of enjoyment, they think desirable, but only for the sake of health. . . . These pleasures are surely the lowest of all as being most adulterated, for they never occur unless they are coupled with the pains which are their opposites. For example, with the pleasure of eating is united hunger—and on no fair terms, for the pain is the stronger and lasts the longer. (p. 177)

The idea that the restorative pleasures are contaminated by being mixed with the opposite pains comes directly from the *Philebus*:

> Whenever, in the process of restoration or destruction, anyone has two opposite feelings, as we sometimes are cold, but are growing warm, or are hot, but are growing cold, the desire of having the one and being free from the other, the mixture of bitter and sweet, as they say, joined with the difficulty in getting rid of the bitter, produces impatience and, later, wild excitement. . . . And such mixtures some-

uation of practical reason are characteristic of humanism (cf. above, p. 41), especially "civic humanism" (see Pocock, pp. 56-57).

times consist of equal pains and pleasures and sometimes
contain more of one or the other. (46C-D; cf. 50D)

As Jones points out (p. 67), More's comic picture of the person
who "thinks that his felicity consists in this kind of pleasure,"
and who must therefore "admit that he will be in the greatest
happiness if his lot happens to be a life which is spent in perpetual
hunger, thirst, itching, eating, drinking, scratching, and rub-
bing," derives from similar passages in the *Philebus* (46A; 46D;
47B), which also use (twice) the example of itching and scratching. For Plato, these adulterated pleasures have no part in the
best life (63D-64A; 66A-D)—though it is hard to see how they
can be entirely excluded. The Utopians, however, though holding that such pleasures "should not be highly valued and only
insofar as they are necessary," nonetheless "enjoy even these pleasures and gratefully acknowledge the kindness of mother nature
who, with alluring sweetness, coaxes her offspring to that which
of necessity they must constantly do." But they agree with Plato
that the unadulterated bodily pleasures of sight, sound, and smell
are much to be preferred to those associated with restoration (*Ut.*,
p. 177; *Phlb.* 51).

Aristotle constructs a similar hierarchy of pleasures. In the
Nicomachean Ethics he says that the various pleasures can be
ranked in accordance with the dignity of the faculty to which
they pertain: "sight is superior to touch in purity, and hearing
and smell to taste; the pleasures, therefore, are similarly superior,
and those of thought superior to these" (x.1175b-1176a). Thus
not only are mental pleasures superior to bodily pleasures, but
it is also the case that "within each of the two kinds some are
superior to others" (1176a). As the highest mental pleasure, "the
activity of philosophic wisdom is admittedly the pleasantest of
virtuous activities; at all events the pursuit of it is thought to
offer pleasures marvellous for their purity and their enduring-
ness, and it is to be expected that those who know will pass their
time more pleasantly than those who inquire" (1177a).

From the ranking of pleasures it follows, for the Utopians as

for Plato and Aristotle, that the best life, while mixing various
mental and bodily pleasures, will be a mixture in which the
highest pleasures predominate. This point is not explicit in the
Philebus but is treated fully in the *Republic*. There Socrates maintains that each of the three elements of human nature has "its
own particular pleasures" (IX.586E), and that reason should serve
as guide to the pleasures of all three: "if our desire for gain and
our ambition will follow the guidance of knowledge and reason,
and choose to pursue only such pleasures as wisdom indicates,
the pleasures they achieve will be the truest of which they are
capable" (586D). Mental pleasures are the keenest: "Of the three
types of pleasure, . . . the pleasantest is that which belongs to
the element in us which brings us knowledge" (583A; cf. 585D-
586C). Accordingly, "the man in whom that element is in control
will lead the pleasantest life." The intelligent man will value only
those studies that form "a character in which self-control and
fair-mindedness are combined" (591B): "And as for his physical
condition and training—he won't live merely with brutish and
irrational pleasures in view, indeed he won't even make health
his primary concern; strength and health and good looks will
mean nothing to him unless self-control goes with them, and we
shall always find him keeping physical values in tune with moral
and intellectual" (591C-D). He will also "observe the same principle of harmony and order in acquiring wealth," and with respect
to "honours, private or public" (591D, 592A). Thus it is the
philosopher-ruler, the perfectly just man, who will lead "the
most pleasant of lives" (587B). Similarly, the Athenian denies
that there is any difference between "the life of supreme justice
. . . [and] the life that gives most pleasure" (*Laws* II.662D):
"That is why we should praise the noblest life—not only because
it enjoys a fine and glorious reputation, but because (provided
one is prepared to try it out instead of recoiling from it as a
youth) it excels in providing what we all seek: a predominance
of pleasure over pain throughout our lives" (v.732E-733A; see
also 728D, III.697B).

In the *Nicomachean Ethics* Aristotle also says that the life of philosophic contemplation "is best and pleasantest, . . . [and] therefore is also the happiest" (1178a). "In a secondary degree," however, "the life in accordance with the other kind of virtue [i.e., active virtue] is happy." It must also be granted that, "being a man, one will also need external prosperity [in order to achieve happiness]; for our nature is not self-sufficient for the purpose of contemplation, but our body also must be healthy and must have food and other attention" (1178b-1179a):

> Still, we must not think that the man who is to be happy will need many things or great things, merely because he cannot be supremely happy without external goods; for self-sufficiency and action do not involve excess, and we can do noble acts without ruling earth and sea; for even with moderate advantages one can act virtuously (this is manifest enough; for private persons are thought to do worthy acts no less than despots—indeed even more); and it is enough that we should have so much as that; for the life of the man who is active in accordance with virtue will be happy.

Similarly, in the *Politics* we read that "the highest pleasure, derived from the noblest sources, will be that of the man of greatest goodness" (VIII.1338a). Thus "felicity—no matter whether men find it in pleasure, or goodness, or both of the two—belongs more to those who have cultivated their character and mind to the uttermost, and kept acquisition of external goods within moderate limits, than it does to those who have managed to acquire more external goods than they can possibly use, and are lacking in the goods of the soul" (VII.1323b). In the *Politics*, however, Aristotle places more stress on the life of virtuous action than in the *Ethics*, and such action appears to be as important a component of happiness as philosophic contemplation. He refers to the *Ethics* for the claim "that a truly happy life is a life of goodness lived in freedom from impediments" (IV.1295a),[42] but whereas in the

---

[42] Cf. Barker's gloss: " 'Freedom from impediments,' if we interpret it positively, means the possession of an adequate 'equipment' of wealth, health, and material resources."

Ethics "perfect happiness is a contemplative activity" (x. 1178b), in the *Politics* "the amount of felicity which falls to the lot of each individual man is equal to the amount of his goodness and his wisdom, and of the good and wise acts that he does" (VII. 1323b).[43]

Likewise the Utopians, as we have seen, "cling above all to mental pleasures," though they also welcome the pure pleasures of the senses and the adulterated pleasures of bodily restoration. They have, moreover, a method—the application of the hedonic calculus—for determining the correct proportions of the various pleasures in the mix that constitutes the best life. In general, More seems much more keenly aware than Plato and Aristotle of the fact that the necessarily limited nature of the individual's resources and capacities must bring even true pleasures into conflict with one another. The evidence of his awareness is the heavy emphasis on the hedonic calculus throughout the section on moral philosophy. The final statement of the principles of the calculus comes at the end of the discussion of the Utopians' relative valuation of pleasures, where we read that "in all [their pleasures] they make this limitation: that the lesser is not to interfere with the greater and that pleasure is not to produce pain in aftermath" (p. 177). Applying these principles to the Utopian hierarchy of pleasures, the conclusion clearly follows that the way to achieve the life of most pleasure is to devote just so much of one's resources to bodily pleasure as will assure the key pleasure of health (insofar as it *can* be assured) and to concentrate all other resources on the acquisition of mental pleasures, and particularly on the practice of virtue, which produces the greatest pleasure, "the consciousness of a good life." The life of greatest pleasure—which according to the Utopians is the best life—is thus the life of virtue.

[43] The *Politics* does, however, say that "the part of the soul which has rational principle" "may . . . be divided . . . into two parts. . . . Rational principle . . . is partly practical, partly speculative. . . . We may add that as the parts of the soul have their hierarchy, so, too, have the activities of those parts" (VII. 1333a)—that is, the activity of the speculative part of the rational principle is higher than the activity of the practical part.

There is, then, a considerable correspondence of views on the best life between the Utopians and the Greek theorists. Within this general harmony, however, profound differences arise from the Utopians' different understanding of the requirements for the consciousness of a virtuous life and their different relative valuation of the mental pleasures.

The most striking characteristic of the Greek treatments of the life of virtue lies in the fact that the enjoyment of this life is regarded as compatible with—indeed as dependent on—the grossest social and economic inequities. In the ideal polis of the *Republic*, the most important component of the good life, philosophic contemplation, is restricted to the Guardians. The artisans, though full citizens, seem in general to be excluded from the pleasures of development of the rational faculty (though gifted children of this class are promoted to the Guardians [III.415A-C]), since, whether by design or accident, no provision is made for their education. And although Plato says nothing on the subject, the Republic presumably includes, like all Greek city-states, a large class of slaves, who, as inherently inferior beings, are excluded from the life of virtue—a circumstance that does not appear to cloud the serene consciousness either of the Guardians or of their creator. In fact it is clear that the existence of laboring classes is a necessary condition for the Guardians' philosophic leisure. In the *Laws*, all citizens are barred from industry and trade, and their virtuous lives are made possible by the labor of the classes of resident aliens and slaves.

Plato nowhere discusses the highly restricted availability of the best life; presumably he regards the justice and necessity of such restriction as self-evident. Aristotle, in his thorough and explicit fashion, unapologetically confronts the fact that the virtuous life in his ideal polis is restricted to one group of inhabitants. For Aristotle, a sufficient cause of such restriction is entailed in his view that the practice of virtue has substantial material preconditions. "In the state," Aristotle says, "as in other natural compounds, the conditions which are necessary for the existence of the whole are not organic parts of the whole system which they serve" (*Pol.* VII. 1328a). In particular, "property . . . is not a part of the state." This property "includes a number of animate beings [i.e., slaves], as well as inanimate objects":

> But the state is an association of equals, and only of equals; and its object is the best and highest life possible. The highest good is felicity; and that consists in the energy and perfect practice of goodness. But in actual life this is not for all; some may share in it fully, but others can only share in it partially or cannot even share at all.

Moreover, since the object of the polis is the best life of its citizens, and since the best life demands leisure, "both for growth in goodness and for the pursuit of political activities" (1329a), the class of artisans is incapable of the best life, and so (to avoid the inconsistency of the *Republic*) must be excluded from citizenship. Leisured property-owners "are citizens—they, and they only. The class of mechanics has no share in the state; nor has any other class which is not a 'producer' of goodness."[44]

In sharp contrast, the Utopians conclude that individual felicity is incompatible with special privilege. Reason tells us not only "to lead a life as free from care and as full of joy as possible" but also, "because of our natural fellowship, to help all other men, too, to attain that end" (*Ut.*, p. 163). Nature, whose dictates are inferred by reason, "surely bids you take constant care not so to further your own advantages as to cause disadvantages to your fellows" (p. 165). And while the Utopians have slaves, slavery, as White points out, "is not instituted in Utopia to provide leisure for the citizens, but to punish immoral actions" (1976, p. 661). All Utopians share in agriculture and the crafts.[45] Thus every inhabitant has the same opportunity for happiness.

[44] The idea that neither resident aliens nor natives engaged in base occupations are fit for citizenship is echoed in Renaissance Italian theory and practice. See Pocock, pp. 117-18, 312.

[45] Officials and scholars are excepted, but the syphogrants participate voluntarily, and any scholar who does not live up to expectations is "reduced to

The Utopian revision of the relative valuation of the mental pleasures has the same thrust. Whereas Plato and Aristotle maintain that philosophic contemplation is the highest of pleasures (but see above, pp. 174-75), the Utopians relegate this pleasure to a secondary position. For them, to be sure, the mental pleasures include "intelligence" and "the sweetness which is bred of contemplation of truth," as well as "the pleasant recollection of a well-spent life and the sure hope of happiness to come." But, as we have seen, they regard the "principal part" of mental pleasure as arising not from the contemplation of truth but from "the practice of the virtues and the consciousness of a good life." Moreover, it is clear that in philosophy the Utopians concentrate their attention on those branches that have practical bearing on life. Moral philosophy is obviously a central interest. In "music, dialectic, arithmetic, and geometry they have made almost the same discoveries as those predecessors of ours in the classical world" (p. 159). They are "most expert . . . in the courses of the stars and the movements of the celestial bodies," and they are accomplished meteorologists (p. 161). Medicine they regard "as one of the finest and most useful branches of philosophy" (p. 183). But they are uninterested in "the inventions of our modern logicians"—"have discovered not even a single one of those very ingeniously devised rules about restrictions, amplifications, and suppositions" and are "so far . . . from ability to speculate on second intentions that not one of them could see even man himself as a so-called universal" (p. 159).

This relative de-emphasis of philosophic contemplation has the effect of making the highest component of the good life available to all men. If felicity depends on philosophic wisdom, then only those possessed of the requisite natural ability, the proper education, and sufficient leisure can attain felicity. But any man can (at least according to the rather Pelagian views of Christian humanists) enjoy "the consciousness of a good life."

---

the rank of workingman" (pp. 131-33). The Manuels note that "More's rehabilitation of the idea of physical labor was a milestone in the history of utopian thought, and was incorporated into all socialist systems" (p. 127).

If the notions that a "natural fellowship" unites all men and that *negotium* is superior to *otium* are foreign to Greek ethical thought, they are central to Roman Stoicism and the Christian-Stoic tradition that descends from it (above, pp. 90-92). By introducing these ideas into the ethical arguments of the first step of the best-commonwealth exercise, then, More makes the Greek exercise support conclusions of Christian-Stoic theory—as he had in Hythloday's arguments in Book I (above, pp. 106-11). In turn, these conclusions about the best life of the individual have (as we shall see) profound implications for the subsequent steps of the exercise.

One should also note that the Utopian moral philosophers' emphasis on the hedonic calculus as a way of choosing between competing pleasures similarly reflects More's interest in Stoic ethics (though the calculus itself is Epicurean). In *De officiis*, Cicero devotes much attention to the problems of resolving conflicts between different *officia*, different *utilia*, and, finally, conflicts between *officia* and *utilia* (I.iii.9-10, xliii.152-xlv.161, II.xxv.88-89, III; see above, pp. 51-53, and Chap. 2, n. 65). The third problem is solved by the argument that conflicts between duties and expedients are only apparent, never real. Careful analysis shows (as Hythloday argues with reference to political questions in Book I) that "if anything is morally right, it is expedient, and if anything is not morally right, it is not expedient" (III.iii.11; cf. vii.34, xii.49-50). This is, in effect, also what the Utopians conclude: for the individual, if not the commonwealth, the dictates of self-interest and morality are identical. But if there are no real conflicts between *officia* and *utilia*, there are certainly conflicts between different *officia* and between different *utilia*. It is to Cicero's credit that he recognized and formulated these problems, which were not, he says, treated in previous ethical theory.[46] Having raised the problems, however, Cicero is woefully inadequate to deal with them. The treatment of conflicting

[46] Rhetorical theory, though, offers some attention to problems of choosing between different goods or expedients, and between goods and expedients (e.g., Aristotle, *Rh.* I.1363b-1365b; Cicero, *Part. Or.* xxv.89-90; Quintilian III.viii.30-33).

officia centers in an attempt to prove that "those duties are closer to Nature [and therefore to be given precedence] which depend upon the social instinct than those which depend upon knowledge" (i.xliii. 153): but the argument by which this conclusion is reached is blatantly fallacious. The exceedingly brief treatment of conflicting *utilia* simply lists types of such conflicts, without offering any guidance to their resolution (ii.xxv.88-89). But since the Utopians prove that *officia* equal *utilia* equal (true) pleasures, the Epicurean criteria for choosing between competing pleasures become the general principles needed for the solution of Cicero's problems.[47] This line of thought, too, has implications on the collective, political level.

In summary, for More as for the Greek best-commonwealth theorists purely rational considerations lead to the conclusion that the best life is that of virtue, which is also the most pleasurable life. For the individual, at least, the expedient and the moral are identical. More also agrees with the Greek theorists that the best life includes both mental and bodily pleasures, and that mental pleasures are the superior class. He differs from these theorists, however, and echoes the views of the Roman Stoics, in regarding the highest mental pleasure as deriving from virtuous action rather than from philosophic contemplation, and in insisting that mental pleasure is incompatible with the knowledge that one's pleasures are dependent on the deprivation of other men. More is keenly aware, like Cicero and unlike Plato and Aristotle, of the potential for conflict between goods (pleasures) that are in themselves legitimate, an awareness that is reflected in the heavy emphasis he places on the importance of the Epicurean calculus

---

[47] More may have been helped toward this solution by the fact that Valla's Epicurean spokesman emphasizes the close relation between the pleasurable and the expedient—both of which, however, he separates from the moral: "For the expedient coincides with the pleasurable, whereas the rightful coincides with virtue [Idem enim utile est quod voluptuosum, rectum quod honestum]; although there are some who distinguish the advantageous from the pleasurable, their ignorance is too manifest to need refutation" (i.xiv. 1; cf. xxxiii. 1-xxxv. 1; ii.xiv. 2).

as a means of determining which of competing pleasures should be chosen. Since mental pleasures are superior to bodily pleasures, the calculus dictates that we prefer the former, so the best life is relatively abstemious. The individual's first priority, however, lies in securing the bodily pleasure of health, since this pleasure is not only the highest bodily pleasure but a precondition for all other pleasures. Whenever (true) pleasures do not conflict, of course, one should participate as fully as possible in the whole range of them.

This ethical position, like that of classical Epicureanism, anticipates the ethics of utilitarianism. More precisely, as Seebohm recognized, it anticipates J. S. Mill's revision of Benthamite utilitarianism, which was effected, like the Utopian revision of Epicureanism, by erecting qualitative distinctions among pleasures:

> in Utopian philosophy, utility was recognised as a criterion of right and wrong; and from experience of what, under the laws of nature, is man's real far-sighted interest, was derived a sanction to the golden rule. And thus, instead of setting themselves against the doctrine of utility, as some would do, on the ground of a supposed opposition to Christianity, they recognised the identity between the two standards. They recognised, as Mr. Mill urges, that Christians ought to do now, "in the golden rule of Jesus of Nazareth, the complete spirit of the ethics of utility." (p. 224; Mill, *Utilitarianism*, p. 218)

III

Since the close connection between *Utopia* and the *Republic* has always been recognized, since Plato's reasonings about the best form of the polis are based directly and explicitly on conclusions about man's nature and best life, and since in the *Politics* (the connection of which with *Utopia* has also, though less widely, been recognized) Aristotle's treatment of the best polis opens with a discussion of the fact that conclusions about this subject depend on conclusions about the best life, it should always have been clear that at least the main aspects of the Utopian constitution must in some way follow from the Utopian conclusions about the best life. In fact precisely the opposite view has dominated criticism: the section on Utopian moral philosophy has normally been regarded as having little or nothing to do with other sections of Book II, except for that on religion.

A hundred years ago Kautsky observed that "the philosophy and religion of *Utopia* have mostly interested our Liberal historians, who have devoted long treatises to this subject, while dismissing the communism with a few phrases as vain imaginings. The philosophy and religion of *Utopia* constitute an important corroboration of More's literary and scientific [i.e., secular and rationalistic] attitude, . . . but they have no organic connection with the communism of his ideal commonwealth" (p. 229). Kautsky at least thought the section on moral philosophy important in its own right; later scholars who regard economic and social policy as central to Utopia not only deny that Utopian philosophy has anything to do with Utopian communism but ignore or denigrate the section itself. Ames says nothing about Utopian philosophy. Hexter regards its elaboration as merely playful: More and Giles, constructing Utopia in conversation, "sometimes, as in the case of the pseudo-Epicureanism of Utopian philosophy[,] . . . embroidered a pattern and ran it more or less consistently through their speculation in a spirit of intellectual play" (*Ut.*, p. xl). Caspari briefly summarizes the section on philosophy and notes its relation to that on religion (pp. 124-25).

Scholars who regard the section on moral philosophy as important are equally unable to relate it to other parts of the Utopian construct, and especially to Utopian communism. As Hexter observes, they usually seek either "to make More's views on private property vanish altogether . . . [or] to minimize the importance of those views for the general significance of *Utopia*" (1952, p. 48). In particular,

Authors in "the hagiographic tradition of More scholarship"
[Ames, p. 105] have achieved . . . [the latter] end by
suggesting that More's encomium of community of property
and goods was a manifestation of More's conservatism and
medievalism against the onrush of capitalist aggression, essentially a defense of the monastic orders—those "rightest
Christian companies," which practiced community of property and goods—against the greedy, grasping hands of the
rising middle class [cf. Chambers, pp. 137-38]. Having
tidied up this little point, . . . [they] concentrate their
attention on the sections dealing with Utopian philosophy
and religion almost to the exclusion of those on Utopian
social and economic policy. (pp. 48-49)

As the highest achievement of this line of interpretation, Hexter
cites one of the studies of R. P. Adams (1945), an essay "that
derives More's philosophy and his social theory from late classical
Stoicism, and that from beginning to end does not directly mention his democratic egalitarianism or his attack on private property at all" (p. 49). In *The Better Part of Valor* (1962), which
represents the culmination of Adams's studies of More and his
circle, Adams does relate Utopian moral philosophy to other
aspects of the construct, suggesting indeed that this "philosophy
is . . . at the basis of the Utopian way of life," and that "all the
major features of that life are logically expressive of it—e.g.,
community of property, planning of agriculture and industry,
of city and country life, marriage and population control, the
system of justice and government, penology and slavery, education, war, and religion itself" (p. 134). But Adams's treatment
of the section on moral philosophy is so inadequate (he reduces
it, by quotation out of context, to a set of Stoic norms) and his
relation of this philosophy to the institutions of Utopia so general
(amounting to little more than the repeated observation that these
institutions reflect Stoic ideals of rationality and the brotherhood
of man) that Hexter's charge still applies to him.

Surtz, though a member of the "hagiographic tradition," can

hardly be charged with concentrating on philosophy and religion to the exclusion of other aspects of Utopia, for he wrote extensively on all its aspects. And indeed, while at one point he lamely suggests that the purpose of the section on moral philosophy is "to incite and provoke to serious thought careless Christians who are behaving as if wealth or glory, not God, were the end of life" (1957a, p. 21), Surtz has considerable insight into the connection between this section and Utopian communism, which he says "is intrinsically and intimately related to Utopian hedonism" (p. 152):

> In a word, the Utopians prefer public ownership to private property in order to secure an equitable and just participation of all the people in the matter of pleasure. . . . Communism, not private property, . . . is the answer of the Utopians to the division of goods among their citizens—so that all might attain a maximum of pleasure and a minimum of pain during their earthly life. (p. 155; cf. p. 199)

Unfortunately, this insight is vitiated by the fact that Surtz goes on to argue (pp. 180-91) that Hythloday's and the Utopians' views on this matter are, as More wishes us to recognize, incorrect, because they do not take into account "human nature as it actually exists" (p. 183). Only if men were perfect Christians would communism be workable. Utopian moral philosophy, that is, is related only spuriously to the most conspicuous feature of the Utopian constitution. Surtz, then, falls into Hexter's category of those who, while not seeking to make Utopian communism disappear altogether, "nevertheless tend to minimize" its importance "for the general significance of *Utopia*." Nor does Surtz have much to say about the relation of Utopian philosophy to other aspects of Utopia, although he does note that the principle that one man's pleasure should not be gained at another's expense is "the basis for the superb justice, both commutative and legal, of the Utopians" (p. 38).[48]

---

[48] Fleisher (pp. 5-60) has many interesting remarks about the section on moral philosophy, but his conclusions do not constitute a significant advance beyond Surtz's position.

The truth is that there is no need to dismiss either the moral philosophy or the communism or indeed any other substantial feature of Utopia. The Utopian construct certainly includes some playful elements, but these are small and local. All conspicuous features of the Utopian constitution derive from the conclusions of the section on moral philosophy, when these conclusions are applied to the problem of determining the particular form that should be given to the components of the self-sufficient polity. Indeed, More's gifts as a political theorist appear most clearly in the perspicacity and precision with which he realizes the implications of his conclusions in the first step of the best-commonwealth exercise (the determination of the best life of the individual) for the subsequent steps.[49]

The second step of the exercise is the determination of the overall goal and the contributory goals of the commonwealth. As we have seen, Plato and Aristotle conclude, though not without considerable confusion deriving from the fallacy of regarding the polis as a big man with goals of his own, that the goal of the polis is the provision of the best life—happiness—for its members. Although More does not directly enunciate this principle, it is implicit in a number of passages[50] and clearly underlies the design of Utopia. Indeed, it is precisely the fact that Utopia provides for the happiness of all its members that enables Hythloday to say that it is the only polity "which can rightly claim the name of a commonwealth" (*Ut.*, p. 237; cf. n. 106 below).

The implications of the conclusions of Utopian moral philosophy for the specific formulation of the overall goal and the contributory goals of the commonwealth are clear, and it is also clear that More grasps these implications. Since happiness resides in pleasure, the goal of the commonwealth must be to secure the

---

[49] Cf. Hexter: "More displays immense skill at devising specific and practical methods to attain envisaged ends within the Utopian commonwealth (as a planner More is way out in front of Plato and Marx)" (1952, pp. 58-59; cf. pp. 62-63).

[50] White (unpubl. paper) calls attention to them: *Ut.*, pp. 87.11-15, 95.32-33, 105.18-21, 109.19-20, 179.20-22, 237.14-17, 241.36-39. One may add p. 135.19-24.

maximum amount of pleasure for its members. Since health is
the most important pleasure (being a condition of all others), the
first contributory goal, and that of highest priority, must be to
secure (insofar as it can be secured) the health of all. This goal
in turn implies a raft of others: the provision of adequate food,
clothing, shelter, and medical care for all members of the commonwealth, and the guaranteeing of national security. But since
mental pleasures are keener than bodily pleasures, the pleasure
of the citizens will be maximized if, once health is secured, all
other communal resources are devoted to the supply or facilitation
of mental pleasure. This is, in fact, the order of priority of goals
that is apparent in Hythloday's one explicit statement on the
matter. The Utopian authorities "do not keep the citizens against
their will at superfluous labor since the constitution of their commonwealth looks in the first place to this sole object: that for all
the citizens, as far as the public needs permit, as much time as
possible should be withdrawn from the service of the body and
devoted to the freedom and culture of the mind. It is in the latter
that they deem the happiness of life to consist" (p. 135). More
precisely, it is in the latter that they deem the *principal* happiness
of life to consist: we know that they regard bodily pleasure as
genuinely contributing to happiness. And of course the authorities
should not and do not interfere with indulgence in any pleasure,
provided that such indulgence does not conflict with the attainment of superior pleasures. Hythloday calls attention to this principle. Commenting on the Utopians' practice of including various
sensory delights as accompaniments to their suppers, he notes
that "they are somewhat[51] inclined to this attitude of mind: that
no kind of pleasure is forbidden, provided no harm comes of it"
(p. 145; cf. p. 161.25-29).

The Utopians, then, have a clear hierarchy of communal goals,
even as they have a clear hierarchy of individual ones. In both
cases, the establishment of a hierarchy assumes special importance

[51] I have deleted "too much" from the Yale translation, since, as Miller
points out (1966, p. 58), the phrase has no warrant in the Latin.

in the light of the realization that, since resources, whether individual or communal, are limited, the simultaneous pursuit of
different valid goals (true pleasures) must result in some conflicts.
More's awareness of this fact is, as we have seen, implicit in the
heavy emphasis on the Epicurean principles of selection in the
section on moral philosophy, and it is clear that an application
of these principles on the collective, political level underlies the
allocation of communal resources in Utopia. (Here too, as in his
treatment of ethics, More anticipates utilitarianism.)

More's thinking in this part of the best-commonwealth exercise—the elaboration of the contributory goals of the commonwealth—is in fact much clearer than that of Plato and Aristotle.
In the first place, the Greek theorists constantly draw spurious
implications from the organic metaphor. The basis of argument
in the *Republic*, which attempts to deduce the nature of the just
man from that of the just polis, lies in the contention that "the
qualities that characterize a state must also exist in the individuals
that compose it" (IV.435E), so that, for example, "if there are
five types of society, there must presumably be five types of
individual character" (VIII.544E). Correspondingly, Plato frequently treats the contributory goals of the polis as being identical
to the requisites for individual happiness, rather than as being
what they logically are, namely, the conditions that must be
satisfied if the individual members of the polis are all to have
the best possible opportunity for happiness. In particular, the
best polis will, like its citizens, "have the virtues of wisdom,
courage, discipline, and justice" (IV.427E). Similarly, Aristotle
concludes that "the felicity of the state is the same as that of the
individual" (*Pol.* VII.1324a; cf. 1323b, 1334a). Thus the contributory goals of the polis become, as in Plato, the cardinal
virtues (1334a), and "the fortitude of a state, and the justice and
wisdom of a state, have the same energy, and the same character,
as the qualities which cause individuals who have them to be
called brave, just, and wise" (1323b). To be sure, at other points
Aristotle states clearly that the contributory goals of the polis are
those entailed in the provision of the requisites of happiness for

its members, and that the hierarchy of these goals should reflect
the relative importance of these requisites: "The legislation of
the true statesman must . . . cover the different parts of the soul
and their different activities; and . . . it should be directed more
to the higher than the lower, and rather to ends than means"
(1333a). And in his discussion of education in the best polis,
Aristotle anticipates the Utopians in recognizing that, despite the
superiority of mind to body, the guarantee of physical health
must be the first priority of the legislator:

> Children's bodies should be given attention before their
> souls; and their appetites should be the next part of them to
> be regulated. But the regulation of their appetites should
> be intended for the benefit of their minds—just as the at-
> tention given to their bodies should be intended for the
> benefit of their souls. (1334b)

But even when not confused by the organic metaphor, the
Greek theorists' elaboration of the contributory goals of the polis
suffers from their failure to realize that there must always—even
in the ideal polis—be some limit to resources, that conflicts therefore arise in the pursuit of valid goals, and that accordingly some
formula for the allocation of resources to different goals must be
devised. Thus Plato and Aristotle determine the question of the
amount of material goods to be supplied to the members of the
polis purely on the basis of ethical considerations: what amount
of such goods is best for the individual? The possibility that the
optimal amount might not be attainable without forfeiting some
part of the optimal amount of spiritual goods never occurs to
them—in part, at least, because they assume that any desired
amount of material goods can be supplied by the labor of those
inhabitants (slaves or members of the class of artisans) whose
happiness is not a goal of the polis. Correspondingly, More's
realization of the potential for conflicts among valid communal
goals, and his application of the Epicurean principles of selection
as a formula for the allocation of resources whenever such conflicts

occur, constitutes a signal advance in the technique of the best-commonwealth exercise and, more generally, in the technique of political analysis.

The final steps of the best-commonwealth exercise involve the determination of the particular array of physical and institutional components that will best promote the achievement of the various goals of the commonwealth. The theorist, that is, must make particular recommendations about the optimal size and nature of the territory of the commonwealth, about the nature of its central city, and about the size and nature of its population. Moreover, it is important that he not neglect to provide for the performance of any essential social function. To preclude the possibility of such neglect, both Plato and Aristotle offer checklists of the occupational functions that must be performed in the self-sufficient polis. In the *Republic*, Socrates points out that the polis must include producers of food, shelter, and clothing, traders to exchange domestic goods for necessities available only from other nations (and shipbuilders and sailors if the trade must be overseas), merchants to act as middlemen in the exchange of goods among citizens, and soldiers and governors (II.369D-375C). Aristotle opens his discussion of the particular features of the ideal polis with the observation that "an ideal constitution is bound to require an equipment appropriate to its nature":

> We must therefore assume, as its basis, a number of ideal conditions, which must be capable of fulfilment as well as being ideal. These conditions include, among others, a citizen body and a territory. . . . The primary factor necessary, in the equipment of a state, is the human material; and this involves us in considering the quality, as well as the quantity, of the population naturally required. The second factor is territory; and here too we have to consider quality as well as quantity. (*Pol.* VII.1325b-1326a)

Specification of the best form of these components is followed by a checklist of necessary occupational functions:

The first thing to be provided is food. The next is arts and crafts; for life is a business which needs many tools. The third is arms: the members of a state must bear arms in person, partly in order to maintain authority and repress disobedience, and partly in order to meet any threat of external aggression. The fourth thing which has to be provided is a certain supply of property, alike for domestic use and for military purposes. The fifth (but, in order of merit, the first) is an establishment for the service of the gods, or, as it is called, public worship. The sixth thing, and the most vitally necessary, is a method of deciding what is demanded by the public interest and what is just in men's private dealings [i.e. some system of deliberation and jurisdiction]. (1328b; Barker's interpolation)

Finally, Aristotle like Plato devotes attention to another topic of obvious importance in the ideal polis: the provision of institutions, including a system of formal education and a set of rules governing foreign contact, designed to assure that citizens develop and maintain the pattern of behavior that the constitution of the polis requires.

If the theorist does not regard goals as conflicting, completion of the best-commonwealth exercise requires only the determination of the particular forms of the physical and institutional features that will flesh out his structural schema and the provision of arguments to show that these forms will lead most directly to the attainment of the various goals of the commonwealth. Particular forms can be appropriated from actual polities or the designs of previous theorists, or they can be created by ratiocination or by rationally-justified modification of the features of other polities. Plato borrows many institutions of the Republic and the Magnesia of the *Laws* from various Greek poleis, especially Sparta. Some of these institutions are modified in ways that seem to him desirable. Still others are pure inventions. Aristotle borrows, and frequently modifies, numerous features not only from a variety of actual polities but also from Plato's best-commonwealth exercises, especially the *Laws*.

Although More's decision to present the results of his best-commonwealth exercise as a fictionalized model precludes explicit discussion of the underlying schema of his construct, it seems clear, as White suggests (1976, pp. 643-47), that he is guided by Aristotle's treatment. We hear first about the geography of Utopia—about its territory and its cities (*Ut.*, pp. 111-13). Moreover, Hythloday's account of Utopia appears to take its general outline from Aristotle's list of the six necessary functions (cf. Duhamel 1955, p. 239). After his opening remarks on geography, Hythloday turns immediately to agricultural arrangements (*Ut.*, pp. 115-17): the provision of food is the first of Aristotle's functions. The Utopian form of government—Aristotle's sixth function—is treated out of order in the section on officials (pp. 123-25), which follows a description of Amaurotum. "Arts and crafts," the second item on Aristotle's list, is treated in the following section, "De artificiis" (pp. 125-35). The next three sections include the account of Utopian moral philosophy, and discussions of education (pp. 159-61, 181-85) and aspects of foreign relations (pp. 137, 149-51, 153-57, 185, 197-99). After these sections, Hythloday turns to military affairs (pp. 199-217), a topic that corresponds to the third item in Aristotle's list. The treatment of the fourth of these items—"a certain supply of property"—is diffused throughout the narrative. The section following that on military affairs, the final segment of the account of Utopia, "De religionibvs vtopiensivm" (pp. 217-37), corresponds to Aristotle's fifth function, "an establishment for the service of the gods."

It is also clear that More draws on the same types of sources as the Greek theorists for the particular forms of the components of the polity. As his annotators have pointed out, he appropriates, with frequent modifications, many features from Plato and Aristotle, as well as, perhaps, some from Renaissance best-commonwealth theorists such as Patrizi and Pontano. Others are drawn from accounts of "wise and prudent provisions" (p. 53) of various nations; that is, from histories of ancient, and some modern, polities—above all, Plutarch's treatments of Sparta (see Schoeck 1956, pp. 275-80; *Ut.*, pp. clx-clxi).[52] Utopia also

[52] Ames calls attention to some parallels with the Swiss Confederation (pp. 93-95), as well as with the organization of the English guilds (pp. 100-3). On parallels between Utopian institutions and monastic rules, see Chambers, pp. 136-38; Hexter 1952, pp. 85-91; Fenlon, pp. 121-23; Manuel and Manuel, pp. 48-51; and Gordon. Chambers notes that "the religious houses are the one European institution which the Utopians are said to approve" (p. 136; cf. *Ut.*, p. 219).

Since More was obviously interested in Augustine's *City of God* (see above, Chap. 2, n. 24), one might expect the Utopian construct to bear the imprint of that work. In fact the connections are neither numerous nor specific (cf. *Ut.*, pp. clxvi-clxvii; Raitiere). Augustine's distinction of the two cities doubtless stimulated More's interest in the question of the relation between a secular and a Christian commonwealth, and Augustine's qualified admiration of republican Rome (esp. v.18-19) may have helped encourage More to think that a pagan commonwealth could be attractive in many ways. *The City of God* also includes the idea that some pagan accomplishments should shame Christians (v.18); and Augustine's pessimism about the possibility of earthly felicity may be reflected in some melancholy aspects of *Utopia* (see below, pp. 246-47). I have noted a few other parallels in the following pages. But Utopia does not much resemble the city of the world, because the Utopians have arrived at, and have embodied in their constitution, moral and religious principles close to those of Christianity. Thus, whereas Augustine says that the achievements of Rome were fueled by the Romans' love of glory (v.12), the Utopians despise worldly, and particularly military, glory (*Ut.*, p. 201). Augustine strongly emphasizes the point that, even in the period when, according to Sallust, "justice and morality prevailed" among the Romans, many data of Roman history (and legend) preclude thinking of the Republic as just or moral (e.g. *CG* II.17-19). In fact the Roman commonwealth "never existed, because there never was real justice in the community" (II.21), and *no* pagan state can exhibit justice (XIX.23). But these charges hardly apply to Utopia (cf. n. 106 below). Another reason for the limited relevance of *The City of God* to *Utopia* is implicit in Augustine's statement that "as for this mortal life, which ends after a few days' course, what does it matter under whose rule a man lives?" (v.17). For More it evidently matters very much. Augustine's examples of the miseries of earthly life are designed to inspire the reader to turn away from it. More's examples (in Book I and at the end of Book II) reflect, and are surely designed to inspire the reader with, a desire to *alleviate* these miseries.

includes a number of features borrowed from England, as well
as some from accounts of America (see Donner, pp. 27-53; R. P.
Adams 1962, pp. 130-32).[53]

For the student of More's political thought, the last two groups
of features are the least important, since they comprise only
indifferent matters: where rational considerations demand a particular feature but do not determine its particular form, More
often borrows the form from England or America. In this way
he is able to enhance the piquancy and topicality of his best-
commonwealth exercise without any diminution of theoretical
rigor. Theoretical considerations demand that the territory of the
self-sufficient polity be "difficult of access to enemies, and easy
of egress for its inhabitants" (*Pol.* VII.1326b-1327a). More satisfies this requirement by making Utopia an island with a large
bay entered by a strait, and with a coast "everywhere . . . well
defended by nature or by engineering" (*Ut.*, p. 111). Once
theoretical requirements are met in this way, the island may as
well, in indifferent features, resemble England.[54] Even the best

[53] Another account of a primitive people, Tacitus' *Germania*, may be reflected
in several details of Utopian life. See Fyfe.

[54] On some particular geographic features in which Utopia does or does not
resemble England, see Surtz's Commentary, *Ut.*, pp. 384-88, 392-93. White
(unpubl. paper) notes that the territory of the Polylerites, which is isolated and
produces all that the inhabitants require (*Ut.*, p. 75), also satisfies the Greek
criteria for the territory of an ideal polis (cf., esp., *Laws* IV.704A-705B).

A good deal has been written about the symbolism of the strange shape of
Utopia. Two popular views are adumbrated in R. M. Adams's comment that
the island's "likeness to the new moon is perhaps less striking, for a post-
Freudian generation, than its resemblance to a womb" (p. 34n; cf. Prévost
1978, p. 164n). But about More's conscious intention (which is our concern
in the matter) one can only speculate.

The same is true of the suggestive description of the great bay of Utopia
and the account, early in Book I, of the unforeseen mischief entailed in Hythloday's revelation of the compass to the American mariners. Hythloday tells us
that the mouth of the Utopian bay is "rendered perilous here by shallows and
there by reefs. Almost in the center of the gap stands one great crag which,
being visible, is not dangerous. . . . The other rocks are hidden and therefore
treacherous" (*Ut.*, p. 111). The compass causes its new possessors to be "dan-

territory will, as Plato and Aristotle acknowledge (*Rep.* II.370E; *Pol.* VII.1327a), lack some necessary commodity, so Utopia may as well lack iron, like England (*Ut.*, pp. 149, 427n).[55] A city should be "linked to the sea as well as the land," and it should have "a natural supply of waters and streams" (*Pol.* VII.1330a-b). Amaurotum may as well, then, have a tidal river, like the Thames (*Ut.*, p. 119). More decided (for a reason that we will consider later) to make his polity a federation of a number of city-states; the precise number may as well be fifty-four, the number of counties of England plus London (*Ut.*, p. 387n; cf. Heiserman, p. 171). But whenever theoretical considerations dictate a form for a particular feature that differs from the corresponding English form, Utopia is unrelated to England. Theory demands, for example, that the principal city of an ideal

---

gerously confident. Thus, there is a risk that what was thought likely to be a great benefit to them may, through their imprudence, cause them great mischief" (p. 53). I should like the crag to allude especially to Utopian communism, with the submerged rocks suggesting the difficulties of attaining the rational commonwealth and, perhaps, the subtle problems that beset it, and I prefer to think of the difficulties with the compass as intimating the mixed benefits and problems inherent in transplanting institutions from one social context to another. But others will prefer different interpretations.

[55] In fact Utopia owes its nearly self-sufficient status more to the industry of its inhabitants than to the natural advantages of its territory. Hythloday stresses that the Utopians "have not a very fertile soil or a very wholesome climate" (p. 179). But "they protect themselves against the atmosphere by temperate living and make up for the defects of the land by diligent labor. Consequently, nowhere in the world is there a more plentiful supply of grain and cattle, nowhere are men's bodies more vigorous and subject to fewer diseases." These serious defects in the territory, which find no precedent in the Greek best-commonwealth exercises and would not seem to reflect the Old- or New-World analogues of Utopia (p. 464n), were presumably dictated by theoretical considerations. They may reflect More's Aristotelian awareness of the constraints that fact places on theory: it is idle to talk about a freely-chosen, perfect territory. Or More may, as White suggests, have been influenced by the line of thought embodied in the tradition that Plato "deliberately located the Academy in a remote and unhealthy area for the sake of encouraging virtue" (unpubl. paper, citing Porphyry, *De abstinentia* 1.36, Jerome, *Adversus Iovinianum* II.9, and John of Salisbury, *Policraticus* VII.3, VIII.8).

polity be centrally located (*Laws* v.745B; *Pol.* VII.1327a, 1330a), and that its layout be according to a preconceived plan (*Pol.* 1330b-1331a): accordingly, Amaurotum does not resemble London in these respects.

Similarly, Utopia incorporates features of accounts of America only when theoretical considerations allow a free choice within a rationally-determined range. Utopia must be somewhere, so it may as well be in the extremely topical Americas. Utopian priests need vestments that symbolize their special function in the community.[56] These vestments cannot be "interwoven with gold or set with precious stones" (*Ut.*, p. 235), since the symbolic significance of these materials derives from a false conception of value. Instead, they are "wrought with the different feathers of birds," a choice that evidently reflects Vespucci's observation that the riches of the Indians "consist of variegated birds' feathers" (quoted *Ut.*, p. 554n). In the same way, one of the Utopian stratagems for reinforcing the proper attitude toward gold—the use of it to make "chamber pots and all the humblest vessels" (p. 153)—may derive from Peter Martyr's tale of an Indian community that used "kitchen and other common utensils made of gold" (quoted *Ut.*, p. 429n). But, as I pointed out earlier (n. 10), More is not in any way constrained by the accounts of America: his Utopians hardly exhibit the lust, ferocity, and generally low level of culture that Vespucci attributes to the Indians. And though his consideration of the nature of a non-Christian, rational commonwealth may have been stimulated by Vespucci's report of the hedonistic and communistic elements in the culture of the Indians, the hedonism and communism of Utopia certainly derive from theoretical considerations.

A more interesting class of Utopian features consists of those adopted from Plato and Aristotle.[57] The fact that More is able

[56] The symbolism of vestments is a topic of considerable interest to Erasmus (and presumably to More). See *The Praise of Folly*, pp. 97-98, and, on the vestments of the prince, *ECP*, p. 152.

[57] The following discussion was from its inception indebted to White's "Aristotle and *Utopia*," which the reader may see for additional parallels. After

to appropriate without change a considerable number of items from the best-commonwealth exercises of the Greek theorists reflects his large area of agreement with them both about various contributory goals of the commonwealth and about the best means for realizing these goals. Aristotle observes that health is "the most indispensable" consideration in choosing a site for the central city of the polis. This consideration dictates that the city "slope towards the east, and . . . [be] exposed to the winds which blow from that quarter, [which] are the healthiest" (*Pol.* VII.1330a). For the same reason, the city ought to have "a natural supply of waters and streams." The latter feature is also desirable as an enhancement of military security, a consideration that, moreover, demands that the city be walled (1330b-1331a). Health is the Utopian goal of highest priority; it implies the additional goal of national security. Accordingly, one is not surprised to find in Hythloday's description of Amaurotum these same features (cf. White 1976, p. 646), presented in the same order. Amaurotum is "situated on the gentle slope of a hill" (*Ut.*, p. 117); it has two rivers (pp. 117-19); it is "surrounded by a high and broad wall with towers and battlements at frequent intervals" (p. 119). Hythloday does not give the rationale for these features. The fictional presentation of More's best-commonwealth exercise inhibits such explanations; the reader is apparently expected to recall the theoretical justification from the *Politics*. The Utopian use of colonies as a way of assuring that the population of the commonwealth remains constant reflects the view of the Greek theorists that there is a particular optimum population for the ideal polis and the stratagem proposed in the *Laws* for assuring the maintenance of that number (*Ut.*, p. 137; *Laws* V.740E). The

my discussion was complete, I was able, through Prof. White's generosity, to read drafts of his forthcoming study of Plato and *Utopia* (*Journal of the History of Philosophy*; see also his dissertation). I am pleased to find that he offers independent confirmation of my view that *Utopia* is directly and heavily indebted, in ways large and small, to Plato's political works and, in particular, much more closely related to the *Laws* than has been recognized. White also supplements my findings at several points, some of which I note below.

Utopian practice of premarital physical inspection apparently also derives from the *Laws*, where, as in *Utopia*, the practice is a means toward assuring stable marriages. Plato's Athenian says that

> when people are going to live together as partners in marriage, it is vital that the fullest possible information should be available about the bride and her background and the family she'll marry into. One should regard the prevention of mistakes here as a matter of supreme importance—so important and serious, in fact, that even the young people's recreation must be arranged with this in mind. Boys and girls must dance together at an age when plausible occasions can be found for their doing so, in order that they may have a reasonable look at each other; and they should dance naked, provided sufficient modesty and restraint are displayed by all concerned. (VI.771E-772A)

Similarly, the Utopians present prospective couples naked to each other and marvel that the people of other nations, "in the choice of a wife, an action which will cause either pleasure or disgust to follow them the rest of their lives, . . . are so careless that, while the rest of her body is covered with clothes, they estimate the value of the whole woman from hardly a single handbreadth of her" (*Ut.*, p. 189). From Plato also More derives the rule that seeking public office disqualifies a citizen for it (p. 193). As in the account of the situation of Amaurotum, Hythloday records this fact without explanation. The reader is evidently expected to recall Plato's argument that those who are suited to rule—true philosophers—will shun political power, while the "morally impoverished . . . hope to snatch some compensation for their own inadequacy from a political career" (*Rep.* VII.521A). In military affairs, the *Republic* provides a precedent for the Utopian custom of having soldiers accompanied to battle by their families (*Ut.*, pp. 209-11), a practice justified, Socrates says, by the fact that "any animal fights better in the presence of its young" (v.467B).[58] The Utopian requirement that an atheist not "argue in support of his opinion in the presence of the common people" but that he be encouraged to do so "before the priests and important personages" (*Ut.*, p. 223) echoes the provision of the *Laws* that "no citizen must come into contact with them [i.e., unbelievers] except the members of the Nocturnal Council, who should pay visits to admonish them and ensure their spiritual salvation" (x.909A). In both cases, the policy of isolating heretics reflects the conviction that, since moral behavior depends on religious belief (*Ut.*, pp. 221-23; *Laws* x.885B, 888B), the spread of atheism constitutes a grave social danger.

More also agrees with the Greek theorists about the necessity for institutions to ensure that the citizens develop and maintain the pattern of behavior that is required for the realization and preservation of the goals of the rational polity. And he largely agrees with them about the particular nature of these institutions, which comprise a system of formal education, the legal prohibition of certain kinds of bad behavior, a network of positive and negative reinforcements to encourage proper behavior, and a system of criminal justice.

Plato and Aristotle devote more space to education than to any other topic in their best-commonwealth exercises. The justification for this emphasis lies in the decisive effect, for better or for worse, of education on the polis. In the *Republic* Plato says that bad education results in bad discipline, which "makes itself at home and gradually undermines morals and manners; from them it invades business dealings generally, and then spreads into the laws and constitution without any restraint, until it has made complete havoc of private and public life" (iv.424D-E). On the contrary, if children "learn orderly habits from their education, it produces quite the opposite results and corrects any previous flaws there may have been in the society" (425A). Accordingly, Plato's ideal polis would include a carefully-designed system of physical and mental education, compulsory for all children of the Guardian class, male and female. Education is also a major

[58] There is also a precedent in Tacitus' *Germania* (viii; *Ut.*, p. clxii).

topic of the *Laws* (see, e.g., II.653A-B, VI.782D-783A, VII.808D). Aristotle places similar emphasis on education, which he characterizes as the means of making the polis "a community and giving it unity" (*Pol.* II.1263b), and as "the greatest . . . of all the means . . . for ensuring the stability of constitutions" (V.1310a). Education is accordingly the "chief and foremost concern" (VIII.1337a) of the legislator. The topic occupies considerably more than half the space Aristotle devotes to the ideal polis, and he is only getting well into the subject of curriculum when the unfinished Book VIII breaks off. Education should be compulsory for all citizens. Given a suitable natural endowment, men become good by means of "the habits we form" and "the rational principle within us" (VII.1332a). Thus education is partly "a training in habits, partly . . . a system of instruction [i.e., rational training]" (1332b).

The Utopians stress education as heavily as the Greek theorists, and for the same reason. The "good opinions" instilled into children's minds are "useful for the preservation of their commonwealth": "When once they are firmly implanted in children, they accompany them all through their adult lives and are of great help in watching over the condition of the commonwealth. The latter never decays except through vices which arise from wrong attitudes" (*Ut.*, p. 229). Accordingly, education is government-controlled and universal—truly universal, since all children, including those of foreign-born slaves, are full citizens (p. 185). As in Plato, full-time advanced study is, however, reserved to those "in whom they have detected from childhood an outstanding personality, a first-rate intelligence, and an inclination of mind toward learning" (p. 159; *Rep.* VII.537B-D). The Utopians entrust education to the priests, who are drawn from the class of scholars (*Ut.*, p. 133) and are also extraordinarily holy (p. 227); one may compare Plato's dictum that the Minister of Education should be "the best all-round citizen in the state" (*Laws* VI.766A).[59] Utopian education, like that proposed by the Greek

---

[59] Since all other officials above the rank of syphogrant are also drawn from the class of scholars (*Ut.*, p. 133), there is no problem of counsel in Utopia. Cf. above, Chap. 2, n. 59, and pp. 122-23, 125.

theorists, has several aspects. The Utopians "regard concern for
their [i.e., the children's] morals and virtue as no less important
than for their advancement in learning" (*Ut.*, p. 229).[60] Education also includes, as in Greek theory, military training for all
citizens, male and female (p. 201; *Laws* VIII.829B; cf. *Pol.*
VII.1329a).[61] As in the *Laws* and the *Politics*, games are a calculated part of education (*Ut.*, p. 129; *Laws* I.643B-C, VII.797A-
B; *Pol.* VII.1336a). In particular, the fact that the Utopians are
instructed in agriculture "from childhood, partly by principles
taught in school, partly by field trips to the farms closer to the
city as if for recreation" (*Ut.*, p. 125), seems to reflect Plato's
observation that a "man who intends to be a good farmer must
play [in childhood] at farming" (*Laws* I.643C).

In the terms of Utopian moral philosophy, education enables
children to distinguish true pleasures from false and to prefer
the former. The Utopian contempt of false pleasure has been
"conceived partly from their upbringing [*partim ex educatione*],
being reared in a commonwealth whose institutions are far removed from follies of the kind mentioned, and partly from
instruction and reading good books [*ex doctrina & literis*]" (*Ut.*,
p. 159). Moreover, education in itself provides the mental pleasure of "contemplation of truth" (p. 173). The success of the
Utopian educational program is supposedly apparent in the fact
that the Utopians "have very few laws because very few are needed
for persons so educated" (p. 195), a circumstance that confirms
Plato's prediction that if the citizens of the polis are properly
educated there will be no need "to legislate for . . . minor
matters": "Good men need no orders. . . . They will find out

[60] The Utopians' educational views coincide closely, on this as on other points,
with More's own views as expressed in his letter to Gonell. See above, pp. 10-
11, and Chap. 2, n. 11. Like More, the Utopians do not share Plato's distrust
of literature as an instrument of moral education. Surtz (*Ut.*, p. clix) calls
attention to the more practical bent of Utopian education as compared to that
in the Republic.

[61] In the *Republic* only the Guardians—male and female (v.466E)—are given
military training.

easily enough what legislation is in general necessary" (*Rep.* IV.425C-D).[62]

In fact, however, good men are not much trusted in either the Republic or Utopia. As I pointed out above (p. 87), Plato says that it would be "a sin" for anything "in our ideal society to take place without regulation" (*Rep.* V.458D-E). In the *Laws*, where he is not counting on the kind of perfect education envisaged in the *Republic*, the regulation of every aspect of life takes the form of detailed legislation. The guiding principle is that "freedom from control must be uncompromisingly eliminated from the life of all men" (XII.942D). The Utopians appear to have even less trust than Plato in the ability of good men to direct their own affairs: their constitution includes both the thorough education in virtue of the *Republic* and the legal prohibition of opportunities for vice—that is, false pleasure—of the polis of the *Laws*. All travel requires a license (*Ut.*, pp. 145-47). The use of leisure hours is supposedly "left to every man's discretion," but a man cannot choose to waste them "in revelry or idleness" (p. 127). If he did choose to do so, he would find the requisite equipment lacking, since there is "no wine shop, no alehouse, no brothel anywhere, no opportunity for corruption, no lurking hole, no secret meeting place" (p. 147). Thus "people are bound either to be performing the usual labor or to be enjoying their leisure

---

[62] Cf. Plutarch, "Lycurgus" XIII. 1-2: "None of his laws were put into writing by Lycurgus, indeed, one of the so-called 'rhetras' forbids it. For he thought that if the most important and binding principles which conduce to the prosperity and virtue of a city were implanted in the habits and training of its citizens, they would remain unchanged and secure, having a stronger bond than compulsion in the fixed purposes imparted to the young by education, which performs the office of a law-giver for every one of them. And as for minor matters, such as business contracts, and cases where the needs vary from time to time, it was better, as he thought, not to hamper them by written constraints or fixed usages, but to suffer them, as occasion demanded, to receive such modifications as educated men should determine." Erasmus says that "a very few laws suffice for a well organized state under a good prince and honorable officials" (*ECP*, p. 221, quoted *Ut.*, p. 489n). Both Utopia and the Republic exclude lawyers (*Ut.*, p. 195; *Rep.* III.405A-B).

in a fashion not without decency." Indeed, all the false pleasures discussed in the section on moral philosophy are either outlawed or simply unavailable as a consequence of some Utopian institution. It is, for example, impossible to take pride in fine clothes in Utopia, since the only clothes produced are the regulation uniforms (pp. 127, 133-35).[63]

In addition to legal prohibitions, the Utopians employ a multitude of positive and negative reinforcements to encourage good behavior and discourage bad. These devices, designed to affect behavior by appeal to the emotions, reflect the conception that human nature includes a large nonrational element. More may have derived his interest in this means of social control from Plato, who exploits it relentlessly in the *Laws*. According to the Athenian, "the influence of the law" must be distinguished from "the educational effect of praise and blame, which makes the individual easier to handle and better disposed towards the laws that are to be established" (v.730B). The ruler must "praise and commend some courses of action and censure others, and in every field of conduct he must see that anyone who disobeys is disgraced" (IV.711B-C).[64] In conformity with this view, More causes the Utopians to make a remarkable number of actions either honorific or disgraceful. They do not merely "discourage crime by punishment but . . . offer honors to invite men to virtue" (*Ut.*, p. 193).[65] Thus "to great men who have done conspicuous service

---

[63] As the Manuels suggest (p. 50), the Benedictine code may also have been a source of the notion, in *Utopia* and other utopian writings, that detailed regulation is a key to the best society.

[64] In the Sparta of Lycurgus, "nothing was left untouched and neglected, but with all the necessary details of life he [Lycurgus] blended some commendation of virtue or rebuke of vice; and he filled the city full of good examples, whose continual presence and society must of necessity exercise a controlling and moulding influence upon those who were walking the path of honour" (Plutarch, "Lycurgus" XXVII.2).

[65] Skinner (1978, pp. 257-58) points out that in Utopia *honor* is always the reward of *virtus*, whereas in Europe it is attached to high birth and wealth (e.g., *Ut.*, pp. 157, 167-69). The stress on *honor* in Book II, then, should also be understood, as Skinner argues, as forming part of More's vigorous

to their country they set up in the market place statues to stand as a record of noble exploits and, at the same time, to have the glory of forefathers serve their descendants as a spur and stimulus to virtue." Similarly, they pay great honor to the virtuous dead, which they regard as "a most efficacious means of stimulating the living to good deeds" (p. 225). Women offer themselves as wet nurses "with the greatest readiness since everybody praises this kind of pity" (p. 143). Whenever "women are anxious to accompany their husbands on military service, not only do they not forbid them but actually encourage them and incite them by expressions of praise" (pp. 209-11). Suicide "counseled by authority is honorific" (p. 187); but "if anyone commits suicide without . . . approval . . . , they deem him unworthy of either fire or earth and cast his body ignominiously into a marsh." Unauthorized travelers not only incur legal penalties but are also "treated with contempt" (p. 147). In cases of premarital intercourse, the fornicators themselves are subject to legal penalties and the parents "in whose house the offense was committed incur great disgrace" (p. 187). There is no legal prohibition against dining privately, "yet no one does it willingly since the practice is considered not decent" (p. 141; cf. "Lycurgus" x.3). Similarly, while the possession of gold and silver is not illegal, the Utopians control the appetite for them by employing "every means in their power . . . [to] make gold and silver a mark of ill fame" (*Ut.*, p. 153). It is a "great disgrace" to maltreat mental defectives (p. 193), and it is "counted as base and disfiguring" to deride disfigured persons. It is also a "disgraceful affectation" to use cosmetics. The priests, who act as "censors of morals" (p. 227), constitute a central agency for negative reinforcement. It is a "great disgrace" even to be rebuked by a priest, and those excluded from divine service by the priests "incur very great disgrace and are tortured by a secret fear of religion" (p. 229).

A related means of encouraging desirable behavior is the de-

critique of the contemporary conception of honor, a critique founded on the Stoic notion that virtue is the only true nobility. See below, p. 242.

liberate provision of good examples by those in authority—a practice that reflects the Stoic and humanist belief in the importance of the example set by rulers. The syphogrants, "though legally exempted from work, yet take no advantage of this privilege so that by their example they may the more readily attract the others to work" (p. 131). Utopus' first act as ruler provided a prototype of the direction of behavior by inspiring example. Having ordered a massive excavation to make Utopia an island, "he set to the task not only the natives but, to prevent them from thinking the labor a disgrace, his own soldiers also" (p. 113; cf. *Laws* IV.711B).

Good behavior is also encouraged by the criminal code. To see severe punishment inflicted on his fellow-citizen for some crime is an excellent "object lesson" ("exemplum") for the Utopian (*Ut.*, p. 185). One reason for the Utopian preference for slavery rather than death as a punishment is that the example of the slave "lasts longer to deter others from like crimes" (p. 191). In the case of a severe offense, "it is to the advantage of public morality to have it punished openly."[66] The criminal code also provides something to do with the social derelicts who, as Plato and More agree, will be found in even an ideal society. In accordance with Plato's views, Utopian criminal justice apportions the severity of punishment to the degree of heinousness of the crime (p. 191; cf. *Laws* XI.933E-934B; Cic., *Off.* I.xxv.89; and see above, Chap. 2, n. 32). The "worst offenses are punished by the sentence of slavery." But incorrigible criminals are, as in the *Laws*, "put to death like untameable beasts that cannot be restrained by prison or chain" (*Ut.*, p. 191; *Laws* IX.862E-863A).

More is also close to the Greek theorists in his handling of some aspects of Utopian foreign relations. Contact with other nations is always problematic for the best commonwealth, because it entails the possibility of contamination by inferior practices:

[66] White (unpubl. paper) observes that a similarly "didactic conception of punishment" is found in *Laws* IX.854E-855A, 862E-863A.

"In the nature of the case, contact between state and state produces a medley of all sorts of characters, because the unfamiliar customs of the visitors rub off on to their hosts—and this, in a healthy society living under sound laws, is an absolute disaster" (*Laws* XII.949E-950A; cf. Plutarch, "Lycurgus" XXVII.3-4). Yet Plato and Aristotle concede that some foreign contact is necessary, since "it is almost impossible to found a state in a place where it will not need imports" (*Rep.* II.370E; cf. *Pol.* VII.1327a). Thus the question how to handle trade relations becomes a part of the best-commonwealth exercise.

The guiding principle is to conduct necessary trade in a way that minimizes contact with foreigners, and especially the admission of foreigners. The Utopians agree with the Greek theorists on this point. There are only a "very few [Utopians] who for a good reason had visited foreign countries" (*Ut.*, p. 155; cf. *Laws* XII.950D-951A), and "few persons . . . come to them in the way of trade" (*Ut.*, p. 185; *Laws* 952D-953A). What could traders bring, after all, except iron, which is "practically the only thing lacking" in Utopia (*Ut.*, p. 149)? "And as to articles of export, the Utopians think it wiser to carry them out of the country themselves than to let strangers come to fetch them" (p. 185; cf. *Pol.* VII.1327a). This policy enables them to "get more information about foreign nations" and to maintain "their skill in navigation," a skill that, as White points out (1976, p. 645), has military applications. The "great quantity of silver and gold" (*Ut.*, p. 149) that the Utopians acquire in trade also has a military application. All this treasure is kept for the "single purpose" of being "their bulwark in extreme peril or in sudden emergency. They use it above all to hire at sky-high rates of pay foreign mercenaries (whom they would jeopardize rather than their own citizens), being well aware that by large sums of money even their enemies themselves may be bought and[67] set to fight

---

[67] I have deleted the unwarranted "sold or" from the Yale translation at this point. See Miller 1966, p. 63.

one another either by treachery or by open warfare" (pp. 149-51; cf. *Rep.* IV.422D).

Contact with other nations is also necessary to the ideal commonwealth in order that it may profit by useful developments that occur elsewhere. In the *Republic* Plato treats the constitution of the ideal polis as perfect and immutable, but in the *Laws* he allows that any good legislator will "realize that his code has many inevitable deficiencies which must be put right by a successor, if the state he's founded is to enjoy a continuous improvement in its administrative arrangements, rather than suffer a decline" (VI.769D). The goal for rulers is to continue to improve the constitution of the "original legislator" until "every detail is thought to have received its final polish. After that, they must assume that the rules are immutable" (772C). A later passage suggests, however, that this happy condition will never quite be reached. Mature citizens should be permitted to survey at leisure "the life lived by foreigners, . . . because no state will ever be able to live at a properly advanced level of civilization if it keeps itself to itself and never comes into contact with all the vices and virtues of mankind":

> In the mass of mankind you'll invariably find a number—though only a small number—of geniuses with whom it is worth anything to associate, and they crop up just as often in badly-ruled states as in the well-ruled. So the citizen of a well-run state, provided he's incorruptible, should go out and range over land and sea to track them down, so that he can see to the strengthening of the customs of his country that are soundly based, and the refurbishing of any that are defective. (XII.951B-C)

In this matter, too, the Utopians' attitude is close to Plato's, though they are a good deal less worried about the possible bad effects of importations than he is. Even after 1,760 years (*Ut.*, p. 121) in which to polish the constitution of their original legislator, the Utopians remain on the lookout for beneficial changes. The importance of a receptive attitude toward new ideas

is drummed into every Utopian in the standard prayer of the
monthly holy days. Each individual prays that "if there is anything better and more approved by God than that commonwealth
[i.e., Utopia] or that religion, . . . that He will . . . bring him
to the knowledge of it, for he is ready to follow in whatever path
He may lead him" (p. 237). And indeed the Utopians are highly
receptive to new sources of ideas: "Whoever, coming to their
land on a sight-seeing tour, is recommended by any special intellectual endowment or is acquainted with many countries through
long travel, is sure of a hearty welcome, for they delight in
hearing what is happening in the whole world" (p. 185). At the
end of Book I, Hythloday tells us that when, twelve hundred
years ago, a ship full of Romans and Egyptians was wrecked on
the island, the Utopians assimilated everything these visitors had
to offer (p. 109).[68] Similarly, they eagerly absorb all the knowledge that Hythloday and his companions bring, including their
religious knowledge (pp. 181-83, 217-19; cf. Nagel, p. 174).

The most interesting connections between Utopia and the Greek
theoretical works, however, occur when More crucially alters or
wholly rejects some important feature of the arrays of institutions
in their ideal poleis. Taken together with the arguments of the
section on moral philosophy, these departures embody More's
critique of the Greek best-commonwealth exercises: since More
and the Greek theorists are performing the same exercise with
the same premises, the departures imply that the Greeks have
drawn incorrect conclusions from their premises. As usual, More
appears to expect a great deal of his readers. Since the departures

[68] One of the first things we hear about Utopia, then, is that this commonwealth has been extraordinarily durable—and this impression is reinforced early
in Book II by the allusion to its 1,760-year history. This durability is surely
intended to suggest the near-perfection of the Utopian constitution. The link
between the excellence and the duration of constitutions is a prominent theme
of Renaissance political thought, embodied especially in the myth of the mixed
constitution of *Serenissima* Venice. See Pocock, esp. pp. 75-76, 99-102; Skinner
1978, pp. 139-42, 171-72. Quintilian says that in the praise of cities "antiquity
carries great authority" (III.vii.26).

are normally introduced without explanation, simply as parts of
Hythloday's descriptive account, the reader is evidently expected
not only to recall the relevant aspects of the Greek works—fair
enough, since the book was directed to humanists—but also to
infer the arguments by which More arrives at his different conclusions. Reconstruction is in fact possible, because the departures
follow logically from the preceding steps of the exercise; for the
most part, from the arguments of the section on moral philosophy,
arguments that More gives in full.

The most conspicuous of the departures from the institutional
arrays of the Greek theorists lies in the matter of Utopian communism. In the *Republic*, Plato makes the life of his Guardians
communistic in every way: they hold wives and children, as well
as all property, in common. The other classes of the population,
however, are in no way communized. In the *Laws*, Plato still
maintains that the best state would be completely communistic
(v.739B-C), although this view has reference only to the relatively small class of full citizens rather than to all the inhabitants
of the polis. He concedes, however, that communism is in practice "too demanding for . . . [people] born and bred and educated
as ours are" (740A). Accordingly, in the "second-best" polis of
the *Laws*, the only communistic institutions are the common tables
(vi.762C, 780E-781A, vii.806E) and the law requiring free
distribution of two-thirds of all agricultural produce to citizens
and slaves (vii.847E-848A).

Aristotle severely criticizes the communism of the *Republic*,
on several grounds. Community of wives and children would
not, as Plato imagines, result in greater harmony but in the
weakening of communal ties: "any and every son will be equally
the son of any and every father; and the result will be that every
son will be equally neglected by every father" (*Pol.* ii.1261b).
Community of property is inadvisable for five reasons (1261b-
1264a). First, it would sap initiative. Second, it would eliminate
opportunities to practice the virtue of liberality. Third, it would
deprive men of the legitimate pleasure of ownership and that
derived from liberality. Fourth, it would not increase concord,

for many of the evils of dissension usually ascribed to private property actually "arise from the wickedness of human nature": "Indeed it is a fact of observation that those who own common property, and share in its management, are far more often at variance with one another than those who have property in severalty." Finally, Plato's scheme restricts communism to the Guardians, leaving the other inhabitants in much the same condition as in actual polities: the "legal complaints, and actions at law, and all the other evils which Plato describes as existing in actual states, will equally exist among them." Nonetheless, Aristotle would divide the property of his ideal polis into privately and publicly owned sections, and he retains the Platonic (and Spartan) institution of the common tables for citizens, to be supported by the public property (VII.1330A; cf. Plutarch, "Lycurgus" x).

Utopian economic communism is as thorough as that proposed for the Guardians. The Utopians resemble the Guardians in having "no private property beyond the barest essentials" (*Rep*. III.416D), nor any "dwelling-house or other property to which all have not the right of entry" (416D; *Ut.*, p. 121); and they share with the Guardians the institution of the common table. More even adds the requirement that all Utopians exchange their houses by lot every ten years (p. 121).

The striking difference between Utopian economic communism and that proposed by Plato lies, of course, in the fact that in Utopia communism extends to all inhabitants of the island. This difference reflects the partly different arguments by which the two thinkers arrive at the conclusion of the necessity of communism.

For Plato, the communism of the Guardians is a necessary but unfortunate consequence of human nature. Men being selfish and private property being the greatest temptation to that selfishness, rulers will "prey upon the rest of the community" (*Rep*. III.416C) unless they are precluded from doing so by being forbidden private property and being deprived of the privacy that might enable them to evade that prohibition. The goal of the polis is

the happiness of its citizens. But the life of the Guardians is hard
and may not be particularly happy: to some extent, their happiness
is sacrificed to the happiness of the community as a whole (420B-
421C).

More, as we have seen, shares Plato's (and Aristotle's) unflattering view of human nature, and he too suggests, through
Hythloday, that removal of opportunity for selfish accumulation
is one reason for Utopian communism. Since communism is
universal in Utopia, Plato's argument for the need to inhibit the
selfishness of a ruling class is recast as an argument for the
necessity of community of property in order to secure distributive
justice (cf. Surtz 1957a, p. 155, quoted above, p. 184). In the
ur-*Utopia*, the reader was evidently left to infer this argument
from the account of Utopia; but in the later-written segment,
More gives it explicit treatment, at the end of Book I. Among
the Utopians, Hythloday says, "affairs are ordered so aptly that
virtue has its reward, and yet, with equality of distribution, all
men have abundance of all things" (*Ut.*, p. 103). By contrast,
in nations where private property exists "good order" is never
achieved—a fact that, Hythloday says, led Plato to refuse "to
make laws for those who rejected that legislation which gave to
all an equal share in all goods":[69]

> This wise sage, to be sure, easily foresaw that the one
> and only road to the general welfare lies in placing everyone
> on an equal footing.[70] I have my doubts that the latter could
> ever be preserved where the individual's possessions are his
> private property. When every man aims at absolute own-
> ership of all the property he can get, be there never so great
> abundance of goods, it is all shared by a handful who leave
> the rest in poverty. . . . I am fully persuaded that no just

[69] This statement evidently derives from Diogenes Laertius (III.23; *Ut.*, p.
379n). Needless to say, it misrepresents Plato, who is never interested in equal
shares for any other group than that of the full citizens.

[70] On the translation, see Chap. 2, n. 83.

and even distribution of goods can be made and that no
happiness can be found in human affairs unless private
property is utterly abolished.[71] (p. 105; cf. pp. 237-43)

But the Utopians have another argument in favor of economic
communism, one that follows from their conclusions about the
best life of the individual and that necessitates the extension of
communism to every inhabitant of the island. The goal of the
commonwealth is, again, to maximize the happiness of its citizens. As we have seen, the Utopian moral philosophers conclude
that individual felicity is incompatible with special privilege.
Therefore, the maximization of the happiness of the citizens
requires that citizenship be extended to all inhabitants[72] and that,
wherever possible, special privileges, including economic privilege and the privilege of status that accompanies it, be avoided.

[71] According to Plutarch, Lycurgus' reasons for undertaking land reform in
Sparta were similar: he divided property equally in order "to banish insolence
and envy and crime and luxury, and those yet more deep-seated and afflictive
diseases of the state, poverty and wealth" ("Lycurgus" VIII. 1-2). Erasmus, who
is extremely sympathetic to the idea of communism, compares Lycurgus to
Christ and praises Spartan communism in terms that recall Hythloday's remarks
here and at the end of Book II:

It was customary [among the Lacedaemonians] to use the slaves of
neighbors, if anyone had need, as one's own. The same held for dogs and
horses, unless their master had occasion to use them. What is more, in
the country, if anyone needed anything, he opened the doors and took
away from its possessor what was necessary for his present task; he merely
marked the place from which he had taken anything and then went his
way. In the midst of customs of this kind, where could insatiable avarice
find a place? where the rapacity of men who appropriate other people's
property as their own? where the arrogance springing from riches? where
the cruelty of robbers who cut the throat of an unknown and innocent
traveler for a few pennies? Would you not say that this was a genuinely
Christian custom if they had obtained Christ, instead of Lycurgus, as a
maker of laws? ("Prisca Lacedaemoniorum Instituta," *Apophthegmata, Opera*,
4:146, trans. Surtz 1957a, p. 173)

[72] Foreign-born slaves are excepted (though their children are not). See *Ut.*,
p. 185.

The obvious way to effect this end lies in the institution of community of property (cf. Surtz 1957a, pp. 153-55, 197; above, p. 184). Thus, far from depriving men of happiness (as in Plato), communism contributes greatly to mental pleasure, the most important component of happiness.

At the same time, More is evidently impressed by Aristotle's objections to communism. Even though communism tends to increase mental pleasure, is it not the case, as the summary of Aristotle's objections at the end of Book I of *Utopia* (p. 107) suggests, that communism would erode the stability and security of the commonwealth by decreasing the efficiency of production and undermining concord and respect for constituted authority? Is it the case, that is, that a conflict exists in this respect between the achievement of the goal of maximizing mental pleasure and that of securing health, which entails the efficient production of necessary commodities and the maintenance of national security? That More does feel that such a conflict exists is evident in the various Utopian arrangements designed to minimize it. Insomuch as conflict arises between the pursuit of health and the pursuit of mental pleasure, the political application of the hedonic calculus requires that mental pleasure be sacrificed to health, the goal of first priority. Accordingly, although they make no exceptions to the rule of community of property, the Utopians do grant special privileges to the officers of the state and the elders of the community. Some of these privileges, such as exemption from the requirement of manual labor (p. 131) and the right of husbands and parents to hear confessions from wives and children (p. 233), are designed primarily to enable the more responsible members of the community to ensure the proper behavior of the less responsible. Other privileges, such as the preferential seating of officials and elders at the common tables (p. 143) and the allotment of the choicest food to the old men (pp. 143-45), serve simply to enhance the authority of these groups by providing symbolic confirmation of it. Utopian social arrangements also seem designed to attain the advantages of the community of wives and children recommended by Plato while avoiding the disadvantages of such community pointed out by Aristotle. A good deal of care is devoted to securing the stability of marriage in Utopia, and every Utopian knows who his children are. But nuclear families are integrated into the extended families of the households, which "as a rule are made up of those related by blood" (p. 135), and these in turn are integrated into the larger families headed by the syphogrants (or phylarchs).[73] Indeed "the whole island is like a single family" (p. 149), a family that is rigidly patriarchal in structure.[74] Hexter, then, is surely correct in suggesting that this elaborate familial organization "is one of the means by which Utopians counteract the possible disruptive effects of their egalitarianism" (*Ut.*, p. xlii; cf. p. xliv).[75]

Another striking departure from the economic arrangements suggested in Greek theory similarly reflects More's awareness of the potential for conflicts between the achievement of different communal goals and his use of the hedonic calculus to determine satisfactory trade-offs where such conflicts occur. Plato insists that each member of the working classes should practice only one profession, a rule that is justified in terms of efficiency (*Rep.* II.370A-C; *Laws* VIII.846D-E). Since efficient production is essential to the economic well-being of the commonwealth, More must also regard it as an important goal. Moreover, since in Utopia everyone (with a few exceptions) is engaged in the labor

---

[73] "Phylarchus" is the Latin form of φύλαρχος, "the head of a tribe" (*Ut.*, p. 389n). Lycurgus divided the Spartan people into φυλαὶ (Plutarch, "Lycurgus" VI.1). White (unpubl. paper) points out that Plato uses φύλαρχος as one of the military ranks in the polis of the *Laws* (VI.755C).

[74] "And it is said that on returning from a journey . . . , as he [Lycurgus] traversed the land just after the harvest, and saw the heaps of grain standing parallel and equal to one another, he smiled, and said to them that were by: 'All Laconia looks like a family estate newly divided among many brothers' " (Plutarch, "Lycurgus" VIII.4).

[75] The various methods of social control discussed above also function to preclude economic inefficiency. See, for example, *Ut.*, p. 147, where the regulations governing travel are explicitly linked with the need to prevent evasion of work.

of production, it is necessary that this labor be performed as efficiently as possible so as to free the maximum amount of time for the cultivation of mental pleasure. But pleasure may also be derived from changing one's profession, or from practicing two professions alternately. And the hedonic calculus demands that no true pleasure be interfered with, so long as it does not conflict with a pleasure of higher priority. Accordingly, the Utopians permit any citizen to acquire a second profession: "if anyone after being thoroughly taught one craft desires another also, . . . permission is given" (*Ut.*, p. 127); quite logically, he may practice whichever profession he prefers just so long as his choice does not compromise the general welfare: "Having acquired both [crafts], he practices his choice unless the city has more need of the one than of the other." Similar calculations underlie the agricultural arrangements of Utopia. In the interest of efficiency, it would obviously be preferable if there were a class of permanent agricultural laborers. But the life of the agricultural worker is unusually harsh (p. 115), and he is deprived of the communal life of the cities (p. 145). Since the hardships of a permanent agricultural class would diminish not only the happiness of the members of that class but also that of all their fellow citizens (since happiness is incompatible with special privilege), the Utopians have instituted a system whereby every citizen is rotated to the farms for two-year periods. (To preclude "anything going wrong with the annual food supply through want of skill" [p. 115], half of the population of each rural household is replaced each year.) But here, too, the principle of not interfering with any legitimate pleasure except when it conflicts with a higher pleasure is applied: "many men who take a natural pleasure in agricultural pursuits obtain leave to stay several years."[76]

---

[76] A parallel example of a calculated trade-off between goals is found in the fact that, although universal military training is part of the egalitarianism of Utopia, those who are timorous by nature are not required to fight, since a timorous soldier "not only will not acquit himself manfully but will throw fear into his companions" (p. 209). In this particular, then, the assurance of national security conflicts with the equal distribution of pleasure (here, the equal sharing

The Utopians also differ radically from the Greek theorists, especially Plato, in their view of war. Plato holds that wars between Greek poleis should be regarded as unfortunate "internal and domestic" (*Rep.* v.470B) quarrels, and that in such wars the Guardians should "fight in the hope of coming to terms": "their object will be to correct a friend and bring him to his senses, rather than to enslave and destroy an enemy" (471A). But non-Greeks are "natural enemies" (470C) to be subjugated by any means. In either kind of war, distinction in battle deserves glorious reward (468B-E); and those who die bravely on active service "we shall reckon as men of gold."[77] Aristotle, who lacks Plato's enthusiasm for war, observes that war is not an end in itself but a means to the good life (*Pol.* VII.1325a). Military training, then, is undertaken not "with a view to enslaving men who do not deserve such a fate":

> Its objects should be these—first, to prevent men from ever becoming enslaved themselves; secondly, to put men in a position to exercise leadership—but a leadership directed to the interest of the led, and not to the establishment of a general system of slavery; and thirdly, to enable men to make themselves masters of those who naturally deserve to be slaves [i.e., non-Greeks]. (1333B-1334A)

The Utopians, however, are innocent of the concepts of natural enemies and natural slaves, and in general they hold that war is "an activity fit only for beasts" and regard it "with utter loathing" (*Ut.*, p. 199). They "count nothing so inglorious as glory sought

---

of pain and danger), and, as always in such cases, the conflict must be resolved in favor of the goal of higher priority.

[77] Lewis Mumford says that "the constitution and daily discipline of Plato's ideal commonwealth converge to a single end: fitness for making war" (p. 274). Cf. *Timaeus*, 19C, 20B (quoted Chap. 2, n. 61). Hexter observes that "with a bit of adaptation . . . [the *Republic*] could very neatly be made to fit the requirements of Europe's military aristocracy." But "More did not conform his imaginary commonwealth to that adaptation of the *Republic* which was becoming the pattern of history in his own day. As Utopia is patriarchal and familial while the Republic is not, so the Republic is a military aristocracy while Utopia is not" (*Ut.*, pp. liii, liv).

in war" (p. 201). These attitudes, which are Stoic commonplaces
(see R. P. Adams 1962, pp. 6-8), follow from the conception
of universal human brotherhood, which the Utopians, like the
Stoics, derive from reason (*Ut.*, p. 163; cf. p. 197.20-23).

Correspondingly, when the Utopians must go to war, their
tactics are governed by the humanitarian considerations that the
Stoics would apply to all wars but that Plato confines to "internal
and domestic" disputes.[78] Plato opposes the practice of "devastating the lands and burning the houses of Greek enemies" (*Rep.*
VI.470A-B; cf. 471A-C). Similarly, the Utopians "do not ravage
the enemy's territory nor burn his crops" (*Ut.*, p. 215; cf. Cic.,
Off. I.xi.34-35, xxiv.82). Plato's Guardians would not "admit
that the whole people of a [Greek] state—men, women, and
children—are their enemies, but only the minority who are responsible for the quarrel" (471A-B). The Utopians "know that
the common folk do not go to war of their own accord but are
driven to it by the madness of kings" (*Ut.*, p. 205), and so they
"are almost[79] as sorry for the throng and mass of the enemy as
for their own citizens."

In summary, More's account of the most rational polity reflects
large areas of both agreement and disagreement with the Greek
theorists. The Utopian construct stands in somewhat the same
relation to the best commonwealths of Plato and Aristotle as
Aristotle's best commonwealth to those of Plato. Aristotle accepts
the general principles of the best-commonwealth exercise and
numerous particular institutional suggestions from Plato, but he
refines the principles and replaces many of Plato's institutions
with others that seem to him better calculated to lead to the
attainment of the goals of the polis. Similarly, More accepts the
principles of construction of the Greek theorists (in the form

---

[78] Indeed the difference between Platonic and Utopian attitudes toward war
is nowhere more sharply defined than in the fact that, whereas the Utopians
extend to all wars the humanitarian tactics recommended by Plato for internecine
strife, Plato urges that when "our citizens . . . are fighting barbarians they
should treat them as the Greeks now treat each other" (*Rep.* V.471B)—i.e.,
viciously.

[79] "Almost" is missing from Yale. See Miller 1966, p. 58.

developed by Aristotle), but he further refines these principles, by formulating more precisely the relation between the goals of the individual and the goals of the commonwealth, and by recognizing the inevitability of conflicts between the achievement of different goals and developing a method (the application to politics of the hedonic calculus of Epicurean ethics) for resolving such conflicts. In the same way, while More adopts numerous particular institutional suggestions from Plato and Aristotle, he modifies or rejects others, thus completing his critique and revision of the Greek best-commonwealth exercises. In general, More's most rational polity, while bearing a strong resemblance to those of the Greek theorists, also reflects Stoic norms, in that it is far more egalitarian and compassionate (though no freer) than the Greeks'. More agrees with Plato that the rational polity would be communistic, though he is impressed by Aristotle's objections to communism and accordingly builds in safeguards against the possibility that communism would, as Aristotle argues, erode the stability and security of the commonwealth. But More differs from Plato in extending communism to all citizens and from both Plato and Aristotle in extending citizenship to all inhabitants (except foreign-born slaves); in both respects, Utopia embodies ideals not of the polis but of the Stoic cosmopolis. More's commonwealth is also—again in accordance with Stoic norms—much more humane and generous in its relations with its neighbors than are the ideal poleis of the Greek theorists, although the foreign policy of Utopia reflects the fear of contamination by outside influences that is inevitably a feature of the best-commonwealth exercise.

As in Book I, then, More uses the methods of city-state theory to provide new underpinnings for some conclusions of Christian-Stoic theory. On the basis of his tortuous proof that one man's pleasure depends on the equal pleasure of all his fellows, he manages to make the best-commonwealth exercise generate a constitution that embodies the central ideals of Christian-Stoic political thought and largely confirms the Stoic thesis that the expedient is, for the community as for the individual, identical to the moral. Above all, the pursuit of perfect expediency does not, as Plato and Aristotle think, dictate the restriction of the good life to a small elite among the inhabitants of the commonwealth. Actual polities may never attain the rational ideal, nor is this ideal the only relevant one. But it remains, as Plato thought it, one standard by which communities may assess and guide themselves. And when their leaders find, as they always do, that actual polities are characterized by inequality and injustice, More would at least forbid them the comfortable conviction, so deleteriously sanctioned by the Greek theorists, that even the most rational polity would share these characteristics.

IV

The fact that some Utopian practices contradict views of the Greek theorists is not surprising: such contradictions are only what we should expect when an Erasmian humanist sets out, with his largely Stoic conceptions of what is rational and just, to revise the conclusions of Plato and Aristotle. What *is* surprising, and constitutes a central interpretive problem, is the fact that others of these practices are at odds with the beliefs and ideals of Erasmian humanists.[80]

To be sure, some of these discrepancies are easily explained, namely, those produced where Utopian practices differ only from what Erasmians regard as uniquely Christian, not from what they regard as rational. Hythloday says that Utopia demonstrates the harmony not only of the prudent and the moral but also of the prudent and the Christian—its institutions are both "prudentissima" and "sanctissima" (*Ut.*, p. 102; see above, p. 129). What this claim means is that one of More's purposes in his best-commonwealth exercise is to explore the degree of harmony between the prudent and the Christian. He concludes, by means

[80] It should go without saying that only those features of Utopia that presumably appeared as defects to More's intended audience—as distinguished from ourselves—are relevant here. Some genuine problems with Utopia are, of course, clearer to us than they could have been to More, who did not, for example, share our experience of rectilinear neighborhoods.

of the dubious arguments of the section on moral philosophy, that the harmony is considerable. The Utopians are led by reason alone to some ethical principles that many theorists (and most modern readers) regard as derivable only from revelation. Since Utopia is built by extrapolating from these ethical principles to their political consequences, in important respects More's purely rational commonwealth behaves like a perfectly Christian one— a point made forcefully by Hexter (e.g., *Ut.*, pp. lxviii-lxxvii). Nonetheless, it is clear to More, as to other medieval and Renaissance thinkers, that unaided reason leads, in some areas, to conclusions quite different from those dictated by revelation, and the account of Utopia includes several passages that remind us of this fact.

Apart from the section on military affairs (to which we shall return), the most conspicuous of these passages are those on euthanasia, divorce, and religious liberty. Contrary to Catholic orthodoxy, the Utopians encourage those in agony from incurable disease to take their own lives (p. 187), permit divorce on several grounds (pp. 189-91), and practice a very considerable degree of religious toleration (pp. 219-23). All three passages have been illuminated by Duhamel, who, in the course of a misguided attempt to prove that *Utopia* is "probably the most medieval of More's works" (1955, p. 234), notes some highly instructive parallels between these passages and Aquinas' explorations of the degree of harmony between reason and revelation.[81] Duhamel cites Aquinas' view that in certain matters reason can reach only probable conclusions, which may be contradicted by revelation (p. 240; see also Surtz 1952, p. 165). Thus men guided by reason alone would conclude, as the Utopians do, that suicide is permissible under certain conditions; but revelation tells us that suicide under any circumstances violates a divine prohibition against the taking of life. Aquinas also "argued that the indissolubility of the marriage bond was a natural quality which had not been recognized until after the promulgation of the New

---

[81] For More's attitude toward Aquinas, see n. 32 above.

Law." Thus the Utopian position on divorce is just what we
should expect in a commonwealth based on reason alone—indeed,
it is partially anticipated in Plato's *Laws* (xi.929E-930A). Similarly, the religious liberty decreed by Utopus is a logical consequence of his realization of the limited degree of certitude on
religious questions attainable by unaided reason. Hythloday tells
us that Utopus took this position because "on religion he did not
venture rashly to dogmatize" (*Ut.*, p. 221). He did not venture,
as Duhamel makes clear (p. 242), because he understood that on
theological questions reason can arrive at only probable conclusions.[82]

[82] In two of these areas, More may even have thought (like Milton) that the
conclusions of reason did not in fact differ as much from the dictates of revelation
as Catholic orthodoxy suggested. Erasmus favored divorce with right of re-
marriage for the deceived party in cases of adultery (*Ut.*, p. 482n), as well as
a high degree of religious toleration (*Adages*, pp. 116-17), and we may wonder
whether More, at this period of "maximum convergence of . . . [their]
trajectories" (Hexter, *Ut.*, p. xxvi), shared these views. More, like Erasmus,
was presumably influenced by the tolerant attitudes of Cusanus (Wind, pp.
220-22) and of Ficino and Pico (Kristeller 1964, pp. 49, 61). Wind (p. 221n;
cf. Prévost 1978, p. 715n) shows how Cusanus' notion of the hidden God
relates to the darkness of the Utopians' temples and their use of "Mythra" (*Ut.*,
pp. 217, 233: Yale has "Mithras"; cf. Prévost, p. 590n) "to represent the one
nature of the divine majesty whatever it be" (*Ut.*, p. 233). The Utopians' ready
acceptance of Christianity (pp. 217-19) should be associated with views like
that of Pico, for whom, as Kristeller says, "religion seems to be a fulfillment
of philosophy: religion helps us to attain that ultimate end for which philosophy
can merely prepare us" (1964, p. 69). (For More's putative views on euthanasia,
see Surtz 1957b, pp. 91-93.)
   The fact that "the feminine sex is not debarred from the priesthood" in
Utopia (*Ut.*, p. 229)—as in Greek and Roman religions—reflects another
discrepancy between the dictates of reason and those of religion. See Surtz
1957b, pp. 162-63. But the fact that Utopian priests are allowed to marry
(*Ut.*, p. 229) reflects the Utopians' ignorance of Catholic tradition rather than
their ignorance of revelation: "Sacerdotal celibacy is a matter of Western ec-
clesiastical discipline, not a decree of divine institution. More clearly recognizes
this feature: 'The Church both knoweth and confesseth that wedlock and priesthood
be not repugnant but compatible of their nature. . . .' " (Surtz 1957b, p. 132,
quoting *Confutation of Tyndale*, p. 307).

Other discrepancies between Utopian practices and Erasmian views cannot, however, be explained in this fashion, since they involve contradictions not only with revealed dictates but also with what Erasmians regarded as the dictates of reason. These discrepancies are implicit in some aspects of Utopian military practice, and in the repressiveness and the drab uniformity of Utopian life.

Of these sets of discrepancies, the first is the most disturbing. The Utopians' detestation of war and martial glory, their compassion for the common citizens of enemy nations, and their attempts to minimize bloodshed are, of course, completely harmonious with Erasmian views (and their Stoic sources). In *The Education of a Christian Prince*, for example, Erasmus says that "a good prince should never go to war at all unless, after trying every other means, he cannot possibly avoid it. . . . if so ruinous an occurrence cannot be avoided, then the prince's main care should be to wage the war with as little calamity to his own people and as little shedding of Christian blood as may be, and to conclude the struggle as soon as possible" (p. 249; cf. Cic., *Off.* I.xi.34-35). The fact that Erasmus regards martial glory as "evil and false" (R. P. Adams 1962, p. 108) is everywhere apparent. But other Utopian attitudes and practices cannot be reconciled with Erasmian views.

Despite their detestation of war, the Utopians are willing to go to war for a number of reasons (cf. Dorsch, pp. 354-55). With the first of these—"to protect their own territory" (*Ut.*, p. 201)—few would quarrel. For all his pacifism, Erasmus grants that some wars are "just and necessary": those that "are, in a strict sense of those words, purely defensive" (*Complaint of Peace*, p. 54).[83] But the Utopians will also go to war "to drive an invading enemy out of their friends' lands or, in pity for a people

---

[83] In *The Education of a Christian Prince*, Erasmus' skepticism about the just war extends even further. The prince should consider "how disastrous and criminal an affair war is and what a host of all evils it carries in its wake even if it is the most justifiable war—if there really is any war which can be called 'just' " (p. 249).

oppressed by tyranny, to deliver them by force of arms from the
yoke and slavery of the tyrant, a course prompted by human
sympathy." Indeed they "oblige their friends with help, not always . . . to defend them merely but sometimes also to requite
and avenge injuries previously done to them." Moreover, we
have learned from an earlier passage that they are willing to go
to war to obtain territory for colonization. If the natives of the
underutilized land selected agree, the Utopian colonists integrate
them with themselves. But "the inhabitants who refuse to live
according to their laws, they drive from the territory which they
carve out for themselves. If they resist, they wage war against
them" (*Ut.*, p. 137).

To be sure, all these excuses for invasive war have some attractive precedent or theoretical justification. Plutarch says that
Lycurgus' Sparta "put down illegal oligarchies and tyrannies in
the different states" ("Lycurgus" XXX.2). Cicero opines that

> as long as the empire of the Roman people maintained itself
> by acts of service, not of oppression, wars were waged in
> the interest of our allies [*pro sociis*] or to safeguard our
> supremacy; . . . and the highest ambition of our magistrates
> and generals was to defend our provinces and allies with
> justice and honour. And so our government could be called
> more accurately a protectorate of the world than a dominion
> [itaque illud patrocinium orbis terrae verius quam impe-
> rium poterat nominari]. (*Off.* II.viii.26-27)

Skinner notes that it was a standard boast of the Florentines that
they fought for others' liberty as well as their own (1978, pp.
77-78). Francisco de Vitoria argues that wars of liberation are
sanctioned by natural law, and he cites the authority of St. Augustine in justification of wars undertaken to avenge wrongs
(Surtz 1957b, pp. 281-82). The Utopians themselves justify
their colonial wars in terms of natural law: "They consider it a
most just cause for war when a people which does not use its soil
but keeps it idle and waste nevertheless forbids the use and pos-

session of it to others who by the rule of nature ought to be maintained by it" (*Ut.*, p. 137).

All the same, it is only too evident to what bad ends such noble-sounding arguments can be, and usually are, applied. In practice Utopian foreign policy seems hard to distinguish from imperialism, a fact that constitutes the central theme of the German interpretive tradition initiated by Oncken, in which, as Ames says, Utopia is regarded as "the very *Urtyp* of all English ethical justification of imperialist *Realpolitik*" (p. 164). Avineri justly observes that it is not "purely accidental that this interpretation flourished and became prevalent in post-Versailles Germany" (p. 271), and he shows that the German claims are overstated and distorting. Yet Avineri himself argues powerfully that there is a core of validity in these views. When the fact that the Utopians undertake wars of liberation is considered in conjunction with the fact that "those liberated people choose Utopian citizens as their rulers, some suspicions creep in whether we are not facing here a phenomenon all too well known from modern Cold War casuistry" (p. 261; cf. *Ut.*, p. 197). Indeed it is clear, as Avineri says, that

> The so-called "friends"[84] are . . . dependent nations, not equal allies. Utopia appears as a center of a loose yet well-ordered community of nations, *not sharing the Utopian social system*, but being utterly dependent upon Utopia in their foreign policy and having Utopians as their rulers. . . . The very historical association expressed by the usage of these terms of *socii* and *amici* seems suggestive more of the Roman empire than of anything else, and when More goes on to relate how the Utopians proclaim war if one of their own or their allies' merchants is being ill-treated somewhere abroad [*Ut.*, pp. 201-3], it is difficult to refrain from thinking about the Saguntines and the Jugurthan Wars. (pp. 261-62)

[84] Actually it is the "allies" ("socii") of Utopia, rather than its "friends" ("amici"), who "seek their administrators from Utopia" (*Ut.*, p. 197).

And if the Germans find a parallel to Utopian policy in British imperialism, John D. Mackie suggests, not without some plausibility, a parallel with Fascist imperialism: More's "planned state was a danger to world-peace—it resembled strangely the Germany of Hitler" (p. 263).

Moreover, the suspect nature of such justifications of invasive war as the Utopians employ was clearly evident to members of More's own circle of humanists. Erasmus observes in *The Education of a Christian Prince* that

> Some princes deceive themselves that any war is certainly a just one and that they have a just cause for going to war. We will not attempt to discuss whether war is ever just; but who does not think his own cause just? Among such great and changing vicissitudes of human events, among so many treaties and agreements which are now entered into, now rescinded, who can lack a pretext—if there is any real excuse—for going to war? (p. 251)

Even in those cases where the prince or the nation has sustained a wrong, the prince "should carefully consider whether . . . [his right] should be maintained by means of catastrophes to the whole world" (p. 253). As R. P. Adams remarks, Erasmus thinks that war is not justified to punish evildoers, since it is "better that a handful of criminals should go unpunished than that innocent thousands suffer untold injury" (1962, p. 106; cf. *Adages*, pp. 339-41). In general, it is true, as Cicero says, that "an unjust peace is far preferable to a just war" (*Adages*, p. 343, quoted R. P. Adams 1962, p. 107; Cic., *Fam.* VI.vi.5). Colet's views are similar. Three years before More wrote Book II of *Utopia*, Colet, according to Erasmus, argued before the king that "an unjust peace was to be preferred to the justest war," and even that "for Christians no war was a just one" (trans. Lupton, in Olin, pp. 188, 190; *EE*, 4:524, 526).

If some of the Utopians' reasons for going to war are at odds with Erasmian ideals, so also are some of their tactics. Here, however, it is important to distinguish between what is repugnant to Christian humanists and what is only repugnant to some modern scholars. In general, the Utopians are extremely unchivalric, and, despite their conception of universal human brotherhood, they value the lives of all other peoples, including their allies, much lower than their own. They prefer to "overcome and crush the enemy by stratagem and cunning" rather than by "strength of body" (*Ut.*, p. 203). Correspondingly, they are "cunning in laying ambushes" (p. 213) and "very clever in inventing war machines" (p. 215). At the beginning of hostilities they arrange that "a great number of placards, made more effective by bearing their public seal, should be set up secretly in the most prominent spots of enemy territory," promising "huge rewards to anyone who will kill the enemy king" (pp. 203-5) and smaller rewards for the heads of other individuals whom they consider to be responsible for the war. (To be sure, these rewards are doubled if the "denounced parties" are brought to them alive [p. 205].) They also "sow the seeds of dissension" among their enemies "by leading a brother of the king or one of the noblemen to hope that he may obtain the throne." "If internal strife dies down, then they stir up and involve the neighbors of their enemies by reviving some forgotten claims to dominion such as kings have always at their disposal." They employ mercenaries to do as much of their fighting as possible; "next to them they employ the forces of the people for whom they are fighting and then auxiliary squadrons of all their other friends. Last of all they add a contingent of their own citizens" (p. 209). Despite their compassion for the common citizens of enemy nations, they enslave the defenders (presumably not all of them professional soldiers) of conquered cities (p. 215). Indeed, they apparently enslave *all* "prisoners of war . . . captured in wars fought by the Utopians themselves" (p. 185).

These practices have upset some defenders of the view of Utopia as a mirror of a reformed Europe, who hasten to explain that this particular segment of the mirror shows Europe as it is, not as it should be. Kautsky dismissed the section on military affairs as "mostly nothing more than scorching satire upon the

war spirit of . . . [More's] time" (p. 232). Donner writes that
the section is "obviously ironical and such a tangible parody of
contemporary European warfare that it seems well-nigh incredible that it should have ever been misunderstood" (p. 44). Surtz
shows that some "dastardly" (*Ut.*, p. cli) Utopian practices correspond to those of European nations of More's time (1957b,
pp. 289-97) and insists that the

> whole section in *Utopia* on bribes, assassins, pretenders, and
> traditional enemies, of course, is not to be taken as expressing
> More's real opinion on international politics. Without doubt
> he himself would wholly disavow Utopian practice. . . .
> But he paints a picture which he knows the Christian of
> Europe will abhor. And then he cries: "Wherefore, thou
> art inexcusable, O man, whoever thou art who judgest. For
> wherein thou judgest another, thou dost condemn thyself.
> For thou who judgest dost the same things thyself" (Romans
> 2:1).[85] (p. 293; cf. *Ut.*, p. 502n)

In fact there is no need to explain away most of the disturbing
tactics of the Utopians, since they are perfectly consistent with
the pacifism of Erasmian humanists. These humanists were deeply
impressed by Stoic criticism of the martial ethic of antiquity (e.g.,
Cic., *Off.* I.xi-xiii, xxiv; Sen., *Ep.* xciv.61-67), and they rou-

---

[85] An easier way of dealing with these embarrassing Utopian practices is to
ignore them. Hexter's argument that Utopia is More's ideal commonwealth is
facilitated by the fact that he says nothing at all about Utopian foreign policy.
Thus when he enumerates the classes of Utopian slaves he simply omits prisoners
of war (1952, pp. 68-69; cf. 1973, p. 52, n. 3), as does Caspari in the course
of a similar argument (p. 137, n. 73). (As Avineri points out [pp. 266-70],
avoiding unpleasant features of Utopia is a common critical maneuver.) Ames
deals with the problem presented by the enslavement of prisoners by the novel
tactic of reversing what *Utopia* says: "More is very careful to explain that
Utopian slavery does not extend to prisoners of war" (p. 170)! As it happens,
the enslavement of captives is allowed by the law of nations, though this
provision had, according to Vitoria, been abrogated among Christian nations
(Surtz 1957b, pp. 263-68). Thus the Utopian practice constitutes another
instance of the imperfect harmony between the conclusions derived from reason
and those dictated by revelation.

tinely apply Stoic techniques of rationalistic debunking to chivalric views of proper tactics and of martial glory that the Middle
Ages had bequeathed to their time (and to ours). Erasmus urges
that the prince, when he hears about "Achilles, Xerxes, Cyrus,
Darius, and Julius Caesar, . . . not be carried away and deluded
by the great names. You are hearing about great raging robbers,
for that is what Seneca has called them on various occasions"
(*ECP*, p. 201; Sen., *De ira* III.xvi.3-4, xxi.1-5). Similarly, he
should avoid "the tales of Arthur and Lancelot, and other tales
of similar nature which are not only about tyrants but also very
poorly done, stupid, and fit to be 'old wives' tales,' so that it
would be more advisable to put in one's time reading the comedies
or the legends of the poets instead of nonsense of that sort" (*ECP*,
p. 200; cf. R. P. Adams 1962, pp. 223-34). As Surtz observes,
"the Utopian views . . . on warfare are the reverse of the contemporary chivalric ethic, which regarded stratagem as con-
temptible and blood-letting as honorific" (*Ut.*, p. 501n). Given
the vehement disavowal of this ethic by Erasmian humanists, this
observation suggests the correct perspective on most Utopian
tactics. The resulting line of argument is forcefully developed
by R. P. Adams. As he shows, More's satiric attack on Brixius
in epigrams of 1513 embodies the "application of a critical . . .
realism to the absurdities of the arts and ideology of chivalric
war" (1962, p. 152; see also pp. 76-78). The section on Utopian
military affairs is to be understood in the same terms. "The
antichivalric Utopian art of war is, in effect, premised upon the
idea that chivalric honor, glory, and falsely heroic war methods
serve the interests only of a small class of decadent men, all
corrupted by vicious custom: tyrannic princes and some of their
noble supporters"; the discussion of Utopian warfare "applies a
kind of witty *realpolitik* against tyranny of both decadent men
and ideas as embodied in traditional chivalry" (p. 152).[86] Utopian
strategy "follows from their rational humanitarianism and hatred

[86] Cf. Lewis, p. 29. Hexter (*Ut.*, pp. l-liv) and Skinner (1978, pp. 257-
60) show that aversion to the values of the European warrior class—the chivalry—
pervades both books of *Utopia*.

of tyranny. It is to use whatever means reason can devise to end
the war with victory but with a minimum of cruelty to and
bloodshed by the common people of the enemy as well as their
own" (p. 153). In turn, "Utopian tactics follow logically from
their broadly humane strategic view of war's nature and purposes":

> Completely avoiding bloodshed of their own people when
> possible, they may "translate" shore beacons on their island
> so that approaching enemy navies may be wholly wrecked
> with ingenious ease [*Ut.*, p. 111]. . . . They use great
> cleverness in devising defenses, armor, and military ma-
> chinery, all intended to hasten the end and lessen the blood-
> shed of the war.[87] (p. 154)

Similarly, the proffer of rewards for the assassination of enemy
leaders can be justified as an attempt to shorten war and restrict
punishment to those responsible for the hostilities.

But this line of argument does not, as Adams thinks, resolve
all the problems of the section on military affairs. It cannot
account for the fact that, contrary to Stoic and Erasmian ideals,
the Utopians value the lives of Utopians more than those of other
men. Nor can it entirely obviate objection to the practice of
encouraging assassinations. As Surtz points out, however much
one wants to justify this practice "as an incitement to legitimate tyrannicide . . . , [two] considerations militate against this
interpretation":

> First . . . , the whole tone of the passage in *Utopia* is realistic
> in its appeal to the venality of the agents. Secondly, if More
> had intended to excuse and defend the behavior of his Uto-
> pians, he would have been much more careful to make clear
> that the rulers among their enemies were viewed as tyrants
> and hence worthy of death.[88] (1957b, p. 291)

[87] One should note, however, that fraudulent tactics are disapproved of by
Cicero (*Off.* I.xiii.41, xix.62).

[88] Cicero justifies tyrannicide (*Off.* III.iv.19, vi.32; above, Chap. 2, n. 65);
but the existence of a state of war does not automatically make the enemy leader
a tyrant:

The practices of sponsoring pretenders to the thrones of enemy nations and stirring up the neighbors of enemies raise similar problems (pp. 291-93). Surtz also makes the telling point that the Utopians' employment of bestial mercenaries is difficult to reconcile with their aim of minimizing bloodshed and plunder: "how the Utopians restrain the Zapoletans is not recorded" (*Ut.*, p. 512n).[89] There is, moreover, the troubling matter of the Utopians' genocidal policy toward the Zapoletans. Hythloday reports that "the Utopians do not care in the least how many Zapoletans they lose, thinking that they would be the greatest benefactors to the human race if they could relieve the world of all the dregs of this abominable and impious people" (p. 209). Although accounts of horrors perpetrated by sixteenth-century mercenaries—including an account by More (*Dialogue Concerning Heresies*, pp. 370-72, quoted R. P. Adams 1962, p. 267)— may make the Utopian attitude more understandable, this policy remains impossible to reconcile with the conception of Utopia as a mirror of a reformed Europe. Finally, Adams's argument, which is based on the parallel between Utopian practices and Stoic and Erasmian humanist recommendations, can hardly account for the fact that the Utopians are willing to go to war for some reasons that Stoics and Erasmians regard as highly suspect.

If these aspects of Utopian foreign policy cannot be accounted

---

Our forefathers have given us . . . [a] striking example of justice toward an enemy: when a deserter from Pyrrhus promised the Senate to administer poison to the king and thus work his death, the Senate and Gaius Fabricius delivered the deserter up to Pyrrhus. Thus they stamped with their disapproval the treacherous murder even of an enemy who was at once powerful, unprovoked, aggressive, and successful. (I.xiii.40)

Later Cicero uses the same episode to illustrate the fundamental point that "nothing can be expedient that is not morally right": "if the mere show of expediency and the popular conception of it are all we want, this one deserter would have put an end to that wasting war and to a formidable foe of our supremacy; but it would have been a lasting shame and disgrace to us to have overcome not by valour but by crime the man with whom we had a contest for glory" (III.xxii.86).

[89] For Erasmus' opposition to the use of mercenaries, see *Adages*, p. 350; and above, Chap. 2, n. 43.

for in terms of the ideals of Erasmian humanists, neither can the
repressive character of the Utopian constitution and the drabness
of Utopian life. Hythloday expresses both the characteristic lib-
ertarianism of humanism and the relatively relaxed attitude of
most humanists toward bodily and esthetic pleasures when he
imagines himself saying in council that a ruler "who cannot
reform the lives of citizens in any other way than by depriving
them of the good things of life must admit that he does not know
how to rule free men" (*Ut.*, p. 97).[90] But Utopian life is highly
regulated, and it exhibits all the grayness that seems an inevitable
corollary of such regulation. Avineri observes that the "totali-
tarianism" of Utopia "comes out in many instances of Utopian
life: the reglementation of daily life, the intellectual indoctri-
nation, the monotonous and uniform daily routine, the strict
control of marriage and divorce, the need for special permits to
move about the country, the standardization of leisure" (p. 287;
cf. pp. 201-2 above). Chambers notes that "even to speak of
State affairs, except at the licensed place and hour, is punishable
in Utopia with death [*Ut.*, p. 125]," and he asks whether "any
State, at any time, [has] carried terrorism quite so far" (p. 137).
And Utopian life is appallingly drab. The cities are as nearly
identical as possible (*Ut.*, p. 113). All citizens of the same sex
and marital status wear identical clothes (p. 127). Moreover, as
James Binder points out, Utopia seems nearly devoid of the arts.
There is music, "but poetry, painting, sculpture, or dancing will
be looked for in vain" (p. 231; cf. Mackie, p. 264).[91]

[90] On humanist attitudes, see Thompson 1955, pp. 176-77; Kristeller 1965,
pp. 26-68; 1972, pp. 129-31; Garin; Baron 1966; Dresden, pp. 87-92.

[91] It is, however, possible to exaggerate the drabness of Utopia: this feature
is to some extent a *trompe-l'œil*. Concentrating, as a political theorist, on institutional arrangements, on what all Utopians have in common, More correspondingly neglects to tell us much about individuality in Utopia, or about
its manifestations in the arts and crafts (cf. Frye, p. 335). But we know that
the Utopians do not share Plato's distrust of the arts, and More does point out,
though the fact is likely to pass unnoticed, that the buildings of Utopia are
handsome (*Ut.*, pp. 121, 231) and that its handicrafts are "of fine workmanship"
(p. 153). The Utopian uniforms, too, are "comely to the eye" (p. 127). In

These dissonances between Utopian practices and humanist ideals, like those implicit in some aspects of Utopian foreign policy, pose a difficult interpretive problem. In particular, they greatly embarrass the interpretation of Utopia as a mirror of a reformed Europe. The principal spokesmen for this view, the humanistic interpreters, have in fact developed a general explanation for these contradictions, which takes the form of suggesting that *Utopia* is a *speculum* of a special, curious kind. While Book I mirrors Europe's current problems without distortion, Book II, the mirror of a reformed society, is partly an ordinary mirror, partly a fun-house mirror, and partly a piece of glass like the troll's eye, which causes him to see black as white, good as bad, and so on. Some parts of the account of Utopia, that is, constitute undisguised recommendations for reform, some are either jokes or distorted or incomplete images that must be discounted, corrected, or completed by the reader, and some Utopian practices must be interpreted as ironic recommendations of their opposites.

The application of this thesis is beset with great practical difficulties. The humanistic interpreters agree that there is no general rule for determining which parts of the mirror exhibit which property; accordingly, the critic must effect this determination by subjecting each part of the account of Utopia to close textual and contextual scrutiny. Having discussed the indirection of *Utopia*, Ames asks "how, with all this dissembling and irony and fantasy, we can decide on a general test for the seriousness of a reformer's views. It is obvious that no over-all rule will be satisfactory, and that each statement must be interpreted concretely in its complex environment" (pp. 84-85). Similarly, Surtz says that "the gravity or levity of each passage must be weighed in itself and in its context to discover if it attacks prevalent abuses or suggests practical reforms" (1957a, p. 4). In cases of the former kind, the interpreter is justified in, as it were, changing

---

the communal halls, moreover, "they burn spices and scatter perfumes and omit nothing that may cheer the company" (p. 145). And the religious festivals that are so important a part of Utopian life offer a good deal of gratification to the senses.

the sign of the passage. Such arguments provide the rationale for the kind of criticism produced by the humanistic interpreters, which typically treats individual segments of the account of Utopia as discrete entities and provides essays on the history of the ideas found in these entities. This approach has proved, as I have said (above, p. 9), useful in illuminating particular passages and in establishing the connection of *Utopia* with the tradition of political theory, but it is, nonetheless, highly problematic.

In practice, the separate "weighing" of each passage seems always to lead to subjectivity. The interpreter is tempted to change the sign of, or dismiss as fantasy, all those passages where the account of Utopia fails to harmonize with his own view of what More should have regarded as serious and important. This problem is illustrated by the fact that interpreters usually accept either Utopian philosophy and religion or Utopian economics as serious, but not both (see above, pp. 182-84). Hexter, as we have seen, dismisses Utopian moral philosophy as "play"; he also finds that More "did not take the religions of the Utopians . . . seriously" (*Ut.*, p. cxxiii; cf. 1952, pp. 51, 56). Clearly the passages that he regards as jokes are those that will not fit into his interpretation.[92] Father Surtz's list of jokes and non-jokes is

[92] In *More's "Utopia,"* Hexter justifies his dismissal of the sections on philosophy and religion on the ground that their meaning is indeterminable:

to regard . . . [these sections] as the key to the interpretation of *Utopia* and to the intent of its author is in effect to surrender at the outset any hope of determining what that intent was. . . . no amount of examination, however close and careful, of the sections on Utopian philosophy and religion can render us certain to what extent the opinions there expressed are More's own. This unresolvable uncertainty is a consequence of the literary form into which More cast *Utopia*. That form is the traveler's tale; the "best state of the commonwealth" is described as a real land existing somewhere on the other side of the earth in More's own time. (pp. 49-50)

Hexter goes on to argue unpersuasively that More was less constrained by accounts of the New World in his description of "secular institutions" than in the description of philosophy and religion, but the reader is bound to wonder why the argument for indeterminableness does not apply equally to all sections of Book II. In fact, although the careful reconstruction by Surtz and others of

more or less the same as Hexter's, but with reversed headings.
For Surtz, Hexter's two dismissible features are the twin sup-
porting pillars of the Utopian commonwealth; correspondingly,
what Surtz tells us More could not have intended as a serious
recommendation is Utopian communism—Hexter's cornerstone.[93]

But the difficulties with the curious-mirror thesis are theoretical as well as practical: it entails a wholly implausible view of
More's intentions and calculations in writing the account of Utopia. If Utopia is a presentation of More's political ideal, why
did he confuse this presentation by the inclusion of jokes, ironic
reversals, and deliberately flawed elements that, as the history of
interpretation shows, are extremely difficult to recognize as such?
The importance and the difficulty of this question for the interpretation of *Utopia* as a *speculum* are vividly illustrated by the
desperation and variety of some of Surtz's attempts to answer it.
1) An ideal commonwealth should include some flaws so as not
to be too discouraging: "All details in his [More's] republic are
not ideal nor perfect. Ideal perfection would defeat his very plea
for a spirit of receptiveness to better things and a spirit of emulation on the part of Europeans" (1957a, p. 4). 2) The flaws
make Utopia credible: "The absurd elements help to impart
verisimilitude to the ideal commonwealth; the wise elements serve
to furnish models for improvement and reform" (*Ut.*, p. 570n).
3) Absurdities are included because unaided reason may produce
absurdities: "If a few institutions in Utopia are labeled absurd,
it is because reason, left to itself, can become logical to the point

---

the intellectual context of individual passages limits the range of possible interpretations more than Hexter thinks, it is true that interpretation via the fun-
house and troll's-eye propositions leads ineluctably toward the conclusion that
Utopia is a kind of pointlessly complicated puzzle, the meaning of which is
impossible to determine with a high degree of completeness. Cf., for example,
the passage from Schoeck quoted above, n. 6, and cf. n. 10.

[93] Avineri calls attention to the arbitrariness of Donner's reading: Donner
brands "as satire those passages whose contents seem objectionable to him, while
considering as 'seriously intended' those with which he happens to agree" (p. 283).

of absurdity" (1957b, p. 12). 4) The inclusion of these features was a mistake: "Unfortunately, for purposes of satire or irony . . . [More] has introduced into his 'philosophical city' institutions which impart an air of realism but which he himself terms silly or even absurd" (1957a, p. 193).

Another answer is that offered by Ames, who suggests that More's purpose in warping his mirror was to protect himself from association with dangerously radical ideas. The argument in support of this position rests on the valid observation that jokes and obscurities, like the book's nature as elaborately self-mocking traveler's tale and the fact that Utopia is praised by Hythloday and partially condemned by the character More, have the effect of distancing or dissociating More from the account of Utopia:

> He partially disowns . . . [*Utopia*] by assigning himself the roles of stenographer and interlocutor, putting the whole of the Utopian plan and the social criticism into the mouth of an invented but life-like character, Hythlodaye, and carefully reserving to himself monosyllables of assent and sentences of protest, particularly protest against the practicability of a community of goods. . . . More's Defoesque realism and fantastic Greek names emphasize the protective paradox. (p. 84; cf. Elliott, p. 329)

But although the effect of these features is to distance More from the Utopian commonwealth, the purpose of this distancing surely cannot be to protect him from association with radical ideas. If this were its function, we should expect distancing techniques to be employed equally in Book I: the ideas of this book are at least as radical as those of Book II, especially in the sense that Book I criticizes existing commonwealths, particularly More's own, whereas Book II deals with an imaginary commonwealth. But while More elaborately dissociates himself from Hythloday's Utopia, he voices strong approval of Hythloday's harsh criticisms of England in Book I: " 'To be sure, my dear Raphael,' I commented, 'you have given me great pleasure, for everything you have said has been both wise and witty' " (*Ut.*, pp. 85-87).

Hexter sums up the matter nicely: "As to attempts to conceal his meaning, no concealed meaning has ever been suggested for any passage of *Utopia* more devastatingly critical of the great and powerful than the explicit statements of a number of passages whose meaning no one has ever disputed or doubted" (1952, p. 12n; cf. Avineri, p. 286). Thus More's dissociation of himself from the Utopian commonwealth, though a fact of importance to interpretation, is of no use to the argument that the account of Utopia is a fiendishly complex mirror of a reformed Europe.

The correct explanation of the discrepancies between Utopian practices and Erasmian ideals, as well as of More's dissociation of himself from Utopia, lies in the fact that Utopia is a strict best-commonwealth exercise and not simply a conglomeration of ideal-sounding features. Indeed the points of *congruence* between Utopian practices and the views of Erasmian humanists and their Stoic predecessors should also be understood in these terms.

The purpose of the best-commonwealth exercise is, as I have said, to determine by reason the constitution of a polity that would act with maximum efficiency to assure that its citizens individually and collectively pursued their real interests. More's idea of what is rational was largely shaped by Stoic and Erasmian views, and there is accordingly considerable harmony between these views and Utopian positions.

Discrepancies between Utopian views and those of Stoic and Christian-Stoic theorists are, however, entailed in the fact that More is acting not as a world-state theorist, whether of the classical or the Christian variety, but as a secular city-state theorist. For example, since Utopia is based on rational, secular premises, the Utopian conception of acceptable military practices is not constrained by revealed Christian imperatives. Moreover, since More is functioning as a city-state theorist, his object is to secure the real interests of the citizens of Utopia, not those of humanity in general. To a large extent, the interests of the Utopians coincide with those of non-Utopians, especially since, as Utopian moral philosophy shows, the keenest mental pleasure depends on one's awareness of not having obtained pleasure at the expense of other men's pleasure. Rational self-interest, then, dictates that, as much as is feasible, the Utopians attempt to secure a good life for all their fellow men. But More, as I have pointed out, is acutely aware of the conflicts that arise in the pursuit of different communal goals. In particular, he is aware of the conflict between achieving the goal of national security and that of equalizing pleasure. Since national security is a contributory goal to the goal of first priority, health, its attainment must take precedence over the attainment of any other goal with which it conflicts. Accordingly, the Utopians can be generous to their neighbors only insomuch as such generosity does not jeopardize their national security: and this, presumably, is the rule that governs their foreign relations. As much as possible, the Utopians implement the ideal of universal brotherhood. But when the implementation of this ideal conflicts with securing the welfare of Utopians, it must be sacrificed.

Precisely where the trade-off between the goal of national security and that of helping all men to a happy life should be established is a matter for the judgment of the theorist. Doubtless the Utopians regret having to act in ways that imply that Utopian lives are more valuable than those of other men, since they know that all men are brothers. But clearly they regard such actions as sometimes necessary to preserve their state, and, as Machiavelli, another city-state theorist, says, "when it is absolutely a question of the safety of one's country, there must be no consideration of just or unjust, of merciful or cruel, of praiseworthy or disgraceful" (*Discourses* III.xli).[94] Doubtless the Utopians, with their hatred

---

[94] As I pointed out earlier (Chap. 2, n. 25), rhetorical theory sanctions the idea that necessity overrides other political considerations. Cicero shows how to argue that a dishonorable course is not dishonorable when necessity demands it: "one should take thought for security in a case in which though honour is lost for the moment while consulting security, it may be recovered in the future by courage and diligence. . . . So in a case of this sort, too, when we seem to consult our security, we shall be able to say with truth that we are concerned about honour, since without security we can never attain to honour" (*Inv.* II.lviii.174). By contrast, Stoic ethical and political theorists establish the trade-

of war, would prefer never to engage in invasive war. But evidently they find it vital to the security of Utopia to assure that their commonwealth is surrounded by stable, friendly, even dependent, neighbors. Happily, Utopian interference in the affairs of neighboring polities often has the added benefit of enhancing the welfare of the citizens of these realms. But even when this is clearly not the case (as in those instances where the Utopians "stir up and involve the neighbors of their enemies"), the Utopians must interfere, if their own security is at stake.

More's sharp awareness of the conflicts between the achievement of different communal goals also provides the explanation for the other major discrepancies between Utopian practices and Erasmian ideals. Utopian repressiveness reflects More's belief that a realistic assessment of man's nature suggests that the goal of freedom conflicts, like the goal of equality (cf. p. 212 above), with the maintenance of stability and efficient production. Since the latter (being contributory to the goal of health) has a higher priority, freedom must, insomuch as there is a conflict, be restricted. Similar considerations account for the drabness of Utopia. The dismal uniformity of Utopian life does not reflect a conviction that such drabness is desirable in itself, for the Utopians believe that "no kind of pleasure is forbidden, provided no harm comes of it" (p. 145; cf. n. 91 above). The proviso here suggests the true explanation, which lies in More's evident conviction that the free development of the material and esthetic delights that would make Utopian life more vivid would seriously inhibit the achievement of more important goals. Labor in Utopia

off at quite a different point. See Chap. 2, n. 65. In his treatment of such conflicts on the individual level, Cicero (here wearing his philosopher's hat) grants that "everybody may prefer to secure for himself rather than for his neighbour what is essential for the conduct of life; but Nature's laws do forbid us to increase our means, wealth, and resources by despoiling others" (*Off.* III.v.22; cf. x.42). Indeed, "for a man to take something from his neighbour and to profit by his neighbour's loss is more contrary to Nature than is death or poverty or pain or anything else that can affect either our person or our property" (v.21; cf. v.26).

is restricted to "only as few crafts as natural needs and conveniences require" (p. 131),[95] in order that as much time as possible be devoted to "the freedom and culture of the mind" (p. 135). One may think that greater diversity in the forms of necessary goods and more production of artistic goods would contribute importantly to mental pleasure, but the Utopians, we recall, hold the principal part of this pleasure to "arise from the practice of the virtues and the consciousness of a good life" (p. 175), and the hedonic calculus demands that no greater pleasure be sacrificed to the attainment of a lesser one. Moreover, there is a potential conflict between the achievement of diversity and the realization of the goals of equalizing pleasure and minimizing opportunities for false pleasure. As Surtz remarks, "the emphasis on uniformity in outward matters in Utopia appears to be motivated by the conviction that individuality in such matters almost inevitably becomes occasion for emulation, vanity, and pride" (p. 387n). Other things being equal, it would, for example, be desirable to give scope to individual taste in dress. But the prohibition of such diversity precludes the possibility of dress becoming a means to false pleasure. Outside Utopia "one man is not satisfied with four or five woolen coats of different colors and as many silk shirts, and the more fastidious not even with ten," but "in Utopia a man is content with a single cape": "There is no reason, of course, why he should desire more, for if he had them he would not be better fortified against the cold nor appear better dressed in the least" (p. 135).

We should note that More does not attempt to conceal the discrepancies between Utopian practices and Erasmian ideals. In the first place, they are rendered conspicuous, like every other feature of Utopia, by More's presentation of the results of his best-commonwealth exercise in the form of a model. Moreover, in some instances he seems particularly to insist on these discrepancies. The dubious nature of some aspects of Utopian for-

[95] I follow Miller (1966, p. 58) in correcting Yale's "as the few needs and conveniences demanded by nature." The Latin is "quam paucas commodus naturae usus postulat."

eign policy is underscored, first, by features of More's rhetoric. The reassuring opening of the section on military affairs, which informs us that the Utopians regard war "with utter loathing" and accordingly "do not lightly go to war," is immediately followed by the disturbingly long list of the "only" reasons for which they *will* go to war.[96] Moreover, the suspicion that some of these reasons would be likely to lead to Utopian involvement in wars of doubtful justice is reinforced by the single particular example of a Utopian war, that "which the Utopians had waged a little before our time on behalf of the Nephelogetes against the Alaopolitans" (p. 201). The account of the cause of this war contains two troubling phrases, which become all the more troubling when we go on to read about the appalling consequences of the war for the vanquished Alaopolitans:

> The Nephelogetic traders suffered a wrong, *as they thought* [ut uisum est ipsis], under pretence of law, *but whether right or wrong* [siue illud ius, siue ea iniuria fuit], it was avenged by a fierce war. Into this war the neighboring nations brought their energies and resources to assist the power and to intensify the rancor of both sides. Most flourishing nations were either shaken to their foundations or grievously afflicted. The troubles upon troubles that arose were ended only by the enslavement and surrender of the Alaopolitans. Since the Utopians were not fighting in their own interest, they yielded them into the power of the Nephelogetes, a

[96] The passage on divorce utilizes the same rhetorical stratagem. We hear first that the Utopians "are satisfied with one spouse [Yale has "wife": cf. Miller 1966, p. 59] and . . . matrimony there is seldom broken except by death" (p. 189), but this opening is immediately followed by a list of additional exceptions. Adultery is a ground for divorce, and so is "intolerable offensiveness" of character ("morum non ferenda molestia"). Moreover, "it sometimes happens . . . that when a married couple agree insufficiently in their dispositions and both find others with whom they hope to live more agreeably, they separate by mutual consent and contract fresh unions, but not without the sanction of the senate" (p. 191). Thus, despite the claim to the contrary, it appears to be as easy to get out of marriage in Utopia as it is to get into war. Cf. n. 82 above, and Dorsch, pp. 356-57.

people who, when the Alaopolitans were prosperous, were
not in the least comparable to them. (p. 201; my emphases)

It is difficult to believe that an ironist of More's sophistication
would offer this account without meaning to prompt his readers
to reflect on the moral irresponsibility inherent in undertaking
such wars for such reasons (cf. Barker, p. 227). Similarly, the
language in which Hythloday describes the Utopians' attitude
toward the Zapoletans is surely designed to suggest the immorality
of this phase of Utopian policy: "The Utopians, just as they seek
good men to use them, so enlist these villains to abuse them
[siquidem ut bonos quaerunt quibus utantur ita hos quoque ho-
mines pessimos quibus abutantur]" (p. 209).

More also decided, in the course of the "second thoughts" that
led to the addition of the dialogue of Book I to the original
Utopia, to emphasize further the unattractiveness of some aspects
of Utopian foreign policy by creating a number of resemblances
between it and the foreign policy of the European rulers scath-
ingly satirized in Hythloday's imaginary meeting of the French
privy council. If the Utopians utilize mercenaries, so do the
French (p. 89). The Utopian policy of sponsoring pretenders to
the thrones of enemy nations also has a French parallel, as do
their attempts to "stir up and involve the neighbors of their
enemies":

Meanwhile the most perplexing question of all comes up:
what is to be done with England? . . . The Scots . . . must
be posted in readiness, prepared for any opportunity to be
let loose on the English if they make the slightest movement.
Moreover, some exiled noble must be fostered secretly . . .
to maintain a claim to the throne.

This passage, composed after the account of Utopian foreign
policy, must surely represent, like other parts of the later-written
segment of *Utopia* that resonate with some aspect of Book II,
More's intention to emphasize "by reiteration or development"

(*Ut.*, p. cxxii; cf. p. 17 above) a point made in the account of Utopia.

Even if such underscoring were not present, it is likely that More's original readers would have been disturbed—and that More counted on their being disturbed—by these aspects of Utopian policy, simply because of their obvious resemblance to the policies of European rulers. English readers, especially, would have been sensitive on the subject of pretenders, since, as Surtz points out, as recently as 1512 "Louis XII had recognized Richard de la Pole as king of England" (1957b, p. 292). Moreover, Richard's brother had a few years earlier "been promised the support of the emperor Maximilian I," and both Maximilian and James IV of Scotland "had furthered the earlier and disastrous schemes of Perkin Warbeck." Louis XII was also adept (like Henry VIII) at stirring up the neighbors of his enemies (p. 293; cf. p. 68 above).

The later-written segment of *Utopia* also invites the reader to question the ideality of Utopia by suggesting that its spokesman, Hythloday, is not an entirely trustworthy assessor (see above, pp. 31, 114-15), and by allowing the character More to call attention to its problematic areas. Presumably More deviated somewhat from the characterizations of his interlocutors in the earlier-written segment (see above, pp. 32-37) precisely so as to give the reader additional guidance in the assessment of Utopia. (We may wish that he had then revised the opening pages of Book I in accordance with this revised view of his characters' functions.) More's preliminary objections to Utopian communism (*Ut.*, p. 107) are, of course, satisfactorily answered. The Utopian constitution has safeguards against the dangers of anarchy and economic disaster that social leveling and common ownership of property entail (cf. above, Chap. 2, n. 88). But at the end of *Utopia*, in a speech that, as Hexter shows (above, p. 13), also forms part of the later-written segment, More again calls attention to problematic aspects of Utopia:

When Raphael had finished his story, many things came
to my mind which seemed very absurdly established in the
customs and laws of the people described—not only in their
method of waging war, their ceremonies and religion, as
well as their other institutions, but most of all in that feature
which is the principal foundation of their whole structure.
I mean their common life and subsistence—without any
exchange of money. This latter alone utterly overthrows all
the nobility, magnificence, splendor, and majesty which are,
in the common opinion,[97] the true glories [*decora*] and
ornaments of the commonwealth. (p. 245)

The final sentence is clearly ironic.[98] It is not necessary to believe
that Utopia represents More's social ideal in order to recognize
that we should not take at face value the character More's concern
at the overthrow of the kinds of "nobilitas, magnificentia, splendor, maiestas" that are commonly thought to be the glories and
ornaments of the commonwealth: these concepts have been harshly
criticized throughout *Utopia*. Skinner is surely correct in regarding the sentence as the "almost desperate[ly]" ironic climax
of More's exploration of the implications of the Stoic notion that
virtue is the only true nobility (1978, p. 259; see above, n. 65).
This nobility, and the true magnificence, splendor, and majesty
that derive from civic virtue, are indeed the "decora atque or-
namenta Reipublicae," and Utopia is rich in these qualities.[99]

[97] I have substituted "in the common opinion" for Yale's misleading "in the
estimation of the common people." The Latin is "ut publica est opinio." See
W. Allen, pp. 116-17; White 1978, p. 140n.

[98] It has been much discussed. See especially Hexter 1952, pp. 35-39; *Ut.*,
pp. lii-liii; 1975; W. Allen; Skinner 1978, pp. 256-59; White 1978; Bradshaw,
p. 25.

[99] White arrives independently at conclusions very similar to Skinner's.
"More no doubt believed that there were such virtues as nobility, magnificence,
splendor, and majesty, but he surely thought that the genuine versions of these
qualities, inasmuch as they could be attributed to a political society, would
depend on goodness and justice" (1978, p. 139). "The Utopian priests are said
to have acquired majesty because of their humanitarian conduct during battles
[*Ut.*, p. 231]. . . . the Utopian city-states are all 'spacious and magnificent'

But the tone of the passage is not uniform. If it is clear that the condemnation of Utopian communism should not be taken literally, it is equally clear that the other aspects of Utopia to which the speech alludes—the Utopians' "method of waging war" and their "ceremonies and religion"—did not entirely correspond to More's ideals, and that he wished to call attention to this fact at the end of his book, even as he wished to provide a final statement on the question of true nobility.

If More could have remedied the defects of Utopia (without violating the rules of the best-commonwealth exercise), presumably he would have: it is hard to imagine why he would play the best-commonwealth game without playing it as well as he could. The fact that he did not remedy these defects, together with the fact that he sometimes appears to go out of his way to call attention to them, suggests that he regarded them (like the discrepancies with Greek conclusions) as important findings—important results, that is, of the tests that he intended the exercise to perform. For these defects make it clear that, although the expedient and the moral are (if we accept the arguments of the Utopian philosophers) identical for the individual, and although they are largely identical for the polity, there are nonetheless several areas in which prudential considerations demand that the commonwealth pursue policies incompatible not only with revealed norms but also with moral norms derivable from reason. If More's model confirms Hythloday's contention that the most rational polity would be communistic, it also shows that his other assertion—that true political prudence is always consistent with morality and religion—is wrong.

[p. 113]. . . . More's idea that nobility and honor depend upon virtue can be seen from his remarks at the beginning of his translation of the life of Pico: '[Learning and virtue] be the things which we may account for our own, of which every man is more properly to be commended than of the nobleness of his ancestors, whose honour maketh us not honourable . . . , for honour is the reward of virtue' " (p. 139n, quoting *English Works*, ed. Campbell, p. 349). White also points out (p. 140n) that More's use of *decora* may reflect Cicero's discussion of *decorum* in *De officiis*. See above, Chap. 2, n. 73.

Doubtless the author of *Utopia* would have preferred that Hythloday be correct. The conclusion that the most rational commonwealth would not always act in accordance with the norms of Christian-Stoic thought must have been profoundly disturbing to him, since it suggests that the truly Christian commonwealth is not even theoretically attainable. For it is not the case, as is sometimes assumed (e.g., Surtz 1957b, p. 308), that the problems with Utopia could be eliminated by adding revealed imperatives to the rational considerations that provide the generative premises of its constitution. Incidental discrepancies between Utopian practices and Christian imperatives—such as those reflected in Utopian divorce and euthanasia—could be easily enough removed. But the major discrepancies arise not from the fact that the premises of Utopia are rational rather than Christian but from conflicts between the achievement of goals—freedom and equality, security and charity—that would presumably be as important to the Christian commonwealth as to the purely rational one. Indeed, the addition of Christian imperatives would only render the theorist's task impossible, since certain resolutions of conflicts that are satisfactory in the rational commonwealth would not be so in a Christian one. Many Utopian expedients in foreign policy, especially, would be unacceptable to a truly Christian commonwealth; yet it seems that the continued existence of the commonwealth depends on occasional recourse to these expedients.

It is not accidental that the most serious problems of Utopia, and the ones to which More most insistently draws attention, are problems of foreign relations. This is always a problematic area in the best-commonwealth exercise, simply because of the systemic nature of its approach to constitutional design. Since the point of the exercise is to secure the good life for those within the system, there must always be differences between the treatment of those inside and those outside its boundaries. The boundaries may be of class as well as of geography. The most disturbing aspects of the best commonwealths of Plato and Aristotle are the discrepancies between the quality of life of the full citizens of the polis and that of its other inhabitants. By extending citizenship to all inhabitants, More eliminates this kind of boundary problem. But the problems at the geographical boundary remain.

Just as the problems of class boundaries can be obviated by extending citizenship to all inhabitants, so the problems at the geographical boundary can be obviated by extending the territory of the system to include the entire world. Such an extension is postulated in Stoic and Christian universal-state theory. But this extension, like the inclusion of Christian imperatives in the set of generative principles, so complicates the systemic equations as to render them insoluble. A number of plausible, durably interesting, solutions for the much simpler—though still very difficult—case of the secular city-state have been produced. But attempts in Christian-Stoic theory (like corresponding attempts in later theory) to produce a plausible detailed design for the world-state seem hopelessly inadequate.

More does not attempt such a solution, but he does extend the geographical boundaries of his best commonwealth beyond those of the city-state, with which the Greek best-commonwealth theorists and their Italian followers had always dealt. Utopia is not a city-state but a federation of fifty-four city-states identical in institutions and size and, as far as geography permits, in appearance (*Ut.*, p. 113). These city-states together occupy a territory the size of England; that is, of a Renaissance nation-state. As Plato and Aristotle provide paradigms for political units of the type characteristic of their political culture, so More attempts the analogous feat for the Europe of his time.[100] This approach to the theory of the nation-state is of dubious value—especially since, as Miller observes (1965-66, p. 308), More's design includes no executive machinery for resolving conflicts of interest among the city-states. For our purposes, however, it is important only to note that although his approach pushes the boundary

[100] There is a precedent of sorts in Plato's account of Atlantis, an island nation divided into ten semi-independent districts (*Critias* 113E-114A). Other parallels between Utopia and Atlantis are discussed by Heiserman, pp. 171-72.

problems out to a considerable distance it offers no solution to
them.

If the dissonances between some aspects of More's most rational
polity and Christian ideals are disturbing, so also is the conclusion, strongly suggested in *Utopia*, that the best commonwealth
or even a good approximation to it cannot be achieved by peaceful,
piecemeal reform—a second point on which Hythloday appears
to be correct. As Plato saw, this conclusion follows from the
systemic view of the polity. Poor education produces poor leaders;
one cannot expect poor leaders to be either willing or able to
reform the polis. The best polis could be realized only by an
absolute ruler (of the right kind), who would begin by eradicating
the existing order: "The first thing our [political] artist must do
. . . is to take human society and human habits and wipe them
clean out, to give himself a clean canvas" (*Rep.* VI.501A). Once
such a man "has power and institutes all the laws and customs
we have described, there's no impossibility in supposing that the
citizens will carry them out" (502B; cf. *Statesman* 296B-E). In
the *Laws*, the Athenian says that "whatever the form of government, the same doctrine holds true: where supreme power in a
man joins hands with wise judgement and self-restraint, there
you have the birth of the best political system, with laws to match;
you'll never achieve it otherwise. . . . though in one sense it is
difficult for a state to acquire a good set of laws, in another sense
nothing could be quicker or easier—granted, of course, the conditions I've laid down" (IV.711E-712A; cf. V.735D).

The same line of thought is, as we have seen, apparent in
Hythloday's arguments in Book I. As a result of poor economic
and educational arrangements, the European ruling class is corrupt. It is foolish to expect that the members of this class will
put into practice the recommendations of political philosophers.
And since the polity is a system of reciprocally-affecting parts,
even when individual reforms are instituted, "while you are intent
upon the cure of one part, you make worse the malady of the
other parts" (*Ut.*, pp. 105-7). There is, of course, the possibility,
left open in the unresolved disagreement at the end of Book I,

that significant reform can be gradually achieved by the "indirect approach"—though even the character More claims only that matters can in this way be made a little less bad.

The unlikelihood of achieving the rational polity by peaceful reform is subtly reinforced in Book II. The constitution of Utopia was not achieved in this way, nor was it created by a native Utopian: it was enacted by Utopus, a foreign conqueror who was (presumably as the result of an appropriate education acquired in some superior political system) a supreme political theorist and statesman (cf. Fleisher, pp. 124, 136).[101] Moreover, Utopus had the best possible materials to work with: a primitive people who constituted a sort of collective tabula rasa and a naturally-defended peninsula that could be sealed off from contamination by turning it into an island. These additional conditions also reflect More's agreement with the Greek theorists. Both Plato and Aristotle emphasize the importance of starting with the best human materials and a suitable territory. But if the rational polity can be achieved only when a foreign conqueror with supreme political ability remolds a primitive people living in a highly favorable territory, then the chances of achieving it are, as Plato allows (*Rep.* IX.592A-B), depressingly small.[102]

[101] The prototypes of Utopus (as of Plato's political artist) are the legendary lawgivers of Greek tradition—Solon, Lycurgus, Pythagoras, and others—who founded or regenerated polities (see Manuel and Manuel, pp. 93-95). Indeed, before the emergence of modern conceptions of the evolutionary or revolutionary formation of constitutions, it was hard to understand their creation in any other terms.

Since Utopia obtained its constitution in this way, and since this constitution so largely determined the stable and prosperous future of the commonwealth, Hythloday's claim (at the end of Book I) that the superiority of Utopia to European commonwealths is owing to the Utopians' "application and industry" and their receptiveness to new ideas (*Ut.*, pp. 107-9) appears to be hardly the whole, or the most important part, of the truth. His overstatement probably reflects More's desire to stress the importance of these traits—just prior to the presentation of the Utopian model with its raft of new ideas.

[102] These considerations largely invalidate Hexter's interpretation of the "structure of More's radicalism," which he summarizes by a quotation from Tawney's *Equality*: "Men have given one stamp to their institutions; they can

More's melancholy conclusions suggest the proper explanation
for the curious fact that he takes the trouble to construct a best
commonwealth, repeatedly hints that he is proud of the construction, and yet dissociates himself from his commonwealth by putting its description into the mouth of Hythloday, by putting
disavowals of it into his own mouth, and by peppering the description with mocking names. More has, and knows he has,
performed the best-commonwealth exercise with unprecedented
sophistication. His results, moreover, embody a profound criticism of the elitist conclusions of earlier theorists and provide an
ideal standard for actual polities that is, from the point of view
of a Christian humanist, much preferable to the standards provided by his predecessors. But his conclusions about the way a
rational polity would act are in some respects strikingly discordant
with his own political ideals, and his conclusions about the near-
impossibility of substantial peaceful reform are at odds with the
reformist impulses apparent in his writings during these years—
including *Utopia* (see R. P. Adams 1962, *passim*). The conclusion
that the rational polity could be created only by a strongman must
also have been disturbing to him. In echoing this Platonic notion,
he is in agreement with most other Renaissance theorists, from
Petrarch to Machiavelli, Vives, and Erasmus, and it is apparent
from the respectful way in which Utopus is treated that More
was to some extent susceptible to the attraction that the figure of
the lawgiver held for other Renaissance political writers.[103] Yet
one cannot believe that More, with his loathing of militarism,
was altogether happy with the conclusion that thorough reform
could come only through force.[104] Since this and the other mel-

give another. They have idealized money and power; they can 'choose' equality"
(p. 269, quoted *Ut.*, p. cxxiv).

[103] On the Renaissance fascination with the lawgiver, see F. Gilbert, pp.
475-76. And see Wilkins, pp. 63-73, 134-35, 142-47 (Petrarch); Skinner
1978, p. 159 (Machiavelli); R. P. Adams 1962, pp. 286 (Vives), 299 (Erasmus).

[104] On More's aversion to militarism, see R. P. Adams 1962, *passim*. Fleisher
(pp. 139-42) shows that revolutionary change was antipathetic to More and
Erasmus. See also Baker-Smith, p. 17.

Since Utopus' invasion of Utopia, which had such good consequences, was ancholy findings of his exercise seem inescapable, they must be presented—but at least he can avoid the appearance of applauding them, by using the various devices of dissociation to keep Utopia at arm's length.

At the same time, the fact that More stresses these conclusions helps to complete the solution of the puzzle of the intended relation between the book and its audience. For in suggesting that *Utopia* is designed as a protest against the ideas of secular theorists, Chambers (pp. 131-33; see p. 111 above) is only half right: it is also designed as a corrective to the naive optimism of More's fellow Christian humanists (more generally, of the Christian-Stoic tradition of political theory as a whole). The lesson that *Utopia* directs to these thinkers is that it is not enough for the normative theorist to function simply as a moralist, criticizing existing practices and institutions and listing ideal alternatives. He must consider not only what should be but what *can* be; consider, that is, the design of plausible means for implementing ideals, and questions of the degree of compatibility of his ideals and of the trade-offs that it may be necessary to make in realizing them.

Hythloday's narrative closes with a peroration that recapitulates most of the themes of *Utopia*. He dilates on the inequities that are at once Europe's worst problem and the cause of other problems. In Europe, while "any nobleman whatsoever or goldsmith-banker or moneylender . . . attain[s] a life of luxury and grandeur on the basis of his idleness or his nonessential work[,] . . . the common laborer, the carter, the carpenter, and the farmer" earn for their vital services "such scanty fare and lead such a miserable life that the condition of beasts of burden might seem far preferable" (*Ut.*, p. 239). Law does not reduce these injustices; indeed, it is manipulated to add to them: "the rich every day extort a part of their daily allowance from the poor not only by private fraud but by public law" (p. 241).[105] In short, in "all

in itself an act hard to reconcile with morality, his career underscores again the nonidentity of the politically prudent and the moral.

[105] Cf. Hanson, p. 182: "Perhaps Holdsworth exaggerated when he said of the [English] fifteenth century that the 'forms of law and physical violence had

commonwealths flourishing anywhere today," one "can see nothing else than a kind of conspiracy of the rich, who are aiming
at their own interests under the name and title of the commonwealth."[106]

The result of this economic injustice is that neither the rich
nor the poor have decent lives: "when these evil men with insatiable greed have divided up among themselves all the goods
which would have been enough for all the people, how far they
are from the happiness of the Utopian commonwealth!" In contrast to Utopia, European life is characterized by "fraud, theft,
rapine, quarrels, disorders, brawls, seditions, murders, treasons,
poisonings, . . . fear, anxiety, worries, toils, and sleepless nights"
(p. 243). Even the rich must "feel that it would be a much better
state of affairs to lack no necessity than to have abundance of
superfluities—to be snatched from such numerous troubles rather
than to be hemmed in by great riches." Thus the unjust policies
of the European nations do not even serve the interests of those
in whose interest they have been developed. Correspondingly,
the truly expedient policy is, Hythloday still insists, identical to
the just, the truly rational to the righteous. Either "a man's regard
for his own interests or the authority of Christ our Savior . . .

---

come to be merely alternative instruments to be used as seemed most expedient
[p. 416],' but it is clear that many great men entertained no scruples and few
qualms in turning the processes of law to their own purposes."

[106] As R. M. Adams (p. 89n) and others have suggested, Hythloday's words
may allude to Augustine's maxim, "Remota . . . iustitia quid sunt regna nisi
magna latrocinia?" (*City of God* IV.4). The assertion that Utopia alone "can
rightly claim the name of a commonwealth" (*Ut.*, p. 237) may also reflect
Augustine, who cites Cicero's *De re publica* to the effect that "a commonwealth
. . . is 'the weal of the community,' and . . . 'the community' . . . [is] not
any and every association of the population, but 'an association united by a
common sense of right and a community of interest.' " Thus a commonwealth
"only exists where there is a sound and just government, whether power rests
with a monarch or with a few aristocrats, or with the people as a whole. But
when the king . . . or the nobles . . . or the people are unjust . . . , then . . .
the commonwealth is not corrupt, . . . but, by a logical deduction from the
definition, it ceases to exist at all" (*CG* II.21, summarizing *Rep.* I.xxv.39,
III.xxxi.43-xxxiii.45).

would long ago have brought the whole world to adopt the laws of the Utopian commonwealth," were it not for pride. And though we have seen that Utopia does not entirely justify the claims that Hythloday makes for it, it is still true, as More ends his book by acknowledging, that "there are very many features in the Utopian commonwealth which it is easier . . . to wish for in our countries than to have any hope of seeing realized" (p. 247).

The key to Utopian felicity lies in the correct approach to social problems that their commonwealth embodies. The superiority of Utopia to Europe derives from the fact that the Utopians "have adopted such institutions of life as have laid the foundations of the commonwealth not only most happily, but also to last forever, as far as human prescience can forecast" (p. 245). Underlying the design of these institutions is the systemic approach to problems, in which root causes, rather than effects, are the objects of attack. If in Europe crimes "are avenged rather than restrained by daily executions" (p. 243), in Utopia "they have extirpated the *roots* of ambition and factionalism along with all the other vices" (p. 245; my emphasis; cf. p. 243.2).

The result is a commonwealth in which the domestic problems of European nations discussed in Book I have been eliminated. There is "no poor man and no beggar" (p. 239) in Utopia, no greed for money, and thus no "fraud, theft, rapine," and so on. Hythloday might have added that in Utopia there is no problem of counsel, since, as we have seen, the institutional arrangements of the commonwealth are such that all high officials are humanist philosophers.

When we see Europe and the model of the alternative commonwealth juxtaposed in this overview, the benefits of a planned, rational society are clear. Yet the enormous attractiveness of a sensibly planned society does not lead More either to underestimate the difficulties of realizing one or to downplay the fact that his model is problematic. Neither Hythloday nor the character More imagines that Europe *will* adopt the laws of the Utopian commonwealth, and More's final criticism of Utopia (p. 245) reemphasizes the questionable aspects of this system.

But if More's model of the rational commonwealth is problematic, this very fact, together with his insistence on the urgency of European problems and his object lesson in the method of developing solutions to them, constitutes a challenge to other thinkers (cf. Johnson, pp. 134-35). Perhaps the disturbing results of More's best-commonwealth exercise stem from errors of play. His recognition of this possibility is embodied in the Utopian prayer, which acknowledges that there may be a better commonwealth than Utopia (*Ut.*, p. 237; cf. p. 207 above).[107] Given the enormous complexity of the best-commonwealth exercise when it is rightly conceived, it is almost impossible to avoid errors. It is not unlikely, then, that the correct solution of the systemic equations is somewhat different. Nevertheless, *Utopia* shows what is appallingly wrong with all existing commonwealths and how to go about developing solutions for their problems. And the model that it includes, though unattractive in some respects, is designed so that no inhabitant of the polity is hungry, no one homeless, and so that virtue rather than vanity and vice is rewarded. Until the theorist can devise a commonwealth in which such blessings can coexist with at least some of the desirable things sacrificed to attain them in Utopia, he has no right to depreciate More's model.

If the primary purpose of *Utopia* was to stimulate political thought in this way, its purpose has been abundantly fulfilled. The challenge of the book has been taken up many times in the subsequent centuries, by a variety of thinkers who grasped with varying degrees of sophistication what More was about. What all grasped was the superiority of his method of presentation of

[107] See also the second letter to Giles, where More says it is not so remarkable that an "unusually sharp" reader "has detected that some little absurdities exist in the institutions of Utopia or that I have devised some things not expedient enough in the framing of a commonwealth. Why should he be so minded as if there were nothing absurd elsewhere in the world or as if any of all the philosophers had ever ordered the commonwealth, the ruler, or even the private home without instituting some feature that had better be changed?" (*Ut.*, p. 249). Cf. Chap. 2, n. 29.

results to that of earlier best-commonwealth theorists. Yet just as the vividness of the Utopian model helps to reveal the shortcomings of More's commonwealth, so also has it helped to reveal the greater weaknesses of the models of his successors. The first Utopia remains the most tantalizing, the most nearly successful.

While we await a more satisfactory comprehensive solution, and wrestle with the problem of how to implement one, we can (as even Hythloday acknowledges) lighten to some extent the "heavy and inescapable burden of poverty and misfortunes" of the greatest and best part of mankind by implementing the kind of partial solutions that Book I shows how to develop. For despite the obstacles to reform implicit in the structure of government, some of these partial solutions *do* get implemented, and some of them result in a modest net improvement in the health of society. As he finished his book, More was about to assume the second possible political role of the humanist philosopher: to try, since he cannot hope to see all turned to good, to make things "as little bad" as possible.

Epilogue
⟨⟩

"Utopia" and Renaissance Humanism

The starting point of this study was the contention that *Utopia* is a product of Renaissance humanism. Its results therefore appear paradoxical. On the one hand, we have seen that the book is characteristic of early sixteenth-century humanism in style and form, that it is even more deeply indebted to the classical works that underlie humanist political thought than has been realized, and that the issues with which More grapples are central to humanist political writing. On the other hand, More's positions on several of these issues dissent sharply from those of other humanists; and I have argued throughout that *Utopia* embodies distinctively modern elements of substance and method that separate More from all but the most advanced humanist political writers. In its very dissent from the positions taken in other humanist writings, however, *Utopia* can be seen to be characteristic of the best work of the humanist tradition. Moreover, it is possible to show that the surprising modernity of More's book derives from his profound grasp of some quintessentially humanist concepts.

The discrepancies between the positions of *Utopia* and those of other humanists has, as we saw in Chapter Three, greatly exercised the humanistic interpreters. Their response to these discrepancies, and the characteristic fault of this critical school, has been a dogged determination to make them disappear.

At least in part, this determination stems from the historically inaccurate conception of Renaissance humanism shared by these scholars. In this conception, which until a few years ago was nearly universal among English-speaking historians, humanism is identified with Erasmian Christian humanism and defined not only in terms of the humanists' classical preferences in literary form and style but also, and primarily, in terms of the philosophic and religious views of Erasmian humanists.[1] Defined in this way, humanism is seen as essentially monolithic and static. Once it is established that *Utopia* is a humanist work (by its embodiment of many of the characteristic humanist elements of form and substance) and that it is a serious work of political theory (by parallels between political views embodied in it and those espoused elsewhere by More and other humanists), this conception encourages and indeed requires the conclusion that More's book must be a kind of fictionalized party manifesto, the literarily sophisticated political plank in the platform of Erasmian humanism.

Recent studies, however, have demonstrated the insufficiency of this view of humanism. Above all, the work of Paul Oskar Kristeller has shown that it is impossible to define humanism as a whole in terms of a shared philosophical or religious position, simply because there is no such position that is common to all humanists (see, e.g., 1962). Kristeller's work is complemented by that of a number of other historians who have, in the past four decades, produced studies of particular phases of the humanist tradition. These studies suggest that the substantive interests of humanists are usually a product of local factors, that it is only particular subtraditions, such as Erasmian humanism, that exhibit a significant homogeneity of substantive interests and positions, and that even these individual subtraditions are fre-

---

[1] The most influential formulation of this conception has perhaps been Douglas Bush's, in *The Renaissance and English Humanism*. See, e.g., pp. 54-57. Bush's conviction that Erasmian positions are characteristic of humanism as a whole reflects especially the influence of Toffanin. To be sure, Bush recognizes, as some of his followers do not, that there were also many nonreligious humanists (pp. 40-41, 57).

The persistence of the identification of humanism with Christian humanism is illustrated in Elton 1977, pp. 12-15.

quently marked by, and are in fact often energized by, lively disagreements over substantive issues (see Bouwsma 1966, 1973). Humanism, as Bouwsma has said, "was a single movement in much the sense that a battlefield is a definable piece of ground" (1975, p. 3).

When one approaches *Utopia* with this plural conception of humanism in mind, the predisposition to establish the identity of More's views with those of all other humanists, and to be embarrassed when such identity cannot be established, does not operate. On the contrary, one is prepared to find that the book, directed as it is primarily to humanists, may be largely concerned with More's disagreements with other humanists, even with those of his own Erasmian subtradition. Thus Quentin Skinner, the first of the humanistic interpreters to have assimilated the lessons of recent studies of humanism, has recognized that *Utopia* is not simply a statement of a humanist orthodoxy.[2] Although More's book has much in common with other northern humanist works, Skinner says, "it also embodies by far the most radical critique of humanism written by a humanist" (1978, p. 256). Interestingly, Skinner specifies the concerns of Machiavelli's *Prince* in much the same way. *The Prince* reflects "the values and preoccupations characteristic of the mirror-for-princes *genre* as a whole" (p. 128) but also Machiavelli's concern "to challenge and repudiate his own humanist heritage" at certain points (p. 129; cf. above, pp. 80-83).

Skinner's application of this approach to the interpretation of *Utopia* is, however, too restricted. He cites only two instances of More's departure from standard humanist positions. First, More attacks "the unduly comfortable social philosophy of his fellow humanists" by insisting "that if we are genuinely concerned to establish a virtuous commonwealth, we must abandon the pretence that our present-day nobles are men of any real nobility,

---

[2] For Skinner's conception of humanism, see the beautifully lucid syntheses in *Foundations*, pp. 35-41, 69-112. Dermot Fenlon also discusses More's disagreements with other humanists. And see Bradshaw, esp. pp. 4-5.

and abolish the entire structure of 'degree' in the name of ensuring that only men of true virtue are treated with due honour and reverence" (p. 259). Second, More radically "parts company . . . with his humanist contemporaries" by insisting that the only way to dismantle "the existing structures of 'degree'·" is to abolish money and private property (pp. 260-61). This critique of humanist views is effected by rigorously following out the implications of the ancient notions, repeated frequently by humanists, that virtue is the only true nobility and that private property is a principal cause of social evils (cf. above, p. 242, and n. 65). But the fact that *Utopia* embodies these radical positions was already clear to Hexter, and Skinner's advance consists only in the recognition that More's emphasis on them amounts to a criticism of the inconsistent views of other humanists. *Utopia* is still regarded, as by the other humanistic interpreters, simply as prescriptive theory, except that two of the central prescriptions are recognized as disputing those of other humanists. Skinner's reading thus makes it more plausible that More should have addressed such a book to humanists (something that is not, as we have seen [pp. 25-26 above], made at all plausible in previous humanistic interpretations), but it leaves the non-ideal features of Utopia as mystifying as before—as Skinner acknowledges.[3]

My own reading of *Utopia* suggests that More's critique of humanist political theory and its classical sources (for it is these sources that he directly engages) is much broader, and that it takes the form of showing how the application of analytic methods appropriated and refined from Greek political theory leads to largely different conclusions from those reached by other theorists. The critique developed in this way is directed at both the

---

[3] "*Utopia* remains an exceptionally puzzling work, with a depth of irony which is sometimes hard to gauge, and a tone which is often disconcertingly variable. Sometimes More manages to strike an apparently effortless note of sweetness and light. . . . But sometimes he appears to be commending a remarkably unimaginative way of life in a strangely solemn style" (p. 256). Skinner, of course, does not think *Utopia* is addressed primarily to humanists. See above, p. 26.

facile idealism of Christian humanists and the facile cynicism of secular humanists.

To Christian humanists, More directs an object lesson in the proper approach to the analysis of social problems, a lesson that suggests the extreme difficulty of achieving solutions to them. This difficulty stems from the structural nature of the problems. It is not enough for the social theorist to elaborate (like the Stoics) the ideals that should inform policy in the area under consideration. He must trace the problem to its roots in the social structure and propose legal and institutional changes that will eliminate these roots. He must also carefully trace the ramifications of his proposed changes, to be sure that in curing one problem he does not create another. Given this view of social problems, moreover, it is foolish to imagine that substantial reform is likely, because the possible instigators of change—rulers and their councils— are themselves, in the current structure of European society, almost inevitably corrupt. Book II provides a model of a comprehensive application of the systemic approach to the ordering of society and in the process suggests that, despite the Stoics' claim that the useful always harmonizes with the good, entirely satisfactory solutions may not be even theoretically possible: there appears to be an inescapable trade-off between the requirements for securing the commonwealth, and the attainment of freedom for its inhabitants and full justice in its dealings with its neighbors. Thus the unattractive features of Utopia signify crucial aspects of More's conclusions.

At the same time, *Utopia* embodies a critique of the *realpolitisch* tendencies of secular humanist theory. This critique takes the form of showing that the dictates of political prudence, though not always identical to those of morality, do not differ from them as much, or as often, as the secular theorists imagine. More establishes this point by demonstrating that the rational pursuit of political expediency, quite independent of moral considerations, normally dictates policies identical to those dictated by morality. The supposedly expedient European solutions to the problems of theft and poverty are in fact as inexpedient as they are immoral, while the pursuit of self-interest by immoral means on the part of monarchs is, as Hythloday's imaginary council meetings suggest, as destructive to the monarchs as to their people. The best-commonwealth exercise of Book II attacks the Greek sources of the notion that the most rational polity would be characterized by gross inequities and militarism. It is true that the rational polity would not always act in ways consistent with Stoic and Christian conceptions of morality, but the exceptions are much less common than Greek theory suggests.

More's disagreements with other humanists, then, should be understood as characteristic manifestations of the internal dialectic of this heterogeneous and lively tradition. Similarly, the modernity of *Utopia* can be accounted for in terms of More's humanism.

This modernity has two elements. First, as is obvious to any twentieth-century reader, the Utopian construct includes a number of features that strikingly foreshadow the modern welfare state. Second, the book embodies, as we have seen, a distinctively modern approach to the analysis of social problems and their possible solutions. More shares with his most advanced contemporaries the conception of the commonwealth as a network of reciprocally-affecting parts and the conviction that the causes of social problems, and the effects of proposed solutions, can be ascertained by rational analysis. He goes beyond these contemporaries, and anticipates the social thought of later times, in suggesting the importance of controlled experimental tests of solutions and in the notion that a partial test can be effected by the construction of an imaginative model.

In a sense, the presence of the first kind of modernity renders the presence of the second unsurprising. We are by now accustomed to the fact that More was amazingly prescient in adumbrating various institutions of modern states: we should expect that these modern results were obtained by methods that also anticipate modern ones, since otherwise it is not clear how More *could* have achieved them. In another sense, however, the fact that *Utopia* embodies modern elements of either kind is both surprising and troubling. How are we to account for the circumstance that an early sixteenth-century thinker on the periphery of Europe managed to produce such an advanced book?

We may begin by observing that the answer is *not* found in More's situation as an Englishman. I have, throughout, said little about the connection between *Utopia* and English political and social realities or previous English political theory—a lack of emphasis that has perhaps been puzzling in a study that claims to offer a contextual approach to More's book. The explanation lies in the fact that my principle has been to include only those matters that elucidate the argument of the book and its significance in intellectual history. I have found that information about English life and theory rarely satisfies this criterion. Although More's thought was of course partly shaped by his experience as an Englishman—something that is especially clear in the Morton episode—the explication of his thought requires only sporadic reference to that experience.

The claim that *Utopia* is related only tangentially to English political reality and political thought finds indirect confirmation in D. W. Hanson's study of English political thought from the Anglo-Saxon period through the seventeenth century. Hanson is exclusively concerned with the kind of thought that *is* connected with its social and political milieu—what he calls "operative political thought," "the ideas and assumptions which accompany and inform the actual political life of the age" (p. 12). In his careful survey, he does not find occasion even to mention *Utopia*. (More himself is mentioned only in connection with his controversy with Christopher St. Germain [pp. 256, 263].) Indeed, reading Hanson's book one is struck by the nearly total absence of anything that helps to explain the nature—or even the existence—of *Utopia*. English politics offers as little help in accounting for the substance of *Utopia* as for its methods. Hanson shows that in the Tudor period the medieval conception of the necessity of a hierarchical ordering of society remained "easily the leading social idea" (p. 17), and that "from the point of view of the history of political thought, the most striking feature of the Tudor era was its exaltation of kingship" (p. 253). Examination of this part of the context of *Utopia*, then, can hardly supply an explanation for the fact that one Tudor thinker was able to (and interested to) envision, and present as at least partly attractive, an egalitarian republic.[4]

All the same, Hanson's study suggests where the explanation *does* lie. "Operative political thought" is defined in distinction to "systematic political theory—grand theory if you will" (p. 12). *Utopia*, a dialogue *de optimo reipublicae statu*, belongs to the tradition of grand theory. This fact not only explains the tangential nature of the connection between *Utopia* and previous English thought but also suggests the source of More's theoretical concerns. As Hanson points out, systematic theory forms a coherent and nearly closed "universe of discourse." Works in this tradition refer primarily to, and consequently are explicable primarily in terms of, other such works. Although they may (like *Utopia*) draw examples and theoretical ideas from their local environments, these materials are normally assimilated to the forms of thought characteristic of the tradition. Moreover, the Renaissance branch of systematic theory to which *Utopia* belongs has no earlier English members: perforce, the literary antecedents of *Utopia* are continental. By the same token, More's theoretical concerns derive from systematic theory. It is doubtless the case, as Hanson claims, that civic consciousness did not become a feature of operative English political thought before the seventeenth century, and yet it is scarcely true that in that century "for the first time since classical antiquity . . . men undertook a completely general discussion of the nature and purpose of society and government from a humanistic standpoint" (p. 310), or that "the very idea of self-conscious, deliberate change of government

---

[4] One way in which More's thought *is* characteristically English is suggested by Elton's remarks on the conservative or restorative nature of the proposals found in English social thought of the early sixteenth century (1977, p. 5). Hythloday criticizes mindless conservatism (*Ut.*, pp. 57-59), and his proposals are radical in means, but sometimes their object is to restore things to a previous condition (e.g., pp. 69-71), and always it is to realize traditional Stoic and Christian ideals.

in accordance with human preferences had been in eclipse since classical antiquity" (p. 329). For these topics are, as Hanson's allusions to antiquity suggest, legacies of systematic theory, and they are present in *Utopia* and some other pre-seventeenth-century works of systematic theory. In particular, the fact that Utopia is a republic rather than an hereditary monarchy reflects the revival, as part of Italian Renaissance political theory (and historiography) of classical theory, in which republicanism is of central interest. Similarly, More's methods are, as we have seen, an extension of those embodied in the theoretical works of Plato and Aristotle.

The connection of *Utopia* with the tradition of systematic theory, then, helps to account both for More's concerns and for the modernity of his thought. If to a considerable extent modern political thought is a revival and extension of Greek thought, then More managed to anticipate some modern conceptions because he was an extraordinarily perceptive and creative responder to the Greek tradition.

But this is as much as to say that the modernity of *Utopia* is explicable in terms of More's humanism: for it is his humanism that leads him to concentrate his attention on, and shape his book in ways suggested by, ancient works of grand theory. Indeed, More's humanism accounts not merely for his focus on the ancient works but also for the particular nature of his response to them. His apprehension and extension of themes of classical theory, and especially of the methods of Plato and Aristotle, was facilitated by the special perspective afforded (to a brilliant man) by features of the humanist tradition.

If humanism cannot be defined in terms of a philosophical or religious position, it can, as Kristeller shows, be defined in terms of its connection with the rhetorical tradition. The professional ancestors of the humanists were the rhetoricians—the *dictatores*, notaries, and public orators—of medieval Italy; the transforming step between *dictator* and humanist occurred in the late thirteenth century, when some of these rhetoricians developed, under the influence of French classicism, the novel idea that "in order to write and to speak well it was necessary to study and to imitate the ancients" (Kristeller 1961, p. 13). Humanism thus originated in a drive to classicize rhetorical practice (cf. above, p. 75).

The connection of humanism with rhetoric has a range of implications for humanist political thought. Most obviously, as we have seen (above, p. 86), it determines the genres of political writing and its permeation with the values of Roman Stoicism, which was, especially through Cicero, entwined with the rhetorical tradition. Less obviously, but at least as important, the connection between humanism and rhetoric is related to the characteristic historical sensitivity of humanist thought and to its civic and pragmatic emphases.

Renaissance humanism is in its nature an historical enterprise. The aim of classicizing rhetorical culture presupposes the conception that rhetorical practice changes over time, and that the practice of a particular era can be codified and resurrected. As the humanists pursued this aim, their skills as historical researchers improved not only by experience but also in consequence of their increasing contact with the classical historians and the comments on historiography and critical method in the classical rhetorical manuals (see Logan, pp. 17-20). The critical techniques revived from classical tradition were in turn supplemented by the humanists' development, in their attempt to recover and order the classical heritage, of various applications of the concept of anachronism (see Burke, esp. pp. 21-49).

One result of these processes was the consolidation of a sophisticated method of historical and philological criticism that, as Kristeller points out (1962, p. 17), became an identifying mark of the Renaissance humanist. The crucial feature of this method is its contextualism. In contrast to the scholastics, who normally treat texts as collections of discrete, isolable sentences, humanists characteristically consider literary works as wholes and within the contexts provided by different kinds of historical knowledge: of the biography of the author, of the nature of his social and cultural milieu, and of the grammatical and rhetorical conventions prevailing when he wrote.

A second, subtler result of the humanists' affiliation with the rhetorical tradition was the permeation of humanism by what Bouwsma calls the "ideological implications" of rhetoric (1976, p. 422n). In ancient and later culture, rhetoric was often regarded as the rival of philosophy. At the base of this rivalry is the fact that these two educational traditions embody fundamentally opposed conceptions of man's nature and the proper use of the mind. Philosophy is concerned with the universal, the unchanging, in human nature and the world. Reason is man's primary faculty, and the highest use of reason lies in the discovery and contemplation of Truth. By contrast, rhetoric is concerned with the changing, the actualities of particular times and places. As Bouwsma writes, rhetoric is "agnostic in regard to general propositions; from its standpoint man . . . [cannot] hope to penetrate to the ultimate order of things but only make particular sense of his immediate experience" (p. 425). Its varied strategies of persuasion imply a view of man as a "complex being, a dynamic and unpredictable bundle of psychic energies, simultaneously sensual, passionate, intellectual, and spiritual" (p. 424; cf. above, p. 160). This being finds fulfillment not "through contemplation but only through active engagement with the demands of life, especially in society" (p. 426; see also Seigel; Struever; Logan, pp. 16-34).

The consequences for Italian political thought of the humanists' immersion in rhetoric have been explored by J.G.A. Pocock. The values of rhetoric are "civic and active" (p. 59); the assumption of these values by Italian humanists encouraged the emergence of the "civic humanism" described by Baron and Garin. At the same time, as Jerrold Seigel shows, Cicero's ambivalence about the relative merits of rhetoric and philosophy— in effect of *negotium* and *otium*—was passed on via Petrarch to later humanists, so that the dialectical confrontation of action and contemplation became a standard theme of humanist writing.

Pocock also explains the difference between Italian and English political thought in the late fifteenth and early sixteenth centuries in terms of the consequences of affiliation with the rhetorical tradition:

rhetoric, occupying a place in Italian thought comparable with that occupied by [the concept of] experience in the thought of Fortescue, is in virtue of its political character far more positive and active; it is forward-looking and per-suades men to do things, whereas experience results only in discovery of what they have already done. A world where rhetoric ranks equal with philosophy is a world of face-to-face political decisions; a world where experience and custom occupy its place is one of institutionalized traditions.

This contrast between Italian and English political thought is generally valid. But we should recall that *Utopia* includes face-to-face discussions about political decisions, that the discussions feature an unresolved debate on the relative merits, for the humanist moral philosopher, of *negotium* and *otium*,[5] and that they open with mockery of traditionalism—characterized by Hythloday as the view that "it would be a dangerous thing to be found with more wisdom on any point than our forefathers" (*Ut.*, p. 59). The explanation for the anomalously "Italian" character of More's book lies in the fact that it is not just Italy where rhetoric ranks equal with philosophy, but wherever there is a humanist. Pocock argues that the themes of Florentine political thought led, when transplanted first to the English seventeenth century and then to the American eighteenth, to the emergence of the modern "Atlantic republican tradition"; like the Italians, More anticipates the development of this tradition in part because his thought, like theirs, is permeated by the inherent attitudes and concerns of the rhetorical tradition.

More's approach to Greek theory is also characteristic of the most sophisticated applications of the humanist critical proce-dures. Whereas the recovery of the works of city-state theory meant for less profound political thinkers, including Erasmus, only the provision of new sources of *sententiae* to be inserted in

[5] Atypically, contemplative withdrawal is advocated in *Utopia* by the repub-lican Hythloday. In Italian political theory, republicanism is normally linked with praise of the active life. See Pocock, pp. 49-80; Baron 1966.

appropriate chapters of their *specula*, More grasps these texts as wholes and is thus able to comprehend their deepest significance, which resides not in the particular observations and recommendations of individual passages but in the holistic and comparative approach to the design and analysis of constitutions that underlies these local features. At the same time, the freedom that he feels in disagreeing with, and venturing to correct, the Greek works also reflects the humanist sense of history. For, as Garin and others have pointed out, the humanists' restoration of classical works to their historical contexts entailed the recognition that these were works of mortal men, who were limited both personally and by their cultural circumstances. As a result, it became thinkable for the first time to disagree with classical authorities, to attempt to move beyond them.[6]

Moreover, the theoretical advances that More effects are characteristically humanist. The essence of the historical sense is the realization that context affects significance. More's appreciation of the systemic approach of Plato and Aristotle in itself reflects this realization, since the notion that a law or institution can be judged only in relation to its social and political context is at the heart of this approach. More's sensitivity to the importance of context is implicit in the comprehensive nature of the approach to reform in Book II and in the careful, appropriate modification, in both books, of ideas and institutions borrowed from previous theory and practice, and it is explicit in Morton's response to

[6] Cf. Petrarch on Aristotle: "I certainly believe that Aristotle was a great man who knew much, but he was human and could well be ignorant of some things, even of a great many things" (*On His Own Ignorance and That of Many Others*, p. 74). Bacon is less respectful: "Men become attached to certain particular sciences and speculations, either because they fancy themselves the authors and inventors thereof, or because they have bestowed the greatest pains upon them and become most habituated to them. But men of this kind, if they betake themselves to philosophy and contemplations of a general character, distort and colour them in obedience to their former fancies; a thing especially to be noticed in Aristotle, who made his natural philosophy a mere bond-servant to his logic, thereby rendering it contentious and well nigh useless" (*New Organon* LIV).

Hythloday's suggestion that England adopt the Polylerite system of criminal justice and in More's criticism of the philosophy that thinks that "everything is suitable to every place."[7] Correspondingly, More's great contributions to the methodology of systemic theory—his realization of the value of experimental tests of proposed solutions to social problems, and the idea that the construction of an imaginative model can serve as a partial test—constitute responses to his sense of the polity as a complex network of reciprocally-affecting parts.

These advances are also characteristic of humanism in another way. Like the heavy reliance on comparative political examples throughout *Utopia*, they reflect the humanist preference for concretion over abstraction, for argument by example over pure dialectics. This preference, which stems in part from the connection of humanism with the pragmatic rhetorical tradition, is also manifest in More's choice of substantive questions for examination. Skinner suggests that it is important to consider not only what a political theorist includes but also what he may be "polemically ignoring" (1978, p. xiii). What More ignores are most of the traditional speculative questions of systematic theory, such as those of the definition of justice and the sources and limits of political authority. Like other humanists, and unlike scholastically-oriented theorists, More is uninterested in such ques-

---

[7] See above, pp. 61-62, 115-17. More's awareness of the principle that context affects significance is also apparent in the fact that the Utopians regard it as appropriate for their "Financial Agents" in other countries "to live there in great style [*magnifice*] and to play the part of magnates" (p. 215)—behavior that would be wholly unacceptable in Utopia itself—and in Hythloday's remark on the Utopians' use of gold and silver to make "chamber pots and all the humblest vessels" (p. 153): this practice, "as it is consonant with the rest of their institutions, so it is extremely unlike our own . . . and therefore incredible except to those who have experience of it" (pp. 151-53). Cf. also More's later statement of the principle: "Hard is it . . . in many maner thinges, to bid or forbede, afferm or denye, reprove or alow, a mater nakidly proponid & put forth or presisely to say this thing is good or this thyng is nought, without consideracion of the circumstaunces" (*A Dialogue of Comfort against Tribulation*, p. 173, quoted Ames, p. 2).

tions—or rather he is uninterested in general, abstract discussion of them. Instead, his attention is focused on particular social problems and the formulation and evaluation of solutions to them.

In the largest terms, More's aim is to fuse city-state theory with universal-state theory by reconciling Aristotle's empirical approach with the idealism of universal-state theory, and by bringing the analytic methods of city-state theory to bear on the problem of realizing Stoic and Christian ideals. This attempt is also typical of the most interesting humanist work, which is often energized by attempts to resolve tensions among the diverse materials— Greek, Roman, Christian—that the tradition incorporates (Bouwsma 1975; Logan, pp. 13-15, 26-34). As I pointed out in Chapter Two, Skinner defines the significance of the work of Machiavelli and Guicciardini in terms of their success in a related attempt. More's results are mixed. The conception of a nation-state made up of a large number of federated city-states is of only academic interest, and the ethical arguments by which he reconciles expediency with morality are of small value. But his application of the methods of systemic theory to the analysis of European problems is highly successful, and his grasp of the constraints imposed on the realization of political ideals by empirical fact and by the conflicts that arise in the pursuit of valid goals represents an impressive accomplishment.

Finally, the complex tone of *Utopia*—that mixture of seriousness and jest that has so confused interpretation—is a humanist characteristic, one that is also closely connected with the sense of history. By suggesting that ideas, like all other cultural manifestations, are conditioned by their social contexts, the sense of history helped to lead more sophisticated humanists of the later Renaissance to the skepticism and relativism apparent in the works of writers such as Erasmus and Montaigne. These attitudes contribute to the humanists' predilection for dialogue and essay, which are genres for tentative, ambivalent thought, and to the growing and increasingly complex use of ironic and fictive modes in their writing. Baker-Smith (pp. 4-11) shows that humanists, especially Erasmian humanists, often believe (like their Stoic predecessors) that they uphold the standard of nature in opposition to the conventions of their time. This belief prompts the kind of irony that Erasmus symbolizes in the Sileni of Alcibiades: "all human affairs . . . have two aspects, each quite different from the other. . . . What at first sight is beautiful may really be ugly; the apparently wealthy may be poorest of all; the disgraceful, glorious; the learned, ignorant. . . . In brief, you find all things suddenly reversed, when you open up the Silenus" (*Praise of Folly*, p. 36). The most complex irony, however, arises from the recognition that one's own view of nature must be colored by convention, and that it is sometimes better to leave the Silenus closed. As Folly says, the suicides of many philosophers suggest that if men saw their situation as it really is "there would be need for some fresh clay and for another potter like Prometheus" (p. 41). In insisting on *all* the conclusions of his best-commonwealth exercise, those that presumably did not please him as well as those that did, More exhibits the same extraordinary objectivity and inclusiveness of vision that we find in *The Praise of Folly*. As in that work also, the ironic fiction in which More embodies his views serves (in addition to its function of sugarcoating the pill of knowledge) to render both the full complexity of these views and the author's own complex attitude toward them. Unfortunately, while this mode of presentation has helped to make *Utopia* an unusually popular work of political theory, it has certainly also acted in one way to lessen its influence. For although More's book has for centuries stimulated the imaginations of political visionaries and revolutionaries, and although its passionate humanity has been widely apprehended, its profound contributions to political theory have passed largely unperceived.[8] In this re-

[8] The Manuels observe that "More's role in the history of utopian thought derives from a surface, simplistic, and fast reading of the text" (pp. 147-48)—a fact that accounts for the curious irony that although his book fathered the literary utopia, and determined many of its narrative conventions, it does not itself belong to that genre (since it does not include the author's ideal commonwealth).

spect the bald overstatements of Machiavelli have proved vastly more effective.

The most significant fact about *Utopia* is the importance and the nobility of what it undertakes. Sabine observes that Aristotle, by treating actual constitutions apart from the ideal constitution, began to sever the link between politics and ethics (p. 108). In *The Prince* Machiavelli announces that the severance is complete. Max Lerner has criticized Machiavelli's assumption that such a dissociation is inevitable:

> Machiavelli sought to distinguish the realm of what ought to be and the realm of what is. He rejected the first for the second. But there is a third realm: the realm of what can be. It is in that realm that what one might call a humanist realism can lie. The measure of man is his ability to extend this sphere of the socially possible. We can start with our democratic values, and we can start also with Machiavelli's realism about tough-minded methods. . . . We may yet find that an effective pursuit of democratic values is possible within the scope of a strong social-welfare state and an unsentimental realism about human motives. (p. xlvi)

The central meaning of *Utopia* lies in its advocacy of just such a humanist realism.

Works Cited

Abbreviations: *EA* = Sylvester and Marc'hadour, ed., *Essential Articles for the Study of Thomas More; JHI* = *Journal of the History of Ideas; JMRS* = *The Journal of Medieval and Renaissance Studies;* LCL = Loeb Classical Library; *RQ* = *Renaissance Quarterly; SP* = *Studies in Philology; SR* = *Studies in the Renaissance*

Adams, Robert M., ed. and trans. *Utopia*, by Sir Thomas More. Norton Critical Editions. New York: W. W. Norton & Company, Inc., 1975.

Adams, Robert P. 1962. *The Better Part of Valor: More, Erasmus, Colet, and Vives, on Humanism, War, and Peace, 1496-1535.* Seattle: University of Washington Press, 1962.

———. 1945. "Designs by More and Erasmus for a New Social Order." *SP* 42 (1945):131-45.

Allen, Don Cameron. "The Rehabilitation of Epicurus and His Theory of Pleasure in the Early Renaissance." *SP* 41 (1944):1-15.

Allen, J. W. *A History of Political Thought in the Sixteenth Century.* 1928. Reprint. London: Methuen & Co. Ltd., 1957.

Allen, Peter R. "*Utopia* and European Humanism: the Function of the Prefatory Letters and Verses." *SR* 10 (1963):91-107.

Allen, Ward. "The Tone of More's Farewell to *Utopia*: A Reply to J. H. Hexter." *Moreana*, No. 51 (1976):108-18.

Ames, Russell. *Citizen Thomas More and His Utopia.* Princeton: Princeton University Press, 1949.

Anglo, Sydney. *Machiavelli: A Dissection.* 1969. Reprint. London: Paladin, 1971.

Apostel, Leo. "Towards the Formal Study of Models in the Non-formal Sciences." In *The Concept and the Role of the Model in Mathematics and Natural and Social Sciences*, edited by Hans Freudenthal. Dordrecht, Holland: D. Reidel Publishing Co., 1961.

Aristotle. *The "Art" of Rhetoric.* Edited and translated by John Henry Freese. LCL. Cambridge, Mass.: Harvard University Press, 1926.

Aristotle. *Ethica Nicomachea*. Translated by W. D. Ross. In *The Works of Aristotle*, edited by J. A. Smith and W. D. Ross, Vol. IX. Oxford: Clarendon Press, 1925.

――――. *Oeconomica* [*Economics*]. Edited and translated by G. C. Armstrong. LCL. Cambridge, Mass.: Harvard University Press, 1935.

――――. *The Politics of Aristotle*. Translated by Ernest Barker. Oxford: Clarendon Press, 1948.

Arnold, E. Vernon. *Roman Stoicism*. Cambridge: Cambridge University Press, 1911.

Augustine, St. *The City of God against the Pagans*. Edited and translated by George E. McCracken et al. LCL. Vol. II. Cambridge, Mass.: Harvard University Press, 1963.

――――. (*CG*) *Concerning the City of God against the Pagans*. Translated by Henry Bettenson, introduction by David Knowles. Harmondsworth: Penguin Books, 1972.

――――. *Confessions and Enchiridion*. Translated by Albert C. Outler. The Library of Christian Classics, Vol. 7. London: SCM Press Ltd., 1955.

Avineri, Schlomo. "War and Slavery in More's *Utopia*." *International Review of Social History* 7 (1962):260-90.

Bacon, Sir Francis. *The History of the Reign of King Henry the Seventh*. Edited by F. J. Levy. Indianapolis: The Bobbs-Merrill Co., Inc., 1972.

――――. *The New Organon*. In *The Works of Francis Bacon*, edited by James Spedding, R. L. Ellis, and D. D. Heath, Vol. IV. London: Longman and Co., 1858.

Baker-Smith, D. *Thomas More and Plato's Voyage*. An Inaugural Lecture given on 1st June 1978 at University College Cardiff. Cardiff: University College Cardiff Press, 1978.

Barker, Arthur. "*Clavis Moreana*: The Yale Edition of Thomas More." In *EA*. Originally publ. *JEGP* 65 (1966):318-30.

Barnes, W. J. "Irony and the English Apprehension of Renewal." *Queen's Quarterly* 73 (1966):357-76.

Baron, Hans. 1966. *The Crisis of the Early Italian Renaissance*. Rev. one-vol. ed. Princeton: Princeton University Press, 1966.

――――. 1938. "Franciscan Poverty and Civic Wealth as Factors in the Rise of Humanistic Thought." *Speculum* 13 (1938):1-37.

――――. 1968. *From Petrarch to Leonardo Bruni: Studies in Humanistic and Political Literature*. Chicago: The University of Chicago Press, 1968.

————. 1971. "Petrarch: His Inner Struggles and the Humanistic Discovery of Man's Nature." In *Florilegium Historiale: Essays Presented to Wallace K. Ferguson*, edited by J. G. Rowe and W. H. Stockdale. Toronto: University of Toronto Press, 1971.

Berger, Harry, Jr. "The Renaissance Imagination: Second World and Green World." *The Centennial Review* 9 (1965):36-77.

Bevington, David M. "The Dialogue in *Utopia*: Two Sides to the Question." *SP* 58 (1961):496-509.

Binder, James. "More's *Utopia* in English: A Note on Translation." In *EA*. Originally publ. *Modern Language Notes* 62 (1947):370-76.

Boewe, Charles. "Human Nature in More's *Utopia*." *The Personalist* 41 (1960):303-9.

Bouwsma, William J. 1976. "Changing Assumptions in the Later Renaissance." *Viator* 7 (1976):421-40.

————. 1973. *The Culture of Renaissance Humanism*. American Historical Association Pamphlets, No. 401. Washington: American Historical Association, 1973.

————. 1975. "The Two Faces of Humanism: Stoicism and Augustinianism in Renaissance Thought." In *Itinerarium Italicum: The Profile of the Italian Renaissance in the Mirror of Its European Transformations*, edited by Heiko A. Oberman with Thomas A. Brady, Jr. Studies in Medieval and Reformation Thought, Vol. XIV. Leiden: E. J. Brill, 1975.

————. 1966. *The Interpretation of Renaissance Humanism*. 2nd ed. Service Center for Teachers of History, Publication No. 18. Washington: American Historical Association, 1966.

Bradshaw, Brendan. "More on Utopia." *The Historical Journal* 24 (1981):1-27.

Burke, Peter. *The Renaissance Sense of the Past*. London: Edward Arnold, 1969.

Bush, Douglas. *The Renaissance and English Humanism*. Toronto: University of Toronto Press, 1939.

Campbell, W. E. *More's Utopia and His Social Teaching*. London: Eyre & Spottiswoode Publishers Ltd., 1930.

Carlyle, R. W., and A. J. Carlyle. *A History of Mediæval Political*

Theory in the West. 3rd ed. Vol. I. London: W. Blackwood & Sons Ltd., 1930.

Caspari, Fritz. *Humanism and the Social Order in Tudor England.* Classics in Education, No. 34. 1954. Reprint. New York: Teachers College Press, Teachers College, Columbia University, 1968.

Cassirer, Ernst. *The Platonic Renaissance in England.* Translated by James P. Pettegrove. 1932. Reprint. New York: Thomas Nelson and Sons, 1953.

————, P. O. Kristeller, and J. H. Randall, Jr., ed. *The Renaissance Philosophy of Man.* Chicago: University of Chicago Press, 1948.

Castiglione, Baldesar. *The Book of the Courtier.* Translated by Charles S. Singleton. Garden City, N.Y.: Anchor Books, 1959.

Catullus. *[Works.]* Edited and translated by F. W. Cornish. 3rd ed. LCL. Cambridge, Mass.: Harvard University Press, 1962.

Chambers, R. W. *Thomas More.* The Bedford Historical Series. London: Jonathan Cape, 1935.

Cicero. *De finibus bonorum et malorum.* Edited and translated by H. Rackham. 2nd ed. LCL. Cambridge, Mass.: Harvard University Press, 1931.

————. *De inventione.* Edited and translated by H. M. Hubbell. LCL. Cambridge, Mass.: Harvard University Press, 1949.

————. *De legibus.* Edited and translated by C. W. Keyes. LCL. Cambridge, Mass.: Harvard University Press, 1928.

————. *De natura deorum.* Edited and translated by H. Rackham. LCL. Cambridge, Mass.: Harvard University Press, 1933.

————. *De officiis.* Edited and translated by Walter Miller. LCL. Cambridge, Mass.: Harvard University Press, 1913.

————. *De oratore.* Edited and translated by E. W. Sutton and H. Rackham. LCL. 2 vols. Cambridge, Mass.: Harvard University Press, 1942.

————. *De partitione oratoria.* Edited and translated by H. Rackham. LCL. Cambridge, Mass.: Harvard University Press, 1942.

————. *De re publica.* Edited and translated by C. W. Keyes. LCL. Cambridge, Mass.: Harvard University Press, 1928.

————. *The Letters to His Friends [Epistulae ad familiares].* Edited and translated by W. G. Williams. LCL. Vol. I. Cambridge, Mass.: Harvard University Press, 1927.

————. *Orator.* Edited and translated by H. M. Hubbell. LCL. Cambridge, Mass.: Harvard University Press, 1952.

Coles, Paul. "The Interpretation of More's *Utopia*." *Hibbert Journal* 56 (1958):365-70.

Colet, John. *Exposition of Romans*. In *Opuscula Quaedam Theologica*, edited by J. H. Lupton. 1876. Reprint. Farnsborough, Hants: Gregg International Publishers Ltd., 1966.

Copleston, Frederick, S.J. *A History of Philosophy*. The Bellarmine Series. Vols. II and III. London: Burns Oates & Washbourne Ltd., 1950, 1953.

Coplin, William D. "Introduction: Simulation as an Approach to the Study of Politics." In *Simulation in the Study of Politics*, edited by William D. Coplin. Chicago: Markham Publishing Co., 1968.

Dawson, Richard E. "Simulation in the Social Sciences." In *Simulation in Social Science: Readings*, edited by Harold Guetzkow. Englewood Cliffs, N.J.: Prentice-Hall, 1962.

Dean, Leonard F. 1943. "Literary Problems in More's *Richard III*." In *EA*. Originally publ. *PMLA* 58 (1943):22-41.

————, ed. and trans. 1946. *The Praise of Folly*, by Desiderius Erasmus. Chicago: Packard and Co., 1946.

Delcourt, Marie. "Le Pouvoir du Roi dans *L'Utopie*." In *Mélanges offerts à M. Abel Lefranc*. Paris: E. Droz, 1936.

Diogenes Laertius. *Lives of Eminent Philosophers*. Edited and translated by R. D. Hicks. LCL. 2 vols. New York: G. P. Putnam's Sons, 1925.

Domingo, Carlos, and Oscar Varsavsky. "Un Modelo Matematico de la Utopía de Moro." *Desarrollo Economico* 7 (1967):3-26.

Donner, H. W. *Introduction to Utopia*. London: Sidgwick & Jackson, Ltd., 1945.

Dorsch, T. S. "Sir Thomas More and Lucian: An Interpretation of *Utopia*." *Archiv für das Studium der Neueren Sprachen und Literaturen* 203 (1966-67):345-63.

Dresden, Sem. *Humanism in the Renaissance*. Translated by Margaret King. World University Library. New York: McGraw-Hill Book Co., 1968.

Duhamel, P. Albert. 1955. "Medievalism of More's *Utopia*." In *EA*. Originally publ. *SP* 52 (1955):99-126.

————. 1953. "The Oxford Lectures of John Colet: An Essay in Defining the English Renaissance." *JHI* 14 (1953):493-510.

Duncan, Douglas. *Ben Jonson and the Lucianic Tradition*. Cambridge: Cambridge University Press, 1979.

Edelstein, Ludwig. *Plato's Seventh Letter*. Philosophia Antiqua, Vol. XIV. Leiden: E. J. Brill, 1966.

Elliott, Robert C. "The Shape of Utopia." *ELH* 30 (1963):317-34.

Elton, G. R. 1977. *Reform and Reformation: England 1509-1558*. The New History of England, 2. London: Edward Arnold, 1977.

————. 1972. "Thomas More, Councillor (1517-1529)." In *St. Thomas More: Action and Contemplation*, edited by Richard S. Sylvester. New Haven: Yale University Press, 1972.

Elyot, Sir Thomas. *The Book named the Governor*. Edited by S. E. Lehmberg. Everyman's Library. New York: Dutton, 1962.

Epictetus. *Discourses*. Edited and translated by W. A. Oldfather. LCL. Vol. I. Cambridge, Mass.: Harvard University Press, 1925.

Erasmus, Desiderius. *Adages*. In Margaret Mann Phillips, *The "Adages" of Erasmus: A Study with Translations*. Cambridge: Cambridge University Press, 1964.

————. *Apophthegmata*. In *Opera*, Vol. IV. Leyden, 1703.

————. *Ciceronianus*. In Izora Scott, *Controversies Over The Imitation of Cicero*. Contributions to Education, No. 35. New York: Teachers College, Columbia University, 1910.

————. *The Complaint of Peace*. Translated by T. Paynell [?]. Chicago: The Open Court Publishing Co., 1917.

————. *The Correspondence of Erasmus*. Vols. I and III. Translated by R.A.B. Mynors and D.F.S. Thomson. *The Collected Works of Erasmus*, Vols. 1 and 3. Toronto: University of Toronto Press, 1974, 1976.

————. *De contemptv mvndi*. Edited by S. Dresden. In *Opera Omnia*, Vol. V, Part 1. Amsterdam-Oxford: North-Holland Publishing Co., 1977.

————. *De copia / De ratione studii*. Edited by Craig R. Thompson, translated by Betty I. Knott and Brian McGregor. *The Collected Works of Erasmus*, Vol. 24. Toronto: University of Toronto Press, 1978.

————. *De libero arbitrio*. In *Luther and Erasmus: Free Will and Salvation*, edited and translated by E. Gordon Rupp in collaboration with A. N. Marlow. The Library of Christian Classics, Vol. XVII. London: SCM Press Ltd., 1969.

————. *(ECP) The Education of a Christian Prince*. Translated by Lester K. Born. Records of Civilization, Sources and Studies. 1936. Reprint. New York: W. W. Norton & Co., Inc., 1968.

——. "The Epicurean." In *The Colloquies of Erasmus*, translated by Craig R. Thompson. Chicago: The University of Chicago Press, 1965.

——, ed. *Novum testamentum*. In *Opera*, Vol. VI. Leyden, 1705.

——. (*EE*) *Opus epistolarum Des. Erasmi Roterodami [Erasmi Epistolae]*. Edited by P. S. Allen, H. M. Allen, and H. W. Garrod. Vols. II and IV. Oxford: Clarendon Press, 1910, 1922.

——. *The Praise of Folly*. Translated by Hoyt Hopewell Hudson. Princeton: Princeton University Press, 1941.

Erikson, Eric. *Childhood and Society*. 2nd ed. New York: W. W. Norton & Co., Inc., 1963.

Fenlon, Dermot. "England and Europe: *Utopia* and Its Aftermath." *Transactions of the Royal Historical Society* 25 (1975):115-35.

Ficino, Marsilio. *Commentaria in Plotinum*. In *Opera*, Vol. II. Basel, 1576.

Fleisher, Martin. *Radical Reform and Political Persuasion in the Life and Writings of Thomas More*. Travaux d'humanisme et Renaissance, CXXXII. Geneva: Librairie Droz, 1973.

Flower, Barbara, trans. "Selection from the letters of Erasmus." In Huizinga.

Frye, Northrop. "Varieties of Literary Utopias." *Dædalus* 94 (1965):323-47.

Fueter, Eduard. *Geschichte der Neueren Historiographie*. Munich: Druck und Verlag von R. Oldenbourg, 1911.

Fyfe, W. H. "Tacitus' *Germania* and More's *Utopia*." *Proceedings and Transactions of the Royal Society of Canada*, 3rd series, 30 (1936):Sec. II, 57-59.

Garin, Eugenio. *Italian Humanism: Philosophy and Civic Life in the Renaissance*. Translated by Peter Munz. 1947. Reprint. Oxford: Basil Blackwell, 1965.

Gewirth, Alan. *Marsilius of Padua: The Defender of Peace*. Vol. I: *Marsilius of Padua and Medieval Political Philosophy*. Records of Civilization, Sources and Studies, No. 46. New York: Columbia University Press, 1951.

Gilbert, Allan H. *Machiavelli's "Prince" and Its Forerunners: "The Prince" as a Typical Book "de Regimine Principum."* 1938. Reprint. New York: Barnes and Noble, Inc., 1968.

Gilbert, Felix. "The Humanist Concept of the Prince and *The Prince* of Machiavelli." *The Journal of Modern History* 11 (1939):449-83.

Gilson, Etienne. *Reason and Revelation in the Middle Ages*. New York: Charles Scribner's Sons, 1938.

Golembiewski, Robert T., William A. Welsh, and William J. Crotty. *A Methodological Primer for Political Scientists*. Chicago: Rand McNally & Co., 1969.

Gordon, Walter M. "The Monastic Achievement and More's Utopian Dream." *Medievalia et Humanistica*, n.s. 9 (1979):199-214.

Greene, James J., and John P. Dolan, ed. *The Essential Thomas More*. New York: The New American Library, 1967.

Guicciardini, Francesco. *Maxims and Reflections of a Renaissance Statesman (Ricordi)*. Translated by Mario Domandi, introduction by Nicolai Rubenstein. New York: Harper Torchbooks, 1965.

Hammond, Mason. *City-State and World State in Greek and Roman Political Theory until Augustus*. Cambridge, Mass.: Harvard University Press, 1951.

Hanson, Donald W. *From Kingdom to Commonwealth: The Development of Civic Consciousness in English Political Thought*. Harvard Political Studies. Cambridge, Mass.: Harvard University Press, 1970.

Heiserman, A. R. "Satire in the *Utopia*." *PMLA* 78 (1963):163-74.

Herbrüggen, Hubertus Schulte. "More's *Utopia* as a Paradigm." In *EA*. Originally publ. *Utopie und Anti-Utopie*. Bochum-Langendreer: H. Pöppinghaus, 1960.

Hermann, Charles F. "Simulation III: Political Processes." In *International Encyclopedia of the Social Sciences*, edited by David L. Sills, Vol. XIV. New York: The Macmillan Co. & The Free Press, 1968.

Herodotus. [*The Histories*.] Edited and translated by A. D. Godley. LCL. Vol. II. Cambridge, Mass.: Harvard University Press, 1921.

Hexter, J. H. 1975. "Intention, Words, and Meaning: The Case of More's *Utopia*." *New Literary History* 6 (1975):529-41.

———. 1952. *More's "Utopia": The Biography of an Idea*. 1952. Reprint with an Epilogue. New York: Harper Torchbooks, 1965.

———. 1973. *The Vision of Politics on the Eve of the Reformation: More, Machiavelli, and Seyssel*. New York: Basic Books, Inc., 1973.

Holdsworth, Sir William. *A History of English Law*. 3rd ed. Vol. II. London: Methuen & Co. Ltd., 1923.

Huizinga, Johan. *Erasmus and the Age of Reformation* [*Erasmus of Rotterdam*]. Translated by F. Hopman. With a selection from the letters of Erasmus, translated by Barbara Flower. 1924 [biography only]. Reprint. New York: Harper Torchbooks, 1957.

Hunt, H.A.K. *The Humanism of Cicero*. Melbourne: Melbourne University Press, 1954.

Huppert, George. *The idea of perfect history: Historical erudition and historical philosophy in Renaissance France*. Urbana: University of Illinois Press, 1970.

Hyma, Albert. *The Youth of Erasmus*. University of Michigan Publications: History and Political Science, Vol. X. Ann Arbor: University of Michigan Press, 1930.

Isaak, Alan C. *Scope and Methods of Political Science: An Introduction to the Methodology of Political Inquiry*. The Dorsey Series in Political Science. Homewood, Ill.: The Dorsey Press, 1969.

Jenkins, Claude. *Sir Thomas More*. Canterbury: Friends of Canterbury Cathedral, 1935.

Jerome, St. *Adversus Jovinianum libri duo*. In *Patrologiae Latinae*, edited by J.-P. Migne, Vol. XXIII. Paris, n.d.

John of Salisbury. *Policraticus*. Edited by Clements C. I. Webb. Vol. II. Oxford: Clarendon Press, 1909.

Johnson, Robbin S. *More's "Utopia": Ideal and Illusion*. New Haven: Yale University Press, 1969.

Jones, Judith P. 1979. *Thomas More*. Twayne's English Authors Series, 247. Boston: Twayne Publishers, 1979.

———. 1971. "The *Philebus* and the Philosophy of Pleasure in Thomas More's *Utopia*." *Moreana*, No. 31-32 (1971):61-69.

Kaplan, Abraham. *The Conduct of Inquiry: Methodology for Behavioral Science*. Chandler Publications in Anthropology and Sociology. San Francisco: Chandler Publishing Co., 1964.

Kautsky, Karl. *Thomas More and His Utopia*. Translated by H. J. Stenning. 1927. (First German ed. 1888.) Reprint with a foreword by Russell Ames. New York: Russell & Russell, 1959.

Kelley, Donald R. *Foundations of Modern Historical Scholarship: Language, Law, and History in the French Renaissance*. New York: Columbia University Press, 1970.

Kennedy, George. *The Art of Persuasion in Greece*. Princeton: Princeton University Press, 1963.

Khanna, Lee Cullen. "*Utopia:* The Case for Open-mindedness in the Commonwealth." *Moreana*, No. 31-32 (1971):91-105.

Kinney, Arthur F. 1979. *Rhetoric and Poetic in Thomas More's "Utopia."* Humana Civilitas, Vol. 5. Malibu: Undena Publications, 1979.

———. 1976. "Rhetoric as Poetic: Humanist Fiction in the Renaissance." *ELH* 43 (1976):413-43.

Knowles, Dom David. *The Evolution of Medieval Thought*. New York: Vintage Books, 1962.

Knox, Father Ronald. "The Charge of Religious Intolerance." In *The Fame of Blessed Thomas More*. London: Sheed and Ward, 1929.

Kohl, Benjamin G., and Ronald G. Witt, ed. and trans. *The Earthly Republic: Italian Humanists on Government and Society*. Philadelphia: University of Pennsylvania Press, 1978.

Kristeller, Paul Oskar. 1964. *Eight Philosophers of the Italian Renaissance*. Stanford: Stanford University Press, 1964.

———. 1972. "The Impact of Early Italian Humanism on Thought and Learning." In *Developments in the Early Renaissance*, edited by Bernard S. Levy. Albany: State University of New York Press, 1972.

———. 1943. *The Philosophy of Marsilio Ficino*. Translated by Virginia Conant. New York: Columbia University Press, 1943.

———. 1979. *Renaissance Thought and Its Sources*. Edited by Michael Mooney. New York: Columbia University Press, 1979.

———. 1961. *Renaissance Thought [I]*: The Classic, Scholastic, and Humanist Strains. New York: Harper Torchbooks, 1961.

———. 1965. *Renaissance Thought II: Papers on Humanism and the Arts*. New York: Harper Torchbooks, 1965.

———. 1962. "Studies on Renaissance Humanism during the Last Twenty Years." *SR* 9 (1962):7-30.

———. 1980. "Thomas More as a Renaissance Humanist." *Moreana*, No. 65-66 (1980):5-22.

Le Guin, Ursula K. *The Left Hand of Darkness*. New York: Ace Books, 1976.

Lerner, Max, ed. *The Prince and the Discourses*, by Niccolò Machiavelli. Modern Library College Editions. New York: The Modern Library, 1950.

Lewis, C. S. *English Literature in the Sixteenth Century Excluding Drama*.

The Oxford History of English Literature, III. Oxford: Clarendon Press, 1954.

Logan, George M. "Substance and form in Renaissance humanism." *JMRS* 7 (1977):1-34.

Lucian. [*Works.*] Edited and translated by A. M. Harmon et al. LCL. Vol. I. Cambridge, Mass.: Harvard University Press, 1913.

McCullough, Peter S. "The Literary Antecedents of Thomas More's *The History of King Richard III.*" Master's thesis, Queen's University, 1975.

McCutcheon, Elizabeth. 1971. "Denying the Contrary: More's Use of Litotes in the *Utopia.*" In *EA*. Originally publ. *Moreana*, No. 31-32 (1971):107-21.

———. 1969. "Thomas More, Raphael Hythlodaeus, and the Angel Raphael." *Studies in English Literature* 9 (1969):21-38.

Machiavelli, Niccolò. *Discourses* and *The Prince*. In *The Chief Works and Others*, translated by Alan Gilbert, Vol. I. Durham: Duke University Press, 1958.

———. *Il Principe*. Edited by L. Arthur Burd, introduction by Lord Acton. Oxford: Clarendon Press, 1891.

McIlwain, Charles H. *The Growth of Political Thought in the West from the Greeks to the End of the Middle Ages*. London: Macmillan and Co., Ltd., 1932.

McKeon, Richard P. "Renaissance and Method in Philosophy." *Columbia Studies in the History of Ideas* 3 (1935):37-114.

Mackie, John D. *The Earlier Tudors, 1485-1558*. The Oxford History of England. Oxford: Clarendon Press, 1952.

Manuel, Frank E., and Fritzie P. Manuel. *Utopian Thought in the Western World*. Cambridge, Mass.: Harvard University Press, 1979.

Marsiglio of Padua. *The Defender of Peace [Defensor pacis]*. Translated by Alan Gewirth. Records of Civilization, Sources and Studies, No. 46. Vol. II. New York: Columbia University Press, 1956.

Mermel, Jerry. "Preparations for a politic life: Sir Thomas More's entry into the king's service." *JMRS* 7 (1977):53-66.

Mill, John Stuart. *Utilitarianism*. Edited by J. M. Robson. In *The Collected Works of John Stuart Mill*, Vol. X. Toronto: University of Toronto Press, 1969.

Miller, Clarence H. 1966. "The English Translation in the Yale *Utopia*: Some Corrections." *Moreana*, No. 9 (1966):57-64.

Miller, Clarence H. 1965-66. Review of *Utopia*, ed. E. Surtz and J. H. Hexter. *English Language Notes* 3 (1965-66):303-9.

Montaigne, Michel de. *The Complete Essays of Montaigne*. Translated by Donald M. Frame. Stanford: Stanford University Press, 1958.

More, St. Thomas. *The Confutation of Tyndale's Answer*. Edited by L. A. Schuster, R. C. Marius, J. P. Lusardi, and R. J. Schoeck. *The Complete Works of St. Thomas More*, Vol. 8. New Haven: Yale University Press, 1973.

————. *The Correspondence of Sir Thomas More*. Edited by Elizabeth F. Rogers. Princeton: Princeton University Press, 1947.

————. *A Dialogue Concerning Heresies*. Edited by T.M.C. Lawler, G. Marc'hadour, and R. C. Marius. *The Complete Works of St. Thomas More*, Vol. 6. New Haven: Yale University Press, 1981.

————. *A Dialogue of Comfort against Tribulation*. Edited by Louis L. Martz and Frank Manley. *The Complete Works of St. Thomas More*, Vol. 12. New Haven: Yale University Press, 1976.

————. *The English Works of Sir Thomas More*. Edited by W. E. Campbell et al. Vol. I. London: Eyre & Spottiswoode Publishers Ltd., 1931.

————. *The Four Last Things*. In *The Workes . . . in the Englysh Tonge*. London, 1557.

————. *The History of King Richard III*. Edited by Richard S. Sylvester. *The Complete Works of St. Thomas More*, Vol. 2. New Haven: Yale University Press, 1963.

————. *The Latin Epigrams of Thomas More*. Edited and translated by Leicester Bradner and Charles A. Lynch. Chicago: The University of Chicago Press, 1953.

————. *Responsio ad Lutherum*. Edited by John M. Headley, translated by Sr. Scholastica Mandeville. *The Complete Works of St. Thomas More*, Vol. 5. New Haven: Yale University Press, 1969.

————. *Selected Letters*. Translated by Elizabeth F. Rogers. *The Yale Edition of the Works of St. Thomas More: Modernized Series*. New Haven: Yale University Press, 1961.

————. *A Treatise upon the Passion*. Edited by Garry E. Haupt. *The Complete Works of St. Thomas More*, Vol. 13. New Haven: Yale University Press, 1976.

————. "Twelve Weapons." In *The Workes . . . in the Englysh Tonge*. London, 1557.

————. *Utopia*. Edited by Robert M. Adams. See under Adams.

————. *Utopia*. Edited by J. H. Lupton. Oxford: Clarendon Press, 1895.

————. *Utopia*. Edited by Edward Surtz, S.J., and J. H. Hexter. *The Complete Works of St. Thomas More*, Vol. 4. New Haven: Yale University Press, 1965.

Morgan, Arthur E. *Nowhere Was Somewhere: How History Makes Utopias and How Utopias Make History*. Chapel Hill: University of North Carolina Press, 1946.

Morris, Christopher. *Political Thought in England: Tyndale to Hooker*. The Home University Library of Modern Knowledge, 225. London: Oxford University Press, 1953.

Mumford, Lewis. "Utopia, the City and the Machine." *Dædalus* 94 (1965):271-92.

Nagel, Alan F. "Lies and the Limitable Inane: Contradiction in More's *Utopia*." *RQ* 26 (1973):173-80.

Nelson, William. "Thomas More, Grammarian and Orator." In *EA* (rev.). Originally publ. *PMLA* 58 (1943):337-52.

Olin, John C., ed. *Christian Humanism and the Reformation: Selected Writings*, by Desiderius Erasmus. New York: Harper Torchbooks, 1965.

Oncken, Hermann. 1922a. *Die Utopia des Thomas Morus und das Machtproblem in der Staatslehre*. Sitzungsberichte der Heidelberger Akademie, Philosophisch-historische Klasse, Jahrgang 1922, Abhandlung 2. Heidelberg: Carl Winters Universitätsbuchhandlung, 1922.

————. 1922b. Introduction to *Utopia*, by Sir Thomas More. Edited and translated by Gerhard Ritter. Berlin: R. Hobbing, 1922.

Panofsky, Erwin. *Renaissance and Renascences in Western Art*. 1960. Reprint. New York: Harper Torchbooks, 1969.

Patrizi, Francesco. *De regno et regis institutione*. Prato, 1531.

Petrarch, Francesco. "The Ascent of Mont Ventoux" [*Familiares* IV. 1]. In Cassirer et al.

————. *Four Dialogues for Scholars* [selections from *De remediis utriusque fortunae*]. Edited and translated by Conrad Rawski. Cleveland: The Press of Western Reserve University, 1967.

————. *On His Own Ignorance and That of Many Others*. In Cassirer et al.

Pfeiffer, Rudolf. *History of Classical Scholarship from 1300 to 1850*. Oxford: Clarendon Press, 1976.

Platina, Baptista. *Principis diatuposis*. Frankfort, 1608.

Plato. *Epistles*. Edited and translated by R. G. Bury. LCL. Cambridge, Mass.: Harvard University Press, 1929.

———. *Critias*. Edited and translated by R. G. Bury. LCL. Cambridge, Mass.: Harvard University Press, 1929.

———. *The Laws*. Translated by Trevor J. Saunders. Rev. ed. Harmondsworth: Penguin Books, 1975.

———. *Phaedo*. Edited and translated by H. N. Fowler. LCL. New York: G. P. Putnam's Sons, 1914.

———. *Philebus*. Edited and translated by H. N. Fowler. LCL. Cambridge, Mass.: Harvard University Press, 1925.

———. *The Republic*. Translated by H.D.P. Lee. Harmondsworth: Penguin Books, 1955.

———. *Sophist*. Edited and translated by H. N. Fowler. LCL. Cambridge, Mass.: Harvard University Press, 1921.

———. *The Statesman*. Edited and translated by H. N. Fowler. LCL. Cambridge, Mass.: Harvard University Press, 1925.

———. *Timaeus*. Edited and translated by R. G. Bury. LCL. Cambridge, Mass.: Harvard University Press, 1929.

Plutarch. *Lives*. Edited and translated by Bernadette Perrin. LCL. Vol. I. New York: G. P. Putnam's Sons, 1914.

———. "How to tell a Flatterer from a Friend." In *Moralia*, Vol. I, edited and translated by Frank Cole Babbitt. LCL. Cambridge, Mass.: Harvard University Press, 1927.

———. "That a Philosopher ought to converse especially with Men in Power." In *Moralia*, Vol. X, edited and translated by Harold North Fowler. LCL. Cambridge, Mass.: Harvard University Press, 1936.

Pocock, J.G.A. *The Machiavellian Moment: Florentine Political Thought and the Atlantic Republican Tradition*. Princeton: Princeton University Press, 1975.

Poggio Bracciolini. *Two Renaissance Book Hunters: The Letters of Poggius Bracciolini to Nicolaus de Niccolis*. Translated by Phyllis W. G. Gordan. Records of Civilization: Sources and Studies, Vol. XCI. New York: Columbia University Press, 1974.

Pomponazzi, Pietro. "On the Immortality of the Soul." In Cassirer et al.

Pontano, Giovanni. *De obedientia*. In *Opera*, Vol. I. Basel, 1556.

Porphyry. *On Abstinence from Animal Food*. Translated by Thomas

Taylor, edited by Esme Wynne-Tyson. New York: Barnes & Noble, 1965.

Post, Gaines. *Studies in Medieval Legal Thought*. Princeton: Princeton University Press, 1964.

Prévost, André. 1964. Review of *Utopia*, ed. E. Surtz. *Moreana*, No. 4 (1964):93-97.

————, ed. and trans. 1978. *L'Utopie de Thomas More*. Paris: Mame, 1978.

Quintilian. *Institutio oratoria*. Edited and translated by H. E. Butler. LCL. Vols. I and IV. Cambridge, Mass.: Harvard University Press, 1921, 1922.

Rabelais, François. *Gargantua and Pantagruel*. Translated by Sir Thomas Urquhart and Peter le Motteux. The World's Classics. London: Humphrey Milford for Oxford University Press, 1934.

Raitiere, Martin N. "More's *Utopia* and *The City of God*." *SR* 20 (1973):144-68.

Reesor, Margaret E. *The Political Theory of the Old and Middle Stoa*. New York: J. J. Augustin Publisher, 1951.

Rhetorica ad Herennium. *[Cicero] ad C. Herennium de ratione dicendi*. Edited and translated by Harry Caplan. LCL. Cambridge, Mass.: Harvard University Press, 1954.

Rice, Eugene F., Jr. *The Renaissance Idea of Wisdom*. Cambridge, Mass.: Harvard University Press, 1958.

Ross, Harry. *Utopias Old and New*. The University Extension Library. London: Nicholson and Watson Ltd., 1938.

Rudat, Wolfgang E. H. 1981a. "More's Raphael Hythloday: Missing the Point in *Utopia* Once More?" *Moreana*, No. 69 (1981):41-64.

————. 1981b. "Thomas More and Hythloday: Some Speculations on *Utopia*." *Bibliothèque d'Humanisme et Renaissance* 43 (1981):123-27.

Sabine, George H. *A History of Political Theory*. 3rd ed. New York: Holt, Rinehart and Winston, 1961.

Salamonio, Mario. *The Sovereignty of the Roman Patriciate [Patritii romani de principatu]*. Rome, 1544.

Sandys, Sir John. *A History of Classical Scholarship*. Vol. II. Cambridge: Cambridge University Press, 1908.

Savonarola, Girolamo. *A Tract on the Constitution and Government of Florence [Trattato circa il reggimento e governo della citta di Fi-*

renze]. In *Prediche sopra Aggeo*, edited by Luigi Firpo. Rome: A. Belardetti, 1965.

Schaeffer, John D. "Socratic Method in More's *Utopia*." *Moreana*, No. 69 (1981):5-20.

Schoeck, R. J. 1956. "More, Plutarch, and King Agis: Spartan History and the Meaning of *Utopia*." In *EA*. Originally publ. *Philological Quarterly* 35 (1956):366-75.

———. 1969. " 'A Nursery of Correct and Useful Institutions': On Reading More's *Utopia* as Dialogue." In *EA*. Originally publ. *Moreana*, No. 22 (1969):19-32.

———. 1967. "Thomas More and the Italian Heritage of Early Tudor Humanism." In *Arts Libéraux et Philosophie au Moyen Age*. Actes du Quatrième Congrès International de Philosophie Médiévale, Université de Montréal, 1967. Montreal: Institut D'Etudes Médiévales, 1969.

Seebohm, Frederick. *The Oxford Reformers: Colet, Erasmus, and More*. Edited by Hugh E. Seebohm. New York: E. P. Dutton & Co., [1914]. (Original version publ. 1867.)

Seigel, Jerrold E. *Rhetoric and Philosophy in Renaissance Humanism: The Union of Eloquence and Wisdom, Petrarch to Valla*. Princeton: Princeton University Press, 1968.

Seneca. *Ad Lucilium Epistulae Morales*. Edited and translated by Richard M. Gummere. LCL. 3 vols. Cambridge, Mass.: Harvard University Press, 1917.

———. *De ira, De otio, De tranquillitate animi*. In *Moral Essays*, edited and translated by John W. Basore. LCL. Vols. I and II. Cambridge, Mass.: Harvard University Press, 1928, 1932.

Sidney, Sir Philip. *An Apology for Poetry*. Edited by Geoffrey Shepherd. Nelson's Medieval and Renaissance Library. London: Thomas Nelson and Sons Ltd., 1965.

Skinner, Quentin. 1978. *The Foundations of Modern Political Thought*. Vol. I. Cambridge: Cambridge University Press, 1978.

———. 1967. "Review Article: More's *Utopia*." *Past and Present*, No. 38 (1967):153-68.

Stapleton, Thomas. *The Life and Illustrious Martyrdom of Sir Thomas More*. Translated by Philip E. Hallett, edited by E. E. Reynolds. London: Burns & Oates, 1966.

Stevens, Irma Ned. "Aesthetic Distance in the *Utopia*." *Moreana*, No. 43-44 (1974):13-24.

Struever, Nancy S. *The Language of History in the Renaissance: Rhetoric and Historical Consciousness in Florentine Humanism*. Princeton: Princeton University Press, 1970.

Surtz, Edward L., S.J. 1952. "Interpretations of *Utopia*." *Catholic Historical Review* 38 (1952):156-74.

———. 1957a. *The Praise of Pleasure: Philosophy, Education, and Communism in More's Utopia*. Cambridge, Mass.: Harvard University Press, 1957.

———. 1957b. *The Praise of Wisdom: A Commentary on the Religious and Moral Problems and Backgrounds of St. Thomas More's "Utopia."* Jesuit Studies. Chicago: Loyola University Press, 1957.

Sylvester, R. S., and G. P. Marc'hadour, ed. (*EA*) *Essential Articles for the Study of Thomas More*. Hamden, Conn.: Archon Books, 1977.

Sylvester, R. S. 1968. " 'Si Hythlodaeo Credimus': Vision and Revision in Thomas More's *Utopia*." In *EA*. Originally publ. *Soundings* 51 (1968), 272-89.

———. 1966. "Thomas More: Humanist in Action." In *EA*. Originally publ. *Medieval and Renaissance Studies*, No. 1. Edited by O. B. Hardison, Jr. Chapel Hill: The University of North Carolina Press, 1966.

Tacitus. *Germania*. Edited and translated by Maurice Hutton. LCL. Cambridge, Mass.: Harvard University Press, 1914.

Tawney, R. H. *Equality*. New York: Harcourt, Brace and Co., 1931.

Thomas Aquinas, St. *In libros politicorum*. In *Opera*, Vol. XXVI. Paris, 1875.

Thompson, Craig R. 1955. "Erasmus as Internationalist and Cosmopolitan." *Archiv für Reformationsgeschichte* 46 (1955):167-95.

———, ed. 1965. *The Colloquies of Erasmus*. See under Erasmus, "The Epicurean."

———, ed. 1974. *Translations of Lucian*, by St. Thomas More. *The Complete Works of St. Thomas More*, Vol. 3, Part 1. New Haven: Yale University Press, 1974.

Toffanin, Giuseppe. *History of Humanism*. Translated by Elio Gianturco. New York: Las Americas Publishing Co., 1954. (Italian ed. 1933.)

Tracy, James D. *Erasmus: The Growth of a Mind*. Travaux d'humanisme et Renaissance, CXXVI. Geneva: Librairie Droz, 1972.

Traugott, John. "A Voyage to Nowhere with Thomas More and Jonathan Swift: *Utopia* and *The Voyage to the Houyhnhnms.*" *Sewanee Review* 69 (1961):534-65.

Trinkaus, Charles. *In Our Image and Likeness: Humanity and Divinity in Italian Humanist Thought.* Vol. I. Chicago: The University of Chicago Press, 1970.

Valla, Lorenzo. *De vero falsoque bono.* Edited by Maristella de Panizza Lorch. Bari: Adriatica Editrice, 1970.

———. *On Pleasure; De voluptate.* Translated by A. Kent Hieatt and Maristella de Panizza Lorch, introduction by Maristella de Panizza Lorch. New York: Abaris Books, 1977.

Van Dyke, Vernon. *Political Science: A Philosophical Analysis.* Stanford: Stanford University Press, 1960.

Weiner, Andrew D. "Raphael's Eutopia and More's *Utopia*: Christian Humanism and the Limits of Reason." *Huntington Library Quarterly* 39 (1975):1-27.

Weiss, Roberto. 1947. *The Dawn of Humanism in Italy.* London: H. K. Lewis, 1947.

———. 1967. *Humanism in England During the Fifteenth Century.* 3rd ed. Oxford: Basil Blackwell, 1967.

White, Thomas I. 1976. "Aristotle and *Utopia*." *RQ* 29 (1976):635-75.

———. 1978. "*Festivitas, Utilitas, et Opes:* The Concluding Irony and Philosophical Purpose of Thomas More's *Utopia*." *Albion* 10 (Supplement, 1978):135-50.

———. "A Study of the Influence of Plato and Aristotle on Thomas More's *Utopia*." Ph.D. dissertation, Columbia, 1974.

Wilkins, Ernest Hatch. *Life of Petrarch.* Chicago: The University of Chicago Press, 1961.

Wilson, K. J., ed. *The Letters of Sir Thomas Elyot.* SP 73, No. 5: Texts and Studies (1976).

Wind, Edgar. *Pagan Mysteries in the Renaissance.* Rev. ed. New York: W. W. Norton & Co., Inc., 1968.

Wooden, Warren W. 1977. "Anti-Scholastic Satire in Sir Thomas More's *Utopia*." *Sixteenth Century Journal* 8, 2 (1977):29-45.

———. 1972. "Thomas More and Lucian: A Study of Satiric Influence and Technique." *University of Mississippi Studies in English* 13 (1972):43-57.

Index

Library of Congress Cataloging in Publication Data

Logan, George M., 1941-
The meaning of More's Utopia.
Bibliography: p.   Includes index.
1. More, Thomas, Sir, Saint, 1478-1535. Utopia.
I. Title.
HX811 1516.Z5L63   1983   321'.07   82-16147
ISBN 0-691-06557-8

George M. Logan is Associate Professor of English
at Queens University, Canada. He has contributed to
such journals as Studies in English Literature,
the Journal of the History of Ideas, The Review of English Studies,
Shakespeare Studies, and The Journal of Medieval
and Renaissance Studies.